Library of Congress Cataloging-in-Publication Data
American Roots Music/edited by Robert Santelli,
Holly George-Warren, and Jim Brown.

      p. cm.

      "A Ginger Group/Rolling Stone Press Book."

      "Based on the PBS Series and a collaboration between: the
Library of Congress, the Smithsonian Institution, the Rock and Roll Hall
of Fame and Museum, Experience Music Project, and Ginger Group
Productions, with major support from the National Endowment for the
Arts, the Public Broadcasting Service, the Corporation for Public
Broadcasting, and AT&T."

      ISBN 0-8109-1432-8 (HNA: hc) / ISBN 0-8109-2139-1 (book
club: pbk.)

      1. Folk music—United States—History and criticism. 2. Popular
music—United States—History and criticism. I. Santelli, Robert.
II. George-Warren, Holly. III. Brown, Jim, 1950–   . IV. American roots
music (Television program)

      ML3551 .A54 2001
      781.62'00973—dc21

Printed and bound in England

Harry N. Abrams, Inc.
100 Fifth Avenue
New York, NY 10011
www.abramsbooks.com

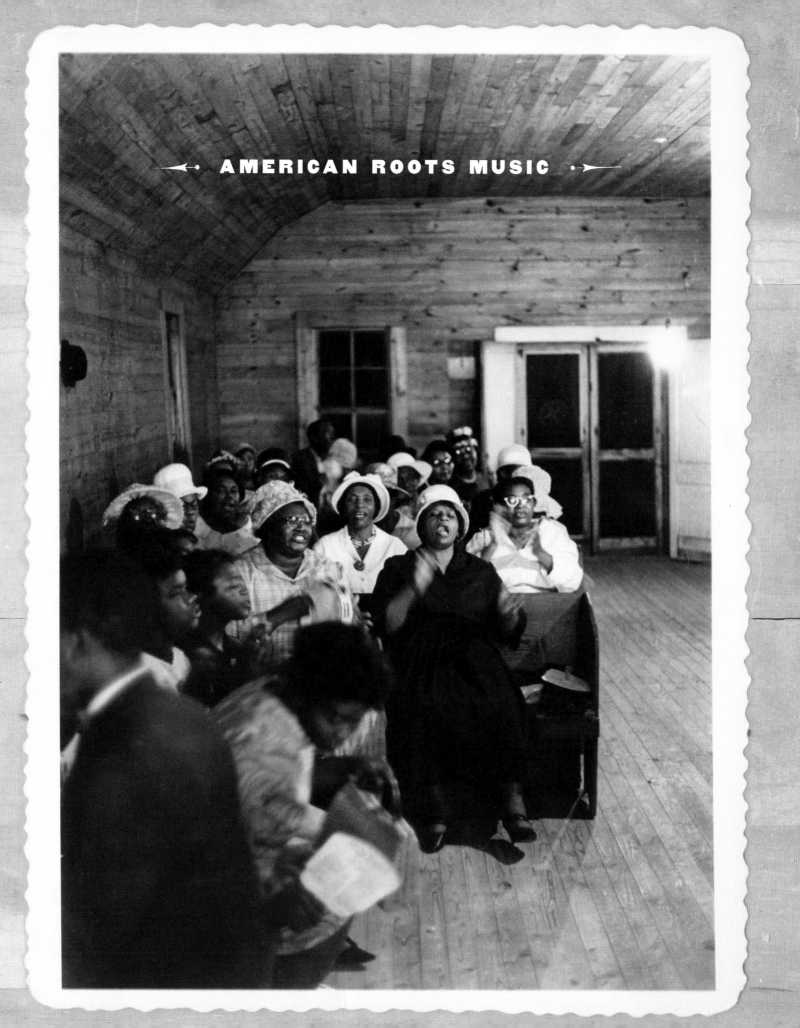
AMERICAN ROOTS MUSIC

A ROLLING STONE PRESS BOOK

CHORUS

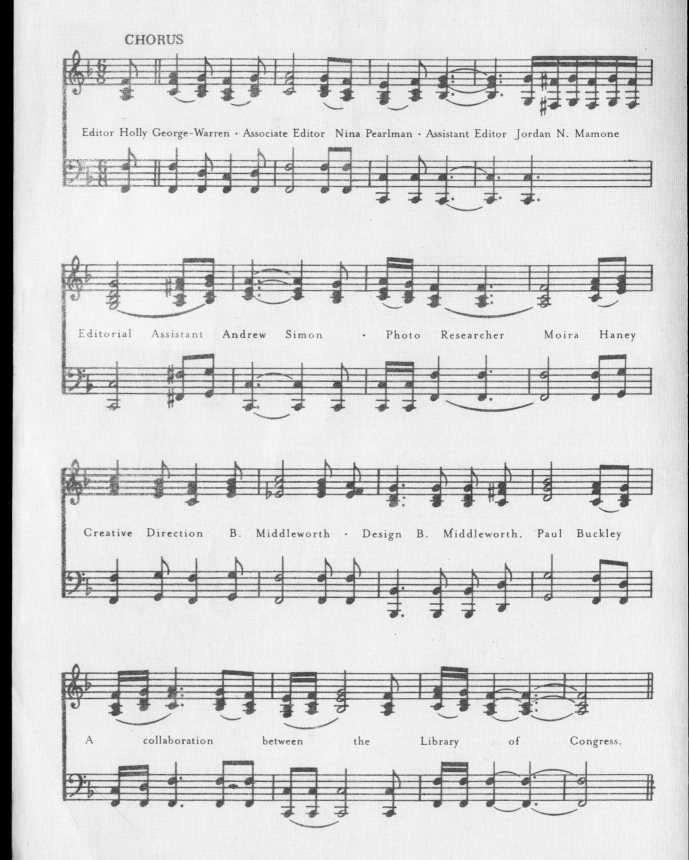

Editor Holly George-Warren · Associate Editor Nina Pearlman · Assistant Editor Jordan N. Mamone

Editorial Assistant Andrew Simon · Photo Researcher Moira Haney

Creative Direction B. Middleworth · Design B. Middleworth, Paul Buckley

A collaboration between the Library of Congress,

VERSES

the Smithsonian Institution, the Rock and Roll Hall of Fame and Museum,

Experience Music Project, and Ginger Group Productions with

major support from the National Endowment for the Arts,

the Public Broadcasting Service, the Corporation for Public Broadcasting, and AT&T.

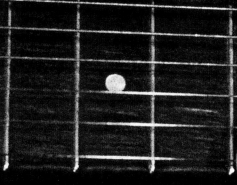

·←· AMERICAN ROOTS MUSIC ·→·

EDITED BY ROBERT SANTELLI · HOLLY GEORGE-WARREN · JIM BROWN

FOREWORD BY BONNIE RAITT

FOREWORD American roots music is at the center of this country's soul. Without roots music, there would be no American music or modern popular culture today. No jazz, no rhythm & blues, no pop music, no rock & roll, no Beatles, no Rolling Stones, no MTV, no rap. Field hollers, work songs, and the old folksongs that people brought with them from the British Isles – these are the earliest sounds of our music heritage and the source of the many great music forms that would follow. Blues, gospel, country, bluegrass, Cajun, zydeco, and Tejano are just some of America's amazing musical expressions. They sounded wonderful when they first entered our musical consciousness, and they still sound that way today.

The roots of this vernacular music stretch across oceans, not only to Africa but throughout Europe and the New World. It was carried to America by slaves and European settlers, each of whom heard and borrowed elements from other cultures to create music that was unique and new. The ancient music of African slaves, for example, was transmogrified with Christianity and gave rise to gospel music, field hollers, work songs, and prison songs. You can see how this music evolved into songs of inspiration for the civil rights and anti-war movements, as well as songs for entertainment in juke joints and nightclubs. You can marvel at how all forms of roots music have found – and continue finding – their way to each of us at different times, through different means – radio, recordings, live performances, music festivals, and television.

With the advent of radio, roots music traveled from one hotbed to another, exposing practically everyone in earshot to the different musics created and enjoyed by people they had never met from places they may never have heard of, much less ever visited. Radio provided the crucial link between the musicians and the music in one farmland, mountain, swamp, or urban community and countless others. People – like a young Elvis Presley – began listening to gospel and black music on Sunday morning radio programs, while at the same time young future rock & roll and soul singers in Detroit, St. Louis, and Philadelphia were tuning in to the Grand Ole Opry broadcast. Beginning back in the 1930s, when radio was still relatively new, it must have seemed like a miracle to dial this magic box, get some wild Appalachian recording, and then turn the dial a little bit more and get some white preacher, then a black preacher, then big-band music, gospel, blues, and the Grand Ole Opry. The resulting cross-pollination gave rise to an amazingly fertile time in music, opening up people's hearts and minds to the possibilities in music, not only for entertainment and personal self-expression, but a way to build or define a community.

Roots music reflects where we've been – politically and sociologically, as well as musically. Early field recordings like those we have from John and Alan Lomax represent such an important contribution to how we can learn about – and celebrate – our past. They tell us where this music really lived, where it came from, and how our own history developed. The evolution of different styles of popular music today can be traced back to those early recordings. They are the most important national resource we have.

When I was fourteen, growing up in Southern California, I heard a record called *Blues at Newport '63*. It changed my life. I got it as a gift, and as a young guitar player I learned every single note on the record and played them until my fingers bled. Later, at college in Cambridge, Massachusetts, there was a great blues program on the Harvard radio station. One night the guests were Son House and Son's manager, Dick Waterman, who had rediscovered Son and had given him a new career. Son House was one of the most ferocious blues players I had ever heard. He tapped into something that was as primal and as painful as anything you could ever hear on Earth. For me, it never got any deeper than Son House. My connection to the blues became permanent and powerful, and I'm forever grateful for that.

There are plenty of other people with the same kind of story as mine and the same kind of passion. For them it might have been Jimmie Rodgers (either one!) or the Carter Family and early country, or maybe Bill Monroe and bluegrass, or Woody Guthrie or Pete Seeger and folk music. When I first started playing, it was folk music and folk festivals that allowed me to experience so many roots musicians and musics firsthand. Early on, at the Philadelphia Folk Festival, I remember listening to the wonderful, earthy blues of Mississippi Fred McDowell and, afterwards, suddenly hearing bluegrass coming from the stage across the way, and wandering over and hearing the amazing Bill Monroe playing "Uncle Pen." Already in love with the blues, I fell in love with Appalachian roots, bluegrass, and folk music, too.

My dream has been for roots music to get into the homes of America and to get its due. And so I'm overjoyed that the *American Roots Music* television series and its book are helping to finally accomplish this. Thank you, thank you, to all those involved in making this happen!

America has an incredibly rich history of roots music; it's one of our greatest gifts. Its ability to tell a story, to speak the truth, to reflect where we've been and why, never goes away. For me, celebrating this music comes naturally. Hopefully, *American Roots Music* will start you on the same kind of journey I've taken. It's a road well traveled and well worth it.

BONNIE RAITT

MARCH 2001

EARLY COUNTRY: TREASURES UNTOLD

BY CHARLES WOLFE One warm afternoon in June 1919, a mule-drawn wagon made its way up the dusty main street toward the town square of Murfreesboro, Tennessee. In the driver's seat was a stocky forty-nine-year-old man with a black vest and a white goatee; on the side of the wagon was the legend MACON MIDWAY MULE AND TRANSPORTATION COMPANY. In the wagon bed were barrels of flour, sacks of meal, and crates of canned peaches and beans. On that particular afternoon, Murfreesboro was as quiet and sleepy as any one of a hundred other midsized southern towns. A couple of miles to the northwest was the site of the Battle of Stones River, one of the ugliest of the Civil War – an indecisive blood bath that had killed more than 24,000 men. On the Murfreesboro square was a monument to the Confederate dead, and there were still enough surviving veterans in the county that every year they donned their old gray uniforms and gathered for a reunion around the monument to listen to fiddle music, speeches, and ceremonial cannon firing. Now, as the wagon pulled onto the square, the driver reached under the seat and pulled out an old, open-backed Slingerland banjo. As he pulled up to one of the square's four grocery stores, he began to sing at the top of his voice and to wham the banjo. "I've brought you corn, corn, corn!" he crowed. "And I've got beans, beans, beans!" The booming voice carried across the square, and the courthouse whittlers and sleepy gaffers looked up and smiled. Uncle Dave Macon was in town, and he was making his rounds. The stock boys soon unloaded the wagon, and the driver turned around and began heading back down Main Street, to his base some eight miles out in the countryside. As he passed under the lush maple trees and the old pre-Civil War houses that lined the street, he began singing a real song.

I'm gwine down town,
Gonna get me a sack of flour,
Gwine to cook it every hour,
Keep my skillet good and greasy
All the time, time, time,
Keep my skillet good and greasy all the time.

I'm going to the hills,
For to get me a jug of brandy,
Gonna give it all to Mandy,
Keep her good and drunk and woozy
All the time, time, time,
Keep her good and drunk
And woozy all the time.

"UNCLE DAVE MACON WAS A LARGER-THAN-LIFE MYTH. HE KNEW EVERY BUTTON TO PUNCH TO MAKE US ALL LIKE HIM. AND, AS IT IS WITH A SHOWMAN, THERE WAS A LOT OF PIZAZZ THERE — THERE WAS A LOT OF POOF AND BLOW DUST, AND WOOFLE DUST, AS ACCORDING TO UNCLE DAVE HIMSELF. BUT HEY, THAT'S WHY WE GO TO SHOWS IN THE FIRST PLACE. WE WANT A LITTLE WOOFLE DUST ON US."
—MARTY STUART

OPPOSITE, FROM LEFT: UNCLE DAVE MACON, 1938; AN EARLY DAVE MACON SONGBOOK, WITH A COVER PORTRAIT FROM 1886.

during Henry Ford's contests, dies at age eighty-three. **1932** WLS moves its Barn Dance to the Eighth Street Theater, a much larger venue. **1933** NBC widely broadcasts a half hour of the WLS Barn Dance as the National Barn Dance. WWVA in Wheeling, West Virginia, airs its first Wheeling Jamboree. On May 26 in New York City, thirty-five-year-old Jimmie Rodgers dies of a tuberculosis-related hemorrhage. **1934** The Decca label rejuvenates record sales; its thirty-five-cent discs, including titles by Stuart Hamblen, Jimmie Davis, and the Carter Family, are far more affordable than the seventy-five-cent standard. The ensuing price war stimulates business. WBT in Charlotte, North Carolina, first airs its Crazy Barn Dance. **1935** America's favorite singing cowboy, Gene Autry, stars in 'Tumbling Tumbleweeds'; the title song is a hit single, one of many Autry will score after 1931's "That Silver-Haired Daddy of Mine." Patsy Montana becomes the first female artist to sell one million records with "I Want to Be a Cowboy's Sweetheart." **1937** Pee Wee King and His Golden West Cowboys first play the Grand Ole Opry. **1939** NBC broadcasts a portion of the Grand Ole Opry as the Prince Albert Show. **1952** Lefty Frizzell releases 'Lefty Frizzell Sings the Songs of Jimmie Rodgers' on the heels of his giant career song, "If You've Got the Money I've Got the Time." **1960** Folklorist Ralph Rinzler discovers Doc Watson in Deep Gap, North Carolina. **1963** Maybelle Carter appears at the Newport Folk Festival. She returns there with fellow Carter Family member and cousin Sara Carter for a performance in 1967. These appearances expose a whole new audience to the Carter Family and help renew interest in oldtime country. **1969** Merle Haggard releases 'Same Train, a Different Time,' an album of Jimmie Rodgers covers. The following year he will release 'A Tribute to the Best Damn Fiddle Player in the World (or, My Salute to Bob Wills).' **1972** California-based, country-folk-rock act the Nitty Gritty Dirt Band releases 'Will the Circle Be Unbroken,' a gold-selling pop hit album that will spend thirty-two weeks on the chart. The double LP features performances by Maybelle Carter, Roy Acuff, Merle Travis, and others. **1997** Bob Dylan produces and assembles 'The Songs of Jimmie Rodgers – A Tribute,' an album of Rodgers covers performed Jerry Garcia, Dwight Yoakam, Steve Earle, U2's Bono, and Dylan himself, among others. The Rock and Roll Hall of Fame and Museum hosts a tribute concert and symposium honoring Rodgers and celebrating the centennial of his birth.

1736 Hanover County, Virginia, hosts America's first fiddling contest. **1830** Virginia native Joel (a.k.a. Joe) Sweeney copyrights the five-string banjo. **1839** Swiss singing group the Tyrolese Rainer Family tours the United States. Their alpine harmonies and yodeling inspire the formation of like-minded singing groups in rural America. **1877** Thomas Edison files patents on the cylinder-playing phonograph. **1887** Emile Berliner, who had earlier invented the microphone, invents the first gramophone, a flat record player with an acoustic horn. **1903** On September 27, a mail train on the Southern Railroad crashes, killing several people. The event becomes the subject of Vernon Dalhart's 1924 single "The Wreck of the Old '97," one of country music's best-selling records. **1919** The Gibson company markets Lloyd Loar's new, easy-to-hold mandolin, which sells extremely well in rural America. **1920** Westinghouse launches commercial radio in Pittsburgh. **1922** On March 16, Atlanta's radio station WSB makes its on-air debut. Fiddle players Eck Robertson and Henry Gilliland make the first country records for New York's Victor label. **1923** On January 4, WBAP in Fort Worth, Texas, broadcasts its first live "barn dance." Robertson becomes the first musician to promote his work via radio; he performs two of his recorded songs on WSB. Fiddlin' John Carson cuts "The Little Old Log Cabin in the Lane," which is arguably the first-ever country record. **1924** On April 19, Chicago's WLS broadcasts a show of live, rural music; the program will turn into the WLS Barn Dance. **1925** The term "hillbilly" is coined by Al Hopkins and his group of mountain musicians. Nashville's WSM radio begins broadcasting a barn dance program. **1926** The National Broadcasting Company launches the NBC Radio Network. Uncle Dave Macon becomes the first star of the WSM Barn Dance. Henry Ford presents several national fiddling contests. **1927** In August, Jimmie Rodgers and the Carter Family audition for Victor Records' Ralph Peer in Bristol, Tennessee; this results in Rodgers's "Sleep, Baby, Sleep" and the Carters' "Bury Me Under the Weeping Willow." George Hay rechristens the WSM Barn Dance the Grand Ole Opry. **1929** The Great Depression flattens the recording industry. Rodgers appears in Columbia Pictures' fifteen-minute film 'The Singing Brakeman.' **1931** Fiddling legend Uncle Jimmy Thompson, who debuted on WSM in 1925 and gained acclaim

Saturday night throughout the South and beyond, particularly in the Twenties, Thirties, and Forties, thousands of households – white and black – listened intently to the program. Musicians counted on learning new songs and picking up ideas from the Opry performers. The number of would-be musicians who were inspired to pick up the guitar or banjo or muster the courage to sing because of what they heard on the radio is impossible to calculate, but the total must be huge. An additional influence on American roots music was the phonograph, which brought music from far away to the intimate confines of one's home. Songs could be played over and over at any time of the day or night and embraced emotionally by everyone in the household, not just the musician in it.

With "roots music" being collected, distributed, and commercialized by a growing number of entrepreneurs and scholars, a profound change occurred in the American music tradition. For decades, folk music had memorialized our history and cultural diversity and helped define our national identity. That task was now also assumed by American roots music.

So what, then, constitutes a roots musician? Such an artist is conscious of being part of the American music tradition. Often he or she feels a personal responsibility to carry on that tradition. The roots artist absorbs the cultural attributes of the music's origins, while eschewing the always shifting swings in contemporary pop culture. He or she adheres to and respects the dress, speech, and social habits that are part of the roots artist's community. Finally, the roots artist writes and sings songs that reflect such themes as gender and class relationships, regional and historical issues, and racial and ethnic tensions. The roots music artist is, essentially, the chronicler of the ongoing story of America told through song.

There are also few fences that separate roots music from the popular music that has evolved from it. For one thing, roots music has always been "popular" within its defined community. And since the advent of the recording industry at the beginning of the last century, more than a few roots musicians have made a decent living by recording their music and offering it up for sale. As far back as the 1920s when the Carter Family, Jimmie Rodgers, and Blind Lemon Jefferson – to name just three American roots music icons – made records, commerce has been a part of the roots music story and continues to be so today. These days it is not uncommon for roots musicians and rock stars to share the same bill, minimizing the differences between popular and roots music. The radio industry uses an equally earthy term to describe roots-influenced music: "Americana."

Thanks to the reissue of hundreds of old, long-out-of-print albums on compact disc – another technological advance that is tied to the roots music story – today there is more of this music available than at any other time. The earliest country recordings, the first jazz and blues records, obscure prison and work songs, black spirituals, and white cowboy songs are stacked in CD megastores near the latest pop, rock, and hip-hop hits. If that certain recording you are searching for is not at your favorite store, it's a good bet you'll find it on the Internet, the most recent technological innovation impacting American roots music. And if all that wasn't enough, what hasn't been

rereleased might have been reinterpreted. Thus, if you can't get a certain roots music song from the original artist, you might be able to find it redone by a contemporary roots musician with the resultant sonic clarity of the modern recording studio.

In the past quarter century, interest in American roots music has risen dramatically. Festivals featuring various roots music forms occur across the country every spring, summer, and fall. The Chicago Blues Festival alone draws more than one hundred thousand fans to Grant Park on the shores of Lake Michigan each June. In New Orleans, the city's annual Jazz and Heritage Festival attracts an equal number of roots music lovers to its fairgrounds and clubs. Fiddlers' conventions in the Carolinas, folk festivals in New Jersey and Pennsylvania, and Native American powwows on reservations, back east and out west, not only celebrate American roots music in the Twenty-First Century but also help to preserve our rich music heritage, despite the increasing encroachment of cultural homogenization.

American Roots Music is surely not an exhaustive version of this country's roots music history. Our book does not try to account for every major artist or musical development that occurred in the Twentieth Century. To accomplish such a goal would take volumes. Instead, *American Roots Music* presents overviews of each of the major roots music genres, featuring artists whose work is emblematic of their times and whose stories are meaningful and historically significant. These musicians' recordings continue to stand out above many others, even though they may have been made fifty or sixty years ago.

If *American Roots Music* is considered a "history," one that documents the past hundred years in musical terms, let it be known that America's roots music history is a living, ongoing history. All of the music forms presented in this book are alive and well; they've lived in the past, they live in the present, and all indications are they will live in the future.

As much as possible, the essays in this book reflect the *American Roots Music* television series. We've asked the writers to translate the general themes of the documentary into words and concise chapters, which, taken together, unfold the American roots music saga. The authors of these essays are among the best and most knowledgeable authorities in American roots music. Their perspective and understanding of its history, as well as their keen ears and deep connection with American music culture, provide a wealth of insight that you, the reader, will no doubt find compelling and valuable. Also in these pages you'll hear from the musicians themselves, who describe their work and the music of those who influenced them.

Ultimately, *American Roots Music* is meant to be a guide to what we, the editors, hope will be your journey through the many roots music forms that came of age in this country last century. We have taken such a journey, and we can attest that the rewards are many.

ROBERT SANTELLI
APRIL 2001

INTRODUCTION The sounds are as sweet as mountain air: the lonesome drift of a fiddle, the easy pluck of banjo strings, the wailing notes from a harmonica, a romping guitar chord, the thump of a homemade drum, a vocal moan. On the surface they seem so simple, even fleeting, as if they were created to celebrate only the moment or to capture a particular emotion, like love or loss. Yet almost always they're drawn from a deeper place and, when bound together, become part of a powerful tradition. These sounds, in all their variety and beauty, are America.

This book is the story of such sounds and the songs they come from and the people who wrote and sang them and the culture that inspired them. It is a story with many twists of plot, countless characters, and settings both rural and urban. In this story, musical strains cross boundaries and influence one another. One artist borrows from another, who borrows from yet another. Songs are reshaped with altered lyrics and fresh solos. Reinventions are plentiful, even unstoppable.

Call this the story of American roots music. Whether it was made on a back porch in a West Virginia holler, at a house party in Chicago, in a Mississippi juke joint, at a bluegrass cutting contest in eastern Kentucky, beyond the bayou in Cajun back country, or in a black Baptist church in North Carolina or Newark, New Jersey, this music has warmed us, enlightened us, informed us, touched us, defined us. We may not buy it in bulk, as we do our popular music. But we respect it and cherish it, much like we do tales told by a family elder or a poem with great meaning. And when we listen to it, we take great pride in its diversity and history, and we allow it to enter our soul and become an indispensable part of us.

Despite this, trying to further define the term "American roots music" is difficult and daunting. After all, since such American music forms as jazz, rock & roll, and hip-hop are practically undefinable,

why would one as vague as American roots music be any different?

Even the term "folk music," which is intimately connected to roots music, is a challenge to define. Pete Seeger, who's called a great American "folksinger," dislikes the term. It has too much baggage, he says, and he's right. Over the years, folklorists have written full-blown essays in prestigious journals describing the music in great detail. Some of them made folk music and its culture seem all too complex and uninviting — at least to the nonacademic audience — and lost the spirit of the music in the process. At the same time, the media routinely labeled anyone playing an acoustic guitar or banjo a "folksinger," in effect abusing the term and making it little more than a cliché.

When music writers realized how badly worn the term "folk music" had become, many abandoned it. In its place they created American roots music in the 1980s and used it as a catchall phrase to describe any American music form that had influenced pop music and was a "root" of rock & roll, or as a simple substitute for folk. Instead of defining American roots music, many journalists just referred to it. The term worked quite nicely in print.

But any book titled *American Roots Music* must proclaim its territory. To start, American roots music might be defined as an updated and expanded evolution of American folk music. Alan Jabbour, one of the essayists in this book, says, "The terms 'folk music' and 'roots music' are loose nets that overlap one another." Noted folk expert John Cohen believes any differences that might exist between folk and roots music "are so blurred as to make them practically meaningless."

Folksongs and folk-music styles are passed on by oral tradition — hearing a song, memorizing it, and recreating it for a specific community. Roots music is passed on in the same way — but it is not the only way. Beginning in the early Twentieth Century, roots music began to embrace technology, using it to popularize itself, commercialize its artists, and become distinctly American in scope and breadth. The term had yet to be created, but the major "roots music" forms — blues, hillbilly, country, zydeco, Cajun, Tejano, Native American, and rockabilly — were either already born or about to be.

Roots music relies on a "directness" in addressing its audience, according to Charles Wolfe, another essayist in the book. The advent of sound reproduction in the form of recordings and of radio, television, and amplification enabled roots artists to be powerfully direct and far reaching. In addition, the mass production of the automobile and the increase of better transportation systems — railroads and highways — made it easy for regional roots musicians to travel and perform far beyond their communities. This new technology and mobility created new audiences for music that previously had been confined by ethnic, racial, and geographic boundaries.

Radio did wonders for roots music, spreading localized sounds far and wide. The influence, for example, of the Grand Ole Opry radio show is astounding. Each

filming Cajun Mardi Gras celebrations in southwest Louisiana, then moved on to other areas including the Mississippi Delta, the Lakota Reservation in South Dakota, the Smoky Mountains of eastern Tennessee, and into cities with strong roots-music traditions such as Chicago, Nashville, Memphis, San Antonio, and New Orleans. Although most of the work days spanned more than fourteen hours, it was a joy to interact with the wonderful musicians who participated in this project. Our job was made easier by the wisdom we received from those consultants who joined us in the field and/or advised us by telephone and e-mail throughout our travels.

For me, *American Roots Music* is a dream come true. Born in 1950, I became interested in music as the folk revival of the early 1960s gained prominence. Beginning at age twelve, I made treks with friends to New York's Greenwich Village, where I was lucky enough to see performances by Mississippi John Hurt and Mississippi Fred McDowell. When I was sixteen, Lee Hays, a founding member of the Almanac Singers and the Weavers, moved to Croton-on-Hudson, where I grew up. His house became my second home. I worked for Lee, mostly as a gardener, but stayed on into the night, listening to incredible stories about Woody Guthrie, Lead Belly, Sonny Terry and Brownie McGhee, the Almanacs, the Weavers, and others.

It was at Lee's house that I met Pete Seeger, a frequent visitor. We first worked together on several small documentaries for New York's public television station, WNET, about the citizens' fight Pete was championing to clean up the polluted Hudson River. Pete and his wife, Toshi, and their family and I have remained friends for the last thirty years. Their grandson Kitama Jackson helped us last summer as an intern and was a wonderful addition to the team.

In 1979, Lee Hays wanted to reunite the Weavers, and my mentor, documentary filmmaker George Stoney, and I joined forces with their manager, Harold Leventhal, to film the reunion of original Weavers members Pete Seeger, Lee Hays, Ronnie Gilbert, and Fred Hellerman at Carnegie Hall, which became the focus of the film *The Weavers: Wasn't That a Time!* Harold had also managed Woody Guthrie, Pete Seeger, and Arlo Guthrie and was one of the most trusted and important impresarios of the folk scene. He let me become involved with his wonderful musical family, and his friendship is one of my greatest joys. Over the next fifteen years, Harold, my wife, Ginger, and I produced a number of television programs together, including the musical documentary *A Vision Shared: A Tribute to Woody Guthrie and Lead Belly,* which helped to raise the money that enabled the Smithsonian Institution to purchase and rerelease the Folkways Records catalogue, one of the most significant storehouses of American roots music.

In 1982, Alan Lomax asked me to serve as his cameraman on the New Orleans and Appalachian legs of one of his final music-collecting trips. Although sometimes a difficult man, Alan was a genius at finding music and getting musicians to talk about their craft. He was perhaps the leading architect of the folk revival and one of the most important figures in realizing the significance of America's folk music. It was a privilege to know and work with Alan, and I am certain that my work on *American Roots Music* was shaped by my brief association with him.

As we continued to shoot and edit the *American Roots Music* series, this book was compiled and edited with loving care by two very trusted members of the *American Roots Music* team: Robert Santelli and Holly George-Warren. A blues expert and longtime chronicler of American roots music, Bob helped orchestrate our first trip through the Mississippi Delta and has been a key advisor to the project since its inception. He served as the vice president of education and public programming at the Rock and Roll Hall of Fame and Museum before moving to Seattle, where he is deputy director of public programs at Experience Music Project. Holly George-Warren is the editor of Rolling Stone Press and an equally knowledgeable authority on American roots music, particularly country & western. Together with talented designer Beth Middleworth and the staff of Rolling Stone Press, they have interpreted the main themes of *American Roots Music* onto the printed page. While the television series is limited by time and the archival footage available, this book can fill in details about the music and performers not covered in the series. Use the book as a compendium to the television series and the CD, DVD, and home video sets, and vice versa.

American roots music doesn't have to be connected to popular music or be called an antecedent of rock & roll to validate its existence. During this project, I learned that many forms of this nation's roots musics continue to thrive in the communities from which they emerged. Thanks to a multitude of clubs, festivals, powwows, and music conventions, as well as independent and major record labels and small magazines, American roots music is within easy reach of us all.

The breadth of American roots music continues to evolve as new immigrant cultures bring new sounds to the "gumbo" of American music. Salsa, which evolved simultaneously in the Caribbean and the United States, had a tremendous influence on the popularization of Latin music on a worldwide basis. Korean music or melodies from Cameroon that are being blended with existing American music forms today could become the blues or bluegrass of tomorrow.

Should you want to further explore *American Roots Music,* please visit the excellent collections housed by our partner institutions for the series. Perhaps the best way to experience this music is live. Festivals and nightclubs often feature American roots music in colorful and contrasting geographic regions throughout the country. As an added bonus, they offer dancing and regional food as well as opportunities to meet and sometimes even play with the musicians. Enjoy.

JIM BROWN
PRODUCER/DIRECTOR,
'AMERICAN ROOTS MUSIC'
MARCH 2001

PREFACE One hundred years ago, few Americans were aware that a musical and cultural explosion was about to take place. At the time, it was not widely recognized that this relatively new nation had a folk music of its own, but as the Twentieth Century progressed, a number of uniquely American genres of folk music such as blues, gospel, country, Western swing, Cajun, zydeco, Tejano, and Native American became recognized and popularized.

By 1920, folk music originally passed on by oral tradition (hearing a song, learning it, and playing or singing it to others) was now being published, recorded, and broadcast on the radio. Simultaneously, American folk music began to be collected, promoted, distributed, and commercialized by an increasing number of entrepreneurs and scholars. Talented folk musicians could now earn a living playing music and were enjoying increased popularity and recognition beyond the geographic and ethnic boundaries of the communities that had fostered their music. These were exciting times that completely changed the way vernacular music was listened to and played and contributed greatly to the new recombinations in what we refer to as American roots music.

Having produced and directed a number of American music documentaries and television concerts during the last twenty-five years, I was aware that many of the great pioneers and innovators of American roots music had been documented on film. Much of their recorded work has been catalogued and reissued by record companies. Unfortunately, the film footage of these musicians lay scattered in various private and public archives around the world. Probably only a handful of filmmakers, collectors, and record producers were aware of the extent of this dispersed body of work, and I feared that future generations might not ever get to see it. Several years ago, I began to talk to friends about ways that this material could be consolidated in a documentary series that would chronicle one of the most exciting developments in American music.

Bill Ivey, chairman of the National Endowment for the Arts and an ethnomusicologist, intimately understood the importance of roots music in American culture. Discussions with Bill in the fall of 1998 led to what at first was a small Chairman's Action Grant from the NEA. This allowed for the formation of a "dream team" of scholars and institutions with expertise in American roots music to collect, evaluate, and help orchestrate this material into a television series. This team includes our partner institutions — the Library of Congress, the Smithsonian Institution, the Rock and Roll Hall of Fame and Museum, the Country Music Hall of Fame and Museum, and Experience Music Project — as well as some of the leading administrators, scholars, and writers in American music, including Barry Jean Ancelet, Horace Boyer, Robert Cantwell, John Cohen, Pete Daniel, David Evans, Ben Filene, Ray Funk, Peter Guralnick, Alan Jabbour, Paul Kingsbury, Guy Logsdon, Bill Malone, Dave Marsh, Manuel Peña, Bernice Johnson Reagon, Robert Santelli, Ann Allen Savoy, Pete Seeger, Tony Seeger, Terry Stewart, Charles Wolfe, and Kyle Young. This project is very much the result of their expertise and experience. As you will see, many of these valued advisors are also the authors of the following chapters.

Nearly every artist we focus on first learned music via the folk tradition within their communities yet eventually went on to have their music commercialized through radio, records, and concerts. Collectively, we decided to adapt a relatively new term, "American roots music," to describe the artists and music featured in the series. American roots music seemed less confusing than the sometimes contradictory definitions that surround American folk music. Regardless of the terminology, the television series and the book focus on the innovators of the unique American music genres that emerged from folk traditions during the last one hundred years and their relationships to the new recording and broadcasting technology.

As the *American Roots Music* project grew, the team began to plan the television series and ancillary components such as this book, CD, DVD, and home video sets, a database, and curricular materials that will take this material into schools and libraries. Interacting with more than 150 archives in the United States and Europe, our head researcher, Barbara Miller, spent most of the last three years locating the historic footage featured throughout the series. The work of the *American Roots Music* project was made easier by *American Folklore Films and Videotapes: An Index,* an important early filmography of American roots music compiled by Judy Peiser and Bill Ferris, the latter a leading blues scholar and champion of American roots music who is now chairman of the National Endowment for the Humanities.

To date, the *American Roots Music* project has been funded by the National Endowment for the Arts, the Public Broadcasting Service, the Corporation for Public Broadcasting, Experience Music Project, AT&T, the New York State Council on the Arts, and the Samuel Rubin Foundation. Also, early in the stages of the project, the visionary entrepreneur Chris Blackwell, who owns RykoPalm, offered his help in making *American Roots Music* available to the public through CD, DVD, and home video releases. Needless to say, none of our work could have gone forward without this important financial support.

Shortly after we began the *American Roots Music* project, Jeff Rosen, a roots-music enthusiast who has represented Bob Dylan for nearly twenty years, agreed to join the team as a producer. Jeff and Bob gave us access to their vast private film and video collection of American roots musicians. Throughout this project, Jeff has contributed his wisdom on a myriad of creative and business matters as well as helped to keep us focused with his logic and humor. My friend Sam Pollard also agreed to come on board as a producer and supervising editor. Sam and I had previously collaborated on several musical documentaries. He is one of the most gifted filmmakers I know and is perhaps best known for his work with Spike Lee, as editor of six of his features and as coproducer of the award-winning documentary *Four Little Girls.* He also was an executive producer for Blackside's wonderful series on African-American culture, *I'll Make Me a World.*

After three years of planning and six revisions of a series outline, we began production of *American Roots Music.* Our tireless associate producer, Sarah Cullen, and I spent most of the year 2000 on the road producing the contemporary performance and interview documentary footage that is used to complement the archival material. We started by

Above: Bonnie Raitt,
Mississippi Fred McDowell,
and friends, Philadelphia
Folk Festival, 1970

Songs and Stories

of

At Age of Sweet Sixteen

Uncle Dave Macon

Uncle Dave Macon

The upstanding townsfolk smiled and shook their heads, amused at the old man whom they regarded as a likeable but eccentric character. They had no idea where Macon had learned such an odd song — he in fact had learned it from a black gristmill worker some ten years before. Nor did they have any idea that Macon would, in five short years, become one of the first southern singers to put his music on phonograph records, or that he would, in 1925, become one of the first stars of a new medium called radio. No one could have guessed that he would help define a new style of art that would be called country music, that he would travel to Hollywood to put his antics on film, or that he would someday have a huge music festival named in his honor that would attract forty thousand fans to Murfreesboro.

People who were young kids when they watched Uncle Dave sing as he delivered grocery supplies would still remember the scene when they were doddering senior citizens in their eighties. It was an example of grassroots music at its most basic — a part of the fabric of everyday life, a little touch of art to brighten for a moment the hard lives of working-class Americans. And it came from the last decade before mass media would inexorably change the face of American music and the way people fit it into their lives. In the 1920s American roots music would collide head-on with the twin forces of radio and phonograph records, and all three would be forever changed.

For much of the Nineteenth Century, most Americans were not aware of anything called "folk music." To be sure, the music was there, scattered in great plentitude in every corner of the land, but most people took it for granted, like wildflowers in the spring or maples turning colors in the fall. But with the dawn of the Twentieth Century, with the closing of the frontier and the raft of new inventions by people like Thomas Edison, Americans were becoming more conscious of their past and of their "heritage." By the second decade of the new century, there were a number of things going on that were calling attention to the musical traditions.

Down in Georgia, fiddlers from all over the state would every fall pack up a plug of old homespun tobacco, gather up their favorite blue tick hound, and head for Atlanta, where they would gather in the Municipal Auditorium and compete for three days in a huge contest to see who could play the best "Mississippi Sawyer" or "Cackling Hen." Over in the Appalachians, a dapper British folksong scholar named Cecil Sharp was traveling around by foot to hamlets like Rocky Fork and Big Laurel and documenting songs like "Barbara Allen" and "Come All You Fair and Tender Ladies," old ballads that the first Scotch-Irish settlers in the mountains had brought with them from across the sea. Out in Texas, people were reading a new book by a young Harvard man

named John Lomax called *Cowboy Songs and Other Frontier Ballads* (1910); it was the first real book-length collection of American folksongs and preserved classics like "Home on the Range" and "The Old Chisholm Trail."

Down in Lawrenceburg, Tennessee, about one hundred miles from where Uncle Dave Macon drove his wagon, a gospel-music publisher named James D. Vaughan was issuing a little paperbacked shape-note songbook called *Praise Evangel* (1919), the most recent in a yearly series of such books that had already sold almost two million copies. To sell his books, Vaughan had hit upon the idea of hiring

well-trained quartets to travel around the country giving free concerts at local churches, and by now people were liking the idea of gospel-quartet singing almost as much as the lively new gospel songs in the books. In the Blue Ridge Mountains around places like Galax, Virginia, young mountain musicians were learning how to play an instrument that many had never seen before, the guitar, and figuring out how to meld it into the classic string band that up until now had often consisted of just the banjo and fiddle. To be sure, many families still got their music when they assembled in the parlor around the old upright piano and sang the newest sheet music hits

"MY DAD WAS A MUSICIAN — HE HAD A BAND THAT SOUNDED
LIKE BLUEGRASS. THEY TRIED TO COPY AND SOUND AN
AWFUL LOT LIKE THE OLD-FASHIONED DELMORE BROTHERS.
HE DIED WHEN I WAS NINE MONTHS OLD. MOTHER SAID
THAT BEFORE HE DIED, HE WAS SITTING AT THE PIANO WITH
ME ON HIS KNEES AND SAID, 'GIVE HER MUSIC LESSONS. I
WANT HER TO PLAY THIS THING WHEN I'M GONE.' I STILL
HAVE MY FATHER'S INSTRUMENTS — A MANDOLIN AND A
GUITAR THAT WAS HIS. MY FATHER AND HIS MOTHER, I
GUESS, WERE MY BIGGEST INSPIRATION. SHE PLAYED ORGAN
AND SHE TAUGHT THE OLD [SACRED] HARP SINGINGS, WHERE
YOU TEACH THE NOTES AND NOT THE WORDS. MY GRANDMA
TAUGHT THE FA-SO-LA SINGINGS, WHICH IS WHERE THEY
TEACH YOU TO SING 'DO-FA-MI-RE' — YOU SING ALL THE
NOTES AND NEVER THE WORDS." —TAMMY WYNETTE

Cat Horn Band

OPPOSITE: INSTRUCTION MANUAL, CIRCA 1880. THIS PAGE: INFORMAL MUSIC GROUPS
FORMED THROUGHOUT THE RURAL SOUTH DURING THE EARLY TWENTIETH CENTURY. MOST
NEVER FOUND AN AUDIENCE OUTSIDE THEIR IMMEDIATE ENVIRONS.

The first shot in the media revolution occurred on November 2, 1920, when the first commercially licensed radio station, KDKA in Pittsburgh, made its debut broadcast by announcing the results of the Harding-Cox presidential election. Within months, new commercial stations were popping up around the country like dandelions after a spring rain. Some were a little bizarre — an early Washington, D.C., station was licensed to a priest and boasted the call letters WJSV: "Will Jesus Save Virginia." Others went to big commercial enterprises, like Chicago's WLS, owned by Sears and standing for "World's Largest Store." Still others were licensed to insurance companies, like Nashville's WSM — standing for "We Shield Millions," the slogan of the owners, the National Life and Accident Insurance Company. By 1922 and 1923, most major cities could boast of a radio station, and in the uncluttered airwaves of the time, people routinely picked up signals from hundreds of miles away.

One effect the popularity of the new radios had was to knock the bottom out of phonograph-record sales. The flat 78 rpm records had been around since the turn of the century, but record companies saw them as playthings for well-to-do families of the time; they featured a lot of light opera, pieces by Sousa's Band, vocal solos by Caruso, and barbershop harmonies by the Peerless Quartet. Now, suddenly, people found they could hear music free on the radio; why buy records for seventy-five cents apiece? Desperate to maintain sales, the record companies began casting about for new markets. They stumbled onto one in 1920, when the Okeh label released a song called "Crazy Blues" by a vaudeville singer named Mamie Smith. It was the first blues record by an African-American artist, and it became a bestseller by appealing to a hitherto untapped record market: black Americans.

In June 1923, the same man who had recorded Mamie Smith — Ralph Peer, a thirty-one-year-old, moon-faced A&R (artists & repertoire) chief who had been born in Kansas City, Missouri, but now worked out of New York — found himself in Atlanta looking for

from New York, or when they went to the local vaudeville theater to see the old song-and-dance men do songs like "I'm Looking for the Bully of the Town." But they were also starting to notice what would later be called grassroots music.

talent. A local dealer promised to buy five hundred copies if Peer would record the town character, Fiddlin' John Carson — a fifty-five-year-old former millworker who had won fame at the Municipal Auditorium's annual fiddling contest. Peer agreed and in a temporary studio recorded Carson playing the fiddle unaccompanied and singing "The Little Old Log Cabin in the Lane." "I thought his singing was pluperfect awful," Peer admitted years later. But he released the record — and was surprised to see it become a modest hit.

Within months, the race was on as the major record companies scrambled to tap into this new market of working-class southerners. At first they didn't even know what to call the music: Some ads mentioned "oldtime southern tunes," others "hill country music," others "oldtime music." Victor called its series "Native American Melodies." In 1924, a Texan singer working in New York, Vernon Dalhart, actually had a nationwide hit with a train-wreck ballad called "The Wreck of the Old '97." He followed this up in 1925 with a topical "broadside" ballad called "The Death of Floyd Collins," about the miner who attracted widespread attention when he was trapped in a Kentucky sand cave; this record sold more than three hundred thousand copies, and if any of the record companies had lingering doubts about the marketability of southern music, these reservations were put to rest.

Following Ralph Peer's lead, the companies began sending talent scouts into the South to hunt up and record on-location fiddlers, singers, banjo players, and gospel quartets. In the summer of 1927, Peer hit pay dirt once again. In an old hat factory doubling as a temporary studio, in the Virginia-Tennessee border town of Bristol, he discovered the two acts that were to dominate country music's first decade: a singing trio called the Carter Family and a former railroad brakeman named Jimmie Rodgers.

The Carters were actually locals; they lived in a lush mountain valley up in southwest Virginia, about thirty miles from Bristol, where they had all grown up and learned the old ballads and gospel songs of their ancestors. They consisted of A.P. Carter; his wife, Sara; and Sara's teenage cousin Maybelle. Sara did most of the lead singing, played a little multistringed mountain instrument called the Autoharp, and played guitar; Maybelle played lead guitar and sang. A.P. "bassed in" on occasion but mainly served as the manager and song-finder. When Ralph Peer first met them, he was not impressed by their plain country dress and manner. But when he heard them sing, his doubts vanished. "As soon as I heard Sara's voice," he recalled years later, "I knew it was going to be wonderful." It was. During that first session, the Carters cut classics like "Bury Me Under the Weeping Willow," "The Storms Are on the Ocean," and "Single Girl." In the months to follow, the group recorded dozens

"THE CARTER FAMILY WAS ONE OF THE FIRST WAYS THAT I STARTED LEARNING OTHER SONGS. I STARTED GETTING SOME OF THEIR RECORDS, AND I'D HEAR THEIR MUSIC ON THE RADIO. AT ONE TIME THEY WERE ON WBT IN CHARLOTTE [NORTH CAROLINA]. SO THAT'S WHERE I GUESS I FIRST GOT EXPOSED TO SOME REAL COUNTRY [MUSIC]. I USED TO PLAY A LITTLE GUITAR AND TRY MAYBELLE'S STYLE OF PLAYING. THEIR PLAYING WAS IMPORTANT AS FAR AS MAKING ME ENJOY MUSIC." —EARL SCRUGGS

BELOW: THE EXTENDED CARTER FAMILY AT THEIR CLINCH VALLEY HOME IN 1941: A.P.: EZRA (MAYBELLE'S HUSBAND); MAYBELLE; ANITA, JUNE, AND HELEN (MAYBELLE AND EZRA'S THREE DAUGHTERS); SARA; FLO MILLARD (A.P. AND SARA'S GRANDDAUGHTER); GLADYS CARTER MILLARD (SARA AND A.P.'S DAUGHTER), MARGARET ADDINGTON (MAYBELLE'S MOTHER), AND JOE (A.P. AND SARA'S SON) (FROM LEFT)

of other songs that would become country and bluegrass standards: "Wildwood Flower," "Wabash Cannonball," "Keep on the Sunny Side," "Little Darling, Pal of Mine," "Worried Man Blues," "Will the Circle Be Unbroken" — a total of almost three hundred sides for every major record company from 1927 to 1941. "They didn't have gold records in those days," said pioneer Nashville music publisher Wesley Rose, "but if they had, the Carters would have had a wall full." It was these records that really created the model for country harmony, and it was Maybelle's guitar runs that defined country guitar playing for generations. (Known as the Carter lick, it involved picking the melody on the lower strings while strumming the chords on the higher ones.) Even after Sara and A.P. split up in the mid-Thirties, the family still performed and recorded together, winning additional fame by playing over-the-border radio "superstations" in the late Thirties. In later years, the Carter dynasty grew to include second, third, and even fourth generations of singers and songwriters, including Maybelle's daughter June, who would marry Johnny Cash.

Jimmie Rodgers, for his part, was anything but a mountain boy. He was born in 1897, hundreds of miles away from the Smoky Mountains, in the steamy flatland of Meridian, Mississippi, in the southeastern corner of the state. It was blues country, not ballad country, and Rodgers was soon trying to adopt African-American Delta blues styles to his own pliant voice. He spent his early days working on the railroad, traveling widely and absorbing all kinds of music of the time: jazz, vaudeville hokum, pop sentimental songs, and "yodel songs." By 1924, he had contracted tuberculosis and was forced to quit railroading; out of desperation, he decided to try to make it in music. Three years later he was singing with a string band in Asheville, North Carolina, when he heard of Peer's auditions. The band journeyed to Bristol but got into an argument the night before the audi-

tion, and its members tried out without Rodgers. With nothing to lose, Rodgers went on and attempted a record by himself — an old story song called "The Soldier's Sweetheart." Peer was not nearly as impressed as he had been with the Carters.

It wasn't until Rodgers appeared again at the Victor studios in Camden, New Jersey, several months later that he recorded what would be his career song: a powerful white blues called "Blue Yodel" but known to most fans as "T for Texas, T for Tennessee." This one did take off — it became one of the very few actual million-selling records from these early days. And during the years from 1928 through 1930, when the Depression stopped most people from buying records, Rodgers became the single biggest-selling artist in country music. His hits included wistful laments like "Treasures Untold" and "My Old Pal" and rough and rowdy send-ups like "In the Jailhouse Now," which had earlier been recorded by blues singer Blind Blake. There was a whole string of "blue yodels," white blues stanzas that, as opposed to Swiss- or cowboy-style yodels, featured a high, falsetto keening that Rodgers could break into with nonchalant ease. Destined to become country standards were "Waiting for a Train," "When the Cactus Is in Bloom," "Peach Picking Time Down in Georgia," and a half dozen others. Rodgers had no regular backup band, but on his records he experimented with all kinds of settings: Hawaiian guitar players, jug bands, black blues guitarists, jazzmen (including Louis Armstrong), small string orchestras, and, on one forgettable occasion, a musical saw player. He toured big-time vaudeville, made a Hollywood short, and did a benefit tour with legendary humorist Will Rogers. With his versatility and charisma, Jimmie Rodgers seemed poised to survive even the Depression and emerge as a

The Singing Brakeman.

"I'M GONNA MAKE THAT OLD GUITAR OF MINE OBEY ME YET, SO IT'LL TALK
WHEN I TALK, AND CRY OR LAUGH WHEN I DO." —JIMMIE RODGERS

OPPOSITE: JIMMIE RODGERS (LEFT) AND THE
CARTER FAMILY (MAYBELLE, A.P., AND SARA, FROM
LEFT), EARLY 1930S. ABOVE: RODGERS'S PUBLICITY
SHOT, LATE 1920S.

2

major singer on the national scene. But he couldn't survive the TB; on May 26, 1933, two days after his last recording session, he collapsed on the street in New York City and died a few hours later. In his wake came dozens of clones, some of whom emerged as major singers of the 1930s and 1940s: Gene Autry, who used his Rodgers imitations as a springboard to cowboy music and Hollywood; Cliff Carlisle, the Kentucky singer who specialized in double-entendre songs and whose blues sounded so authentic that some of his records were released in the "race" series (aimed at an African-American audience); and Bill Cox, whose topical songs like "NRA Blues" sold thousands of records. In later years, Rodgers's admirers included a young Ernest Tubb (who made his first records using Rodgers's guitar), Hank Snow, Lefty Frizzell, Merle Haggard, and Randy Travis. It was little wonder that Rodgers was the first member elected to the Country Music Hall of Fame (in 1961).

Rodgers and the Carters were by no means the only major recording stars in the 1920s and early 1930s. Galax, Virginia, carpenter Ernest Stoneman, whose 1924 recording of "The Titanic" was an early bestseller, recorded prolifically for virtually every major label and started a family dynasty that still survives in the country scene today. A colorful "supergroup" of instrumentalists called the Skillet Lickers took southern string-band music in new and complex directions, and their vocalist, a blind guitarist named Riley Puckett, was for a time the only serious rival to Rodgers. In North Carolina, banjoist and singer Charlie Poole made dozens of influential records like "Can I Sleep in Your Barn Tonight, Mister" and "White House Blues." A group of north Georgia gospel singers called Smith's Sacred Singers had huge sellers with recordings like "Where We'll Never Grow Old." Hundreds of other performers from every corner of the South made only a handful of records and disappeared into the mists of history, leaving behind a rich and complex legacy celebrated in modern collections like Harry Smith's 1952 set, *Anthology of American Folk Music.*

But with typically very low royalty rates, not many first-generation performers were able to make much of a living from their records. To do that, they needed the second new form of mass media: radio. As early as 1922, stations in Fort Worth and Atlanta were broadcasting some country music, and in 1924, WLS Chicago began a regular Saturday night music show that soon became the National Barn Dance. It was a springboard for singers like "the Kentucky Mountain Boy," Bradley Kincaid, who reportedly sang his signature song, the ballad "Barbara Allen," every single Saturday night for more than a year. Also popular on WLS were the Coon Creek Girls, an all-girl string band built around the awesome talents of Lily May Ledford, who played banjo and fiddle. But the radio show that would play the pivotal role in country music's development was founded on Nashville's WSM radio one cold November evening in 1925. On that night a seventy-eight-year-old white-bearded fiddler named Uncle Jimmy Thompson, who bragged that he could "fiddle the bugs off a tater vine," gave an impromptu and unscheduled performance that got station phones ringing off the hook.

By coincidence, WSM had just hired as its station manager George D. Hay, nicknamed "the Solemn Ole Judge," who had won fame as the announcer for WLS's Barn Dance show. One of Hay's biggest problems in downtown Chicago had been finding a supply of fiddlers and country singers, and he had already thought about how easy it would be to find such musicians in the hills and farmlands surrounding Nashville. The success of Thompson and his Civil War–era fiddle tunes convinced him that such a show would work, and in the following days, the mail arriving from all over the South convinced him — and his bosses at National Life — that there was a huge rural audience out there hungry for old-time music. In December 1925, he announced that WSM would start a regular "barn dance feature" every Saturday night. Within a few weeks, the plush WSM studios were awash with local musicians on Saturday evenings, all convinced that they were good enough to be on the show. "It was a good-natured riot," quipped Hay, but gradually the best ones were singled out and became regulars on the show — which in 1927 was renamed the Grand Ole Opry.

Hay was a master at public relations, and he lost no time in playing up the folksy, homespun image of the show. He kept in his desk a list of colorful band names and when a new group won a slot on the show, if its name was not colorful enough, Hay rechristened it. Thus Dr. Humphrey Bate's Augmented String Orchestra became the Possum Hunters. Paul Warmack's Square Dance Band became the Gully Jumpers. Though many of the musicians were factory workers or tradesmen, Hay had them pose for pictures in cornfields dressed in overalls, holding hound dogs or drinking moonshine. Some musicians resented this at first, but when they found that such image-making got them well-paying bookings, they swallowed their

pride and cashed their checks. Soon some of them were actually making a living with their music.

The Opry's first real star was Uncle Dave Macon, who had given up his freight-hauling business when a rival started using newfangled trucks; at the age of fifty-three, Uncle Dave started in show business, dazzling audiences with his banjo-picking styles, wowing them with his stage tricks, and knocking them off their seats with his jokes. "It ain't so much what you got," he liked to say. "It's what you can put out. And, boys, I can put out." He often traveled with Alabama's Delmore Brothers, the other biggest act on the show in the Thirties. Framed in precise, plaintive harmonies and complex guitar picking, the Delmores merged blues and gospel traditions to create master-works like "Brown's Ferry Blues." By the end of the Thirties, almost every act on the Grand Ole Opry was a full-time professional, and during the 1938–39 seasons, the show saw the addition of modern giants like Roy Acuff, Bill Monroe, and Pee Wee King.

Throughout the Depression, radio became the means by which most people heard country music. Few of the performers got on the big national networks headquartered in New York or Los Angeles, but many had regional and local sponsors that helped them pay the bills. Often these were patent medicines and nostrums of dubious pur-pose, such as Crazy Water Crystals, which sponsored dozens of

regional shows and had something to do with "promoting regular-ity." A new style of singing developed, one more suited to the sen-sitive radio microphones; gone was the booming singing of the vaudeville stage or tent show. In its place was the softer, more intri-cate brother-duet style of the Delmores, the Monroe Brothers, Karl and Harty, the Blue Sky Boys, and female counterparts like the Girls of the Golden West. Their songs were often unabashedly sentimen-tal ("I'm Just Here to Get My Baby Out of Jail," sang Karl and Harty) or religious ("What Would You Give in Exchange for Your Soul?" sang the Monroe Brothers). But they spoke to a generation and offered solace in a world of hard hits and hard times. Much had happened to the music in the twenty years since Uncle Dave had sung his ditties as he delivered his freight. But the purpose was still the same: to offer a glimpse of magic in the drudgery of everyday life.

"WE LISTENED TO THE GRAND OLE OPRY EVERY SATURDAY NIGHT. WHEN I WAS ABOUT THREE YEARS OLD, WE HAD A RADIO ON TOP OF THIS SHELF, AND IT PLAYED MUSIC IN THE MORNING. I THOUGHT WHEN WE WEREN'T LOOKING, LITTLE PEOPLE CAME OUT AND GOT INTO THE RADIO AND WOULD PLAY FOR US." —BUCK OWENS

OPPOSITE: ROY ACUFF AND THE SMOKY MOUNTAIN BOYS: LONNIE "PAP" WILSON, JESS EASTERDAY, RACHEL VEACH, ACUFF, BASHFUL BROTHER OSWALD (PETE KIRBY) (FROM LEFT). ABOVE: THE COON CREEK GIRLS, WHO FORMED IN 1937.

SINGING COWBOYS

There really were cowboys, of course, on the Nineteenth-Century frontier, and some of them did sing songs. Some, in fact, were the sources for John Lomax's *Cowboy Songs and Other Frontier Ballads.* But their singing was nothing like the smooth yodeling of later Hollywood cowboys; one early commentator recalled, "I never did hear a cowboy with a real good voice. If he had one to start with, he always lost it bawling at cattle." Nonetheless, a number of genuine cowboy singers made it into the recording studios during the 1920s and 1930s. One of the first was a young man named Carl T. Sprague, who had been raised on his uncle's ranch near Houston. Between 1925 and 1934, he recorded a good many of the old songs he had learned from his uncle for the Victor Talking Machine Company. His 1925 version of "When the Work's All Done This Fall" sold almost a million copies, making it the first hit record of cowboy music. A fellow Texan (born in Waxahachie in 1883) was Jules Verne Allen, who worked as a horse wrangler and a trail drive hand before he turned to show business and began billing himself as "the Original Singing Cowboy." In 1928, Victor's Ralph Peer set up a temporary field studio in El Paso to record Allen's first sides, including what was probably the original recording of "Home on the Range." A third early star was Harry McClintock, "Haywire Mac," whose experience included singing in mining camps in the Nevada gold fields, and whose 1928 recording of "Big Rock Candy Mountain" made it an American folk favorite. Indeed, the record was so pervasive that more than seventy years later it was featured in the soundtrack to the hit film *O Brother, Where Art Thou?*

But the man who came to epitomize the singing cowboy for most Americans was a young Tioga, Texas, native named Orvon Gene Autry. Growing up on the Texas and Oklahoma frontier, Autry never punched cows, but he did learn to sing in his granddad's rural church and while traveling with an oldtime medicine show. After being encouraged by humorist Will Rogers, he made his way to New York City where he began making records, often specializing in imitations of Jimmie Rodgers and in off-color white blues. But his first giant hit was a sentimental song called "That Silver-Haired Daddy of Mine" (1931), and it propelled him to national stardom on Chicago's WLS National Barn Dance. The station was owned by the giant mail-order catalogue company Sears and Roebuck, and soon the catalogues were advertising "Gene Autry Round-Up Guitars" for $9.98, as well as Gene Autry songbooks and Autry records. When Hollywood called him to try some roles for Republic Pictures in 1934, he was ready.

After a bizarre start in a strange science-fiction serial called *The Phantom Empire,* Autry embarked on a series of low-budget "two-reelers" designed for the Saturday matinee crowd. In these he introduced a number of classic songs, such as Billy Hill's haunting "The Last Round-Up," Bob Nolan's "Tumbling Tumbleweeds," and "Back in the Saddle Again," which Autry cowrote with Ray Whitley. Autry's success opened the floodgates to dozens of followers, including Roy Rogers (and his group the Sons of the Pioneers), Eddie Dean, Ray Whitley, Jimmy Wakely, and Tex Ritter. By the end of World War II, the initial impetus had spent its force, though remnants of the singing cowboy tradition survived on early television and on long-running radio shows like Autry's Melody Ranch. Today, such artists as Riders in the Sky and Don Edwards keep alive the music of the great singing cowboys Gene Autry and Roy Rogers.

"GENE AUTRY AND ROY ROGERS FOUND THAT PEOPLE, ESPECIALLY IN THE WEST, CELEBRATE THEIR HERITAGE THROUGH THE MUSIC OF THE WEST. THEY MARK THEIR IDENTITY OUT BY THESE SONGS WHICH, THEY FEEL, SPEAK DIRECTLY TO THEM. AND IT IS BECAUSE IT'S A LAND OF UNBELIEVABLE VARIETY AND SPECTACULAR BEAUTY, AND LAND THAT SEEMS TO PROMISE FREEDOM AND INDEPENDENCE." —DOUG GREEN

ABOVE: AUTRY'S 1936 FILM, 'THE BIG SHOW,' ALSO FEATURED THE WESTERN SINGING GROUP THE SONS OF THE PIONEERS; TEX RITTER'S FILM DEBUT WAS 1936'S 'SONG OF THE GRINGO.' OPPOSITE: AN EARLY AUTRY SONGBOOK, PUBLISHED IN 1932, AFTER "THAT SILVER-HAIRED DADDY OF MINE" (NOTE THE MISSPELLING ON THE SONGBOOK COVER) BECAME AUTRY'S FIRST HIT.

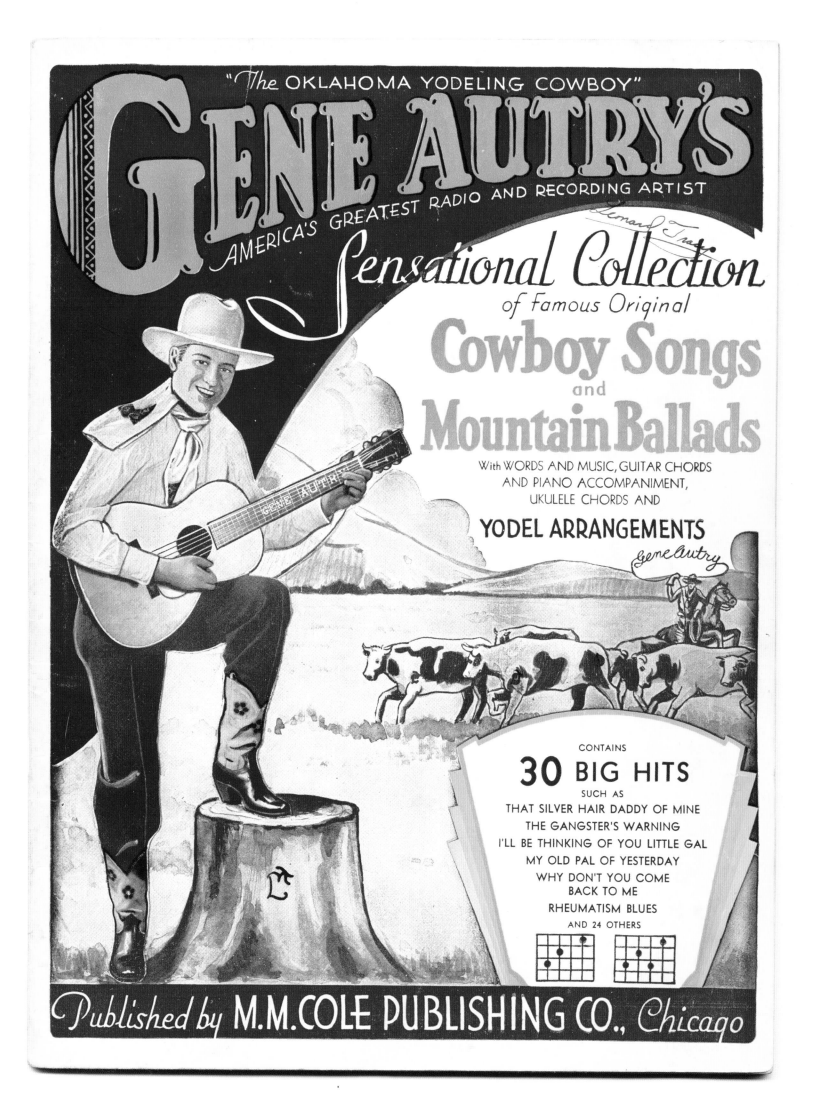

WESTERN SWING

It was a warm September day inside a dusty warehouse in downtown Dallas; Jimmie Rodgers had been dead a little over two years, and the Carter Family were looking at lists of their new records appearing in the fall edition of the Sears catalogue. The new commercial music that some were starting to call "hillbilly" was about to take a tremendous leap. Art Satherley, the head of the American Record Corporation, watched his new band as they unpacked for their first recording session. Here were fiddles and guitars and banjos, to be sure, but here too was a trombone player, and another member had a sax, and one guy had a weird-looking amplified guitar, and there was someone in the corner uncasing a set of drums. This was his new hot "fiddle band"? Satherley went over to the leader, a stocky, dark-haired man named Bob Wills and complained. Wills bristled: "You either want what we got, or you don't want to see me at all."

Satherley backed off, and waited to see what he heard. The band roared into a breakneck version of an old black jug-band tune they called "Osage Stomp." Soon they were into a pop chestnut, "I Can't Give You Anything But Love." Then a lilting fiddle tune they called "Maiden's Prayer." On and on they went, some twelve numbers' worth, and though Satherley didn't know what to call the new music, he liked it. On the record labels he just put "Hot Dance Band," but before long people were starting to call it "Western swing." And they were starting to call the band, Bob Wills and His Texas Playboys, the kings of it.

By the early 1930s, the large, rowdy dancehalls in Texas and Oklahoma were echoing to a new style of music. Based on the old ranch house fiddle dance tunes, mixed with a bit of Mexican music and more than a touch of the blues, the new music also borrowed a lot from the big-band swing that was sweeping the North. Unlike their counterparts in the mountains and the Southeast, the southwestern musicians didn't mind borrowing from the music they heard on the radio and on records by Cab Calloway, Duke Ellington, Glen Gray and the Casa Loma Orchestra, Tommy Dorsey, and Benny Goodman. The result was one of the first great musical stews of modern roots music. Many of the veteran pioneers of the music were quick to point out that while Bob Wills was the most popular star of the new music, its real father was a young jazzy singer and bandleader named Milton Brown. In 1932, he formed a band called the Musical Brownies, which began making a name for itself over Fort Worth radio and through a series of brilliant records.

Introducing such classics as "Right or Wrong"and "Sitting on Top of the World," the Brownies seemed destined to break into national fame. Then, in 1936, Brown was seriously injured in an automobile accident and died soon after. Following in the wake of Brown and Wills came a new generation of southwestern bands, including Bill Boyd and his Cowboy Ramblers, Cliff Bruner, the Light Crust Doughboys, Roy Newman, and, in later years, West Coast incarnations like those led by Hank Penny, Spade Cooley, Tex Williams, Hank Thompson, and Cliffie Stone. Some of the later bands used complex arrangements that were as slick and sophisticated as any New York dance band, but the raw, unvarnished spirit of the old Southwest still shone through at delightful and unexpected turns.

OPPOSITE: BOB WILLS, THE KING OF WESTERN SWING. BELOW: WILLS (FAR LEFT) AND HIS TEXAS PLAYBOYS.

BILL MONROE: *When I was young, I used to hear my older brothers play guitar and fiddle around the home. My mother could play the fiddle, and she was a good dancer. I picked the fiddle up and the guitar and the banjo — the mandolin came in later. I learned the mandolin — nobody else could play the mandolin. My Uncle Pen would come see us and maybe spend a night or two and bring his fiddle along. He was a good uncle and a good fiddle player.*

I'd hear different people play the blues. There was an old black man who would come around our place in Kentucky — his name was Arnold Shultz. He was a good guitar man and played some blues. I'd just sit and listen to him. I listened to Jimmie Rodgers some. He was a good yodeler, a good singer.

I was up in my teens, seventeen or eighteen years old [when I started playing professionally with my brother Charlie] in Indiana. We played some shows in different places. I hadn't wrote anything when me and my brother was together. He just sung oldtime songs — no telling how old they was, that was what he'd sing. And if I wanted to sing tenor with him I could, but he'd be sure he played his [songs] and he'd sing his part and play the guitar. [After the Monroe Brothers broke up] I was putting some music together and working on it and seeing how it would come out. I just wanted to come up with a music of my own and let the people hear it and hope they would like it.

"IF BILL MONROE HADN'T COME ON THE SCENE, WHERE WOULD THE STANLEY BROTHERS BE, WHERE WOULD LESTER FLATT AND EARL SCRUGGS HAVE BEEN? WHERE WOULD DON RENO AND RED SMILEY, THE OSBORNE BROTHERS, JIM AND JESSE BE? YOU CAN SEE FROM THAT TRUNK HOW MUCH FRUIT CAME OFF THE BILL MONROE SPROUT ON THE TREE." —RICKY SKAGGS

RALPH STANLEY: *About the first music that I heard when I was a child was some people like the Carter Family, and then it moved on up to the Monroe Brothers and people like that. That was on phonograph records. I never heard of radio until about 1936.*

My father sang the old ballads like "Pretty Polly" and "Man of Constant Sorrow." He didn't play any music, but he would sing 'em just a cappella. "Pretty Polly" and "Man of Constant Sorrow" are old traditional songs that go way, way back, I guess hundreds of years as far as I know. I really don't know who wrote them, but I would guess they maybe came over from England or somewhere.

Gospel music was real important to me from the start. When I was a little boy I'd even go around and sing the old church songs. My mama played the banjo. She taught me to tune the banjo, and she played what I play now, the claw-hammer style. She taught me a tune called "Shout Little Lily," which was the first that I did on the banjo.

My brother Carter and I used to listen to the Grand Ole Opry on the radio, beginning in '36. And we didn't have any [instruments] to play, so we would cut chestnut kindling to start a fire with and use those sticks for instruments. And when a tune or something would come on the radio, well, we'd play the sticks. And I knew right then that that was my life, if it could be arranged.

Finally, my mama said, "Now you make up your mind, either I'm gonna get you a pig or I'm gonna get you a banjo." So I chose the banjo, and I'm mighty glad that I did.

My favorite on the Grand Ole Opry was Bill Monroe. After my brother and I formed the Stanley Brothers, I got acquainted with Bill real good and Bill helped me on some of my records, and I helped him sing on some of his records. We just became good buddies and got along wonderful for years. Bill Monroe put a little bit of overdrive to the music. [Before that], it was just old-time mountain music.

Opposite: A Stanley Brothers handbill from the early Sixties. This page, from top: Ralph Stanley in a Bristol, Tennessee, theater where the Stanley Brothers frequently performed; Stanley in Nashville, 1998.

1619 The first shipload of American slaves is sold to colonists in Virginia. Field-holler singing subsequently develops. Through the ensuing centuries, African work songs, call-and-response patterns, oral tradition, religious beliefs and practices, and rhythms intermingle with European melodies and eventually white American folk forms. The seeds of the blues are planted. **1833** Christian Friedrich Martin builds his first American-made acoustic guitar. **1843** The first public minstrel show is performed by the all-white Virginia Minstrels in blackface, sparking a desire for "black" entertainment. **1863** The Emancipation Proclamation frees slaves in the Confederate states. In the 1870s, following Reconstruction, southern states will enforce segregation. **1903** Black bandleader W.C. Handy hears Delta-style blues in rural Mississippi. **1910** Outraged by a lynching, W.E.B. DuBois cofounds the National Association for the Advancement of Colored People (NAACP). **1912** Handy publishes "The Memphis Blues," Baby Seals publishes "Baby Seals Blues," and Hart Wand and Lloyd Garrett publish "Dallas Blues." These are the first published compositions with "blues" in the title. **1914** Handy publishes the hit "St. Louis Blues," which throws the genre into the mainstream of American popular music. He is later acknowledged as "the Father of the Blues." **1917** The 'Chicago Defender' calls for blacks to flee the South and seek better lives in the urban North. America enters World War I. **1919** Ratification of the Eighteenth Amendment enacts Prohibition. Illegal, music-filled speak-easies, house parties, and juke joints attract drinkers. Race riots proliferate in the North. **1920** Mamie Smith lays down "Crazy Blues," the first blues recording by a black singer, for Okeh Records. The phonograph replaces sheet music as the blues' chief medium of popularization. The dawn of commercial radio makes music available to people nationwide. **1922** The first International Harvester row tractors arrive, making farm work easier. **1923** Ma Rainey records "Bo-Weavil Blues" for Paramount, and a wave of southern female blues singers, including Bessie Smith, enter the studio. **1925** Blind Lemon Jefferson first records for Paramount. The electrical recording process is introduced, and record companies, pressured by competition from radio, tap new specialty markets such as folk blues. **1927** The Great Mississippi River Flood occurs. **1928** Piano blues arises from southern barrelhouses and Chicago house parties. Clarence "Pine Top"

Smith finds success with "Pine Top's Boogie Woogie." Leroy Carr and Scrapper Blackwell pioneer guitar-and-piano duets. Tampa Red and Georgia Tom Dorsey's "It's Tight Like That" introduces the sexually charged, dance-friendly form of piano blues known as hokum blues. **1929** Black Friday hits, and the Great Depression ensues; phonograph makers and record companies will go bankrupt during the next few years. Bessie Smith appears in the film short 'St. Louis Blues.' Blind Lemon Jefferson freezes to death in a Chicago blizzard. **1930** Bukka White debuts on Victor Records. **1933** Prohibition is repealed. John and Alan Lomax, who begin scouring the South to make folk and blues field recordings, immortalize Lead Belly when they record him at the Louisiana State Penitentiary. Blacks, traditionally Republican supporters, begin to switch voting parties, thanks to President Roosevelt's New Deal and Public Works Administration. The Tennessee Valley Authority creates dams to prevent flooding and erosion while supplying part of the South with cheap electricity. **1936** Robert Johnson makes his first recordings for Vocalion. Two years later he dies in Mississippi, after drinking poisoned whiskey. **1937** Bessie Smith dies in a car crash in Mississippi. **1938** Carnegie Hall hosts the first From Spirituals to Swing concert, which features Big Bill Broonzy, Sonny Terry, and other blues greats. **1949** Lead Belly plays in France and becomes the first solo, male blues artist to tour Europe. **1961** Columbia releases a Robert Johnson retrospective LP 'King of the Delta Blues Singers.' **1964** Recently rediscovered by blues enthusiasts, Son House and Skip James play the Newport Folk Festival. **1976** Singer/songwriter Joni Mitchell visits bluesman Furry Lewis in Memphis. The experience inspires her to write "Furry Sings the Blues," which appears on her 1976 album, 'Hejira.' **1981** Ruby Records releases 'Fire of Love,' the debut album by the Gun Club. The L.A.-based band covers various Delta blues songs, introducing the early blues' restless spirit to a punk audience. **1990** The Robert Johnson CD box set, 'Complete Recordings,' is issued by Columbia; it will eventually go platinum and spend thirty-one weeks on the pop chart. **1999** V2 Records releases 'Play' by electronic-dance artist Moby. The album, which samples the Alan Lomax collection of field recordings, will go platinum and spend more than seventy weeks on the pop chart.

THE BIRTH OF THE BLUES BY DAVID EVANS

Although you can trace the probable roots of the blues, its actual birth remains shrouded in mystery. No one knows precisely who performed the first blues song, or where, or when. There may have been some forgotten "genius" who single-handedly created this powerful and enduring musical genre. Most likely, though, what we now call the blues arose near the end of the Nineteenth Century, the synthesis of different black musical forms evolving concurrently as obscure and long-forgotten musicians performed throughout the South. These early blues musicians were probably of modest talent but were capable of holding an audience on a town's street corner or at a plantation shack's "Saturday night supper." Transitional blueslike songs go back to the 1890s and early 1900s, when now-familiar themes, slide-guitar technique, and the use of the guitar to answer the singer's voice were first heard in Texas, Mississippi, and Georgia, in Memphis and New Orleans, and further up the Mississippi and Ohio Rivers. Not coincidentally, this period also brought forth ragtime, jazz, and gospel music in an unprecedented explosion of black American musical creativity. The music that came from the lowest rung of the social ladder – the blues – would prove to be at the heart of this musical development, which continues today to drive the style, sound, and attitude of popular music.

Now these blues, blues ain't nothing, Lord, but a doggone hungry spell.
Got no money in your pocket and you're sure, Lord, catching hell.
And I went, went to the depot, Lord, I read up on the board.
Said, "Your baby ain't here, she's a long ways up the road."
Now I got to sitting, sitting down studying 'bout my old time used-to-be.
Lord, I studied so hard till the blues crept up on me.
—Ishman Bracey (1929)

⎰ OPPOSITE: LEAD BELLY, 1939; EARLY PARAMOUNT RECORDING BY VAUDEVILLE BLUES STAR MA RAINEY. ABOVE,
⎱ FROM LEFT: RAINEY (WITH TOM DORSEY ON PIANO); ONE OF THE DELTA'S FIRST LOCAL STARS, CHARLEY PATTON.

The blues' development paralleled and reflected the black experience. The decades surrounding the year 1900 were generally the worst for black Americans since the time of slavery. The blues spoke both from and to the heart of an impoverished, disenfranchised population that was either bound to rural poverty through sharecropping and seasonal labor or dislocated by migration to urban areas where work was equally hard. Institutionalized racism had systematically stripped away whatever political rights and economic advances blacks gained during Reconstruction. Substandard education, dead-end employment, Jim Crow laws, and an oppressive, white-defined social etiquette undermined blacks' standing in society. Blacks who objected to or questioned their status in society — or who were believed by whites to have done so — risked harassment, arrest, violence, or incarceration in a prison work farm. Lynching — the ultimate sanction — reached a peak in these years of about three per week in the South, often with participation by mobs numbering in the hundreds.

It was out of this oppressive social and economic environment that the blues arose. They were songs of general dissatisfaction, fundamentally shifting and ambivalent in character, expressed in allusive and elusive language. They rarely discussed the causes of oppression but commented instead on the safer subject of male-female relationships under these pressures, an area within the black community where there was more room to maneuver and express one's individuality.

Got the blues, can't be satisfied.
Got the blues, can't be satisfied.
[If I] keep the blues, I'll catch the train and ride.
—Mississippi John Hurt (1928)

Well, I'm going away, Lord, won't be back till fall, won't be back till fall.
Well, I'm going away, Lord, won't be back till fall.
And if I meet my good gal, mama, won't be back at all.
—Tommy Johnson (1928)

Blues were especially popular in the Mississippi Delta and in southeast Texas. The Delta's population was 80 percent black, and its big plantations were worked mostly by sharecroppers; southeast Texas was a semifrontier area opened up largely in the post–Civil War decades where blacks found work that was plentiful and hard. In this region, they built levees to hold back the spring floods, cut timber, and laid the railroads that carried crops to market. Blues thrived wherever hard work and hardship prevailed — in tobacco, mining, and factory towns; in the industrial cities; in the work camps, the hobo jungles, the prisons; and in the underworld of gambling dens, saloons, and brothels — as well as in the more legitimate environments of house parties, picnics, cafes, barbershops, railroad stations, barbecue stands, parks, and street corners.

In the blues, musical elements and forms that had existed in older types of African-American folk expression merged into something new. Although the early blues singers created lyrics —

FROM TOP: MISSISSIPPI COTTON FIELD WORKERS IN THE 1930S; AN AMATEUR BLUESMAN AND HIS HOME-MADE DIDDLEY BOW.

"[BLUES] COME FROM SLAVERY TIME, HOLLER SONGS IN THE FIELD AND THINGS LIKE THAT. THEY DON'T KNOW NOTHING TO DO BUT SING, AND THEY CALLED IT THE BLUES."
—HONEYBOY EDWARDS

notable for their outstanding folk poetry and their sometimes shocking frankness, particularly in matters of love and sex — they often drew their melodies from other types of solo singing. Perhaps the most important of these was the holler: a song, sometimes mixed with moaning, humming, whistling, and falsetto whooping, sung during solitary work activities, such as plowing with a mule, herding cattle, driving a wagon, chopping cotton, or walking to and from work. Most often, hollers told of the work itself or the singer's love life, with melodies that were melismatic and free flowing, full of "blue notes." Chanted prayers and sermons lent the music a spirit-filled quality that remains today. Blues musicians found creative ways to express blue notes on instruments by using such techniques as bending the strings on the guitar, sliding a knife or bottleneck along the strings, bending notes on the harmonica by redirecting the air flow, and playing adjacent black and white keys on the piano in rapid alternation.

Since Reconstruction, if not before, blacks had been adapting the Anglo-American folk-ballad tradition to their own purposes and had begun creating ballads about black characters, such as John Henry, the spike driver on a railroad construction job who "died with a hammer in his hand" in a victorious contest against a steam drill. Unlike the ballads of whites that were usually sung unaccompanied, many of the black ballads were performed with guitar and other instruments. By the 1890s a three-line ballad form had been created, consisting of two rhymed lines followed by a one-line refrain. Most of these ballads told of "bad" men and women who lived outside the law or acted brashly and against society's norms and restraints. These colorful, heroic characters often paid the ultimate price for their transgressions but gained everlasting fame in song: the train robber Railroad Bill, the gambler and murderer Stagolee, and even the destructive insect the boll weevil, among many others.

Police officer, how can it be?
You can arrest everybody but cruel Stagolee.
That bad man, that cruel Stagolee.
—Mississippi John Hurt (1928)

Blues adopted this three-line form and its characteristic harmonic sequence, changing the verse pattern to AAB and leaving space at the ends of lines for the instrumental response. The blues singer became his or her song's chief protagonist, dramatizing the self to heroic proportions, still living and acting on the margins of society as defined and structured by the "white folks," ready to "catch the train and ride" if trouble arose or opportunity beckoned.

At the turn of the century, the guitar, harmonica, and piano were all relatively new to black folk music. In adopting these instruments, blues players sometimes borrowed techniques from older folk instrumentation. The panpipes contributed to the harmonica tradition, and guitar playing was enriched with ideas from the banjo. Another instrument that contributed elements to blues guitar was one sometimes called a diddley bow, a type of children's homemade device made from a single strand of broom wire or baling wire stretched along a board or the wall of a house. The player would strike the string with a finger or a stick and slide a bottle along its length to create a percussive and whining sound. Found mostly in northwest Mississippi and derived from a Central African prototype, this instrument enabled children to practice basic riff ideas and develop a slide technique that some of them would later transfer to the guitar.

Early-Twentieth-Century folk-blues performers often constructed their songs from a repertoire of lyric, melodic, and instrumental elements or formulas, sometimes piecing together a song while it was performed. Musicians shared these elements with one another in their local communities; some musicians also traveled widely or became regional stars, influencing musicians outside their community and creating chains of stylistic tradition that would span decades. Although whole songs and musical and lyrical elements were transmitted as folk music in an oral tradition, the blues were also commercial music. The earliest performers were paid to play at dances and house parties, and they could earn tips from whatever crowd they might draw at public places. At first no one had the reputation of being strictly a blues singer or bluesman. The blues were just one of several styles in these musicians' repertoires, which might also include ballads, folk-ragtime tunes, versions of popular songs, and spirituals.

Soon, however, musical entrepreneurs and professional entertainers began to see the commercial potential in this marginal folk music. While based in Clarksdale in the Mississippi Delta between 1903 and 1905, black bandleader W.C. Handy first encountered folk blues. Soon after he began arranging such tunes for his band of reading musicians, its bookings increased. Between 1908 and 1912, professional black entertainers who worked a loose circuit of vaudeville theaters in Memphis, New Orleans, and other southern cities and towns started incorporating blues into their acts and also met with success. Meanwhile, songwriters and publishers of sheet music, both black and white, began to exploit this new trend. Though the sheet music found a market among both white and black singers, there were radical differences in how it was performed. Whites viewed the early published blues repertoire as novelty numbers to be performed in dialect and blackface. In contrast, black singers made these songs the basis of a far more personal type of expression, and soon some vaudeville entertainers were recognized as specialists in the blues. Unlike the less formal folk-blues scene that was dominated by male performers playing their own accompaniment, the majority of the vaudeville blues singers were women.

Usually accompanied by a male pianist or a small jazz combo, these new blues stars wore elaborate beaded gowns and diamond necklaces. Beautifully coiffed and holding elegant ostrich plumes or fans, they not only presented a majestic image of "colored folks' opera" to enraptured black audiences but lent an air of urban sophistication to a heretofore rural genre.

In the early 1920s, the phonograph record replaced sheet music as the chief medium for popularizing the blues, and it remained almost the only medium for the music, other than live performance, until the advent of black-format radio three decades later. Unfortunately, by the early 1920s, the American record labels had developed a strategy of selling blues and most of their other music by black artists strictly to the black community, marketed as "race" records. Advertised in black newspapers and sold in stores that catered to a predominantly black clientele, these records went virtually unnoticed for years by the rest of the country until the more democratic radio airwaves of the 1950s made them available to everyone.

In 1920, "Crazy Blues," the first blues recording by a black singer, was released. The song was composed by Perry Bradford, a black songwriter, bandleader, and promoter with a background in vaudeville who had moved from Alabama to New York, the capital of America's entertainment, music-publishing, and recording industries. Bradford persuaded Okeh Records, one of the smaller companies, that there was a market for blues in the black community. He would supply the song and the singer, Mamie Smith — a Cincinnati-born vaudeville veteran who performed a wide range of material that included blues — and would organize the Jazz Hounds to back her up. "Crazy Blues" was structured like a popular tune with an introduction and multiple strains, but one of them was in the twelve-bar form; the lyrics dealt with heartbreak, desertion, and revenge, culminating with the singer's vow to get high on dope and shoot a policeman. The record became a smash, and Bradford would later claim it sold more than a million copies. Whatever its actual sales figures, it made other record companies take notice and begin to sign blues singers from the ranks of female vaudeville stars. The larger Columbia Records even released a rival recording of "Crazy Blues" sung by Mary Stafford. When Columbia's lawyer asked Bradford to waive his publisher's royalties in return for making

ABOVE: THE BEST-KNOWN PHOTOGRAPH OF THE GREAT TEXAS BLUESMAN BLIND LEMON JEFFERSON, CIRCA 1927

his song famous, Bradford wrote back that he didn't "waive" anything but the American flag.

Most of the first blues singers to record were based in the North, particularly around New York. Starting in 1923, a wave of vaudeville singers who had been working the southern circuit for years hit the studios. This wave included Ma Rainey from Columbus, Georgia, and Bessie Smith from Chattanooga, Tennessee, who had both been in vaudeville before 1910; Ida Cox from Toccoa, Georgia; and Sara Martin from Louisville, Kentucky. These singers had a long-standing familiarity with the blues and brought a greater degree of authenticity to the recording studio than did many of their predecessors. On their recordings they were often backed by some of the top jazz artists of the day, such as Louis Armstrong, Sidney Bechet, King Oliver, and Jelly Roll Morton. The biggest stars lived a life of opulence, with Ma Rainey traveling in a private railroad car and Bessie Smith making two thousand dollars a week at the height of her career.

In 1925, with the introduction of the electrical recording process, records had greater fidelity, and the microphone could pick up regional accents and the sounds of the guitar and piano better than the large horn used in the old acoustic recording technique. By this time, the record companies were being forced to seek ever more specialized markets because of the growing competition of radio's "free" entertainment. In 1926, they began to look to the South and the as yet untapped field of folk blues. The companies sent the new, more portable electrical equipment to southern cities with their talent scouts, including Victor's Ralph Peer and Columbia's Frank Walker. In sessions lasting from a few days to a couple of weeks and held in rented hotel rooms, auditoriums, and office spaces, these early A&R men recorded local and regional artists in Dallas, Memphis, Atlanta, and a host of other cities, not only in the blues field but also in gospel, jazz, country, and more mainstream popular music. Often they worked with local scouts who had a good eye and ear for talent and a sense of the public tastes — men like H.C. Speir of Jackson, Mississippi, and Polk Brockman of Atlanta, both owners of furniture stores that sold phonographs and records. Chicago also became an important secondary blues recording center in the late 1920s, and many southern artists were sent there to record. They were supplemented by a vast pool

"THERE WAS SOMETHING TERRIFYING ABOUT WATCHING SON HOUSE. YOU REALLY GOT THE SENSE OF A MAN WHO HAD SEVERAL DIFFERENT PERSONALITIES AT WORK WITHIN HIM." —JOHN SEBASTIAN

of local performers who had migrated to the Windy City, mostly from the middle South. The Paramount Record Company also recorded southern blues artists at its studios in Grafton, Wisconsin, as did Gennett Records in Richmond, Indiana.

One of the first great folk-blues performers to be recorded came from Texas. Singer, guitarist, and composer Blind Lemon Jefferson recorded nearly a hundred blues songs between 1926 and 1929. Jefferson had a strong voice that easily traversed his two-octave range; he attacked his guitar with long staccato runs of notes, almost constantly improvising and varying his performances. He sang about railroads, liquor, jails, violence, extreme poverty, and wild women, displaying a gift for startling themes and novel imagery that seemed to belie his blindness. Growing up in rural poverty in Wortham, Texas, Jefferson performed for tips on the streets of Dallas; by the height of his recording career, he was traveling around the South in a chauffeured sedan, having become a household name in much of black America. Jefferson's success opened the door for many other blues singer/guitarists to record in the late 1920s and on through the 1930s, and he set an almost unapproachable standard that raised the level of performance throughout the genre. Among the many guitarists he influenced was Huddie Ledbetter (Lead Belly), who performed several of Jefferson's songs throughout his career. Jefferson's playing would also amaze and inspire such solo performers as Lightnin' Hopkins, who would adapt a somewhat simplified version of Jefferson's guitar style to the electric guitar in the 1940s, and T-Bone Walker, who would add more complex, jazzy harmonies to Jefferson's foundation, applying it to the electric guitar as a lead instrument in a blues band. As a youth, Walker had been Jefferson's "lead boy" in Dallas, and from the 1940s onward, Walker directly or indirectly influenced almost every lead guitarist in a blues band.

The great Mississippi Delta bluesman Charley Patton was enormously successful on a regional basis from the early 1910s and more widely known once he started recording commercially in 1929 (he died five years later, in 1934). His gruff voice and percussive guitar playing — along with his image as an acrobatic clown during performance — inspired countless bluesmen, who were often equally impressed with his money, clothes, car, fancy guitars, and many female admirers. Among Patton's major disciples who later gained fame themselves were Tommy Johnson, Son House, Willie Brown, Big Joe Williams, and Howlin' Wolf. Among the contemporary black musicians inspired by Patton's blues and gospel was the late Roebuck "Pops" Staples, who had grown up on the same Delta plantation where Patton lived. (Staples and his children would become one of the leading groups in gospel and soul music from the 1950s to the 1990s.) Finally, the commercial records Patton made between 1929 and 1934 influenced the late John Fahey, a popular performer and composer for the steel-stringed guitar in the 1960s. (Fahey would also publish the first study of Patton's life and music in 1970.)

Elements of Patton's style would be passed down from generation to generation through one of his Delta protégés: Son House, who was born in 1902 near Clarksdale, Mississippi. With his deep, soulful, impassioned singing and percussive slide-guitar style, House would prove a key influence for such well-known bluesmen as Robert Johnson and Muddy Waters.

Robert Johnson understudied with House when he was first learning to play guitar. Born in 1911, in Hazlehurst, Mississippi, Johnson soon became known in the Delta for his masterful singing and guitar playing. In fact, he would emerge as the stylistic forefather of great blues artists including Elmore James, Eddie Taylor, Johnny Shines, and Robert Junior Lockwood (Johnson's stepson), all of whom would gain prominence in Chicago in the 1950s. Through his powerful, dark recordings cut in 1936 and 1937 (and their reissue in popular anthologies from the 1960s through the present), the mysterious Johnson would defy time and be discovered and revered by future generations of blues-revival artists. Johnson's haunting, evocative such as "Crossroads Blues," "Me and the Devil Blues," ‸ve in Vain," and "Hell Hound on My Trail" intrigued new ‸enerations who were also taken with his romantic image as the prototypical ill-fated, haunted bluesman.

Son House's other Delta disciple, Muddy Waters, would exert a more direct influence on future musicians. House and Waters both recorded in Mississippi in 1941 and 1942 for Alan Lomax and John Work, who were carrying out a joint research project of Fisk University and the Library of Congress. In 1943, Waters moved to Chicago, where he recorded a catalogue that would essentially define the Windy City's electric blues sound. He eventually adapted House's solo country blues style to the format of a small electric urban ensemble, still retaining Son House's and Robert Johnson's raw power and merging it with his image as the "hoochie-coochie man" who "got his mojo working." Through his recordings and international tours up to his death in 1983, Waters literally took the blues around the world and proved a major influence on 1960s British blues-based rock groups such as the Rolling Stones.

Ironically, Son House outlived both Johnson and Waters, was rediscovered by blues researchers, and had a significant second career from 1964 until the early 1970s performing and touring throughout North America and Europe. Many younger artists from the 1960s on were equally influenced by House and by his arguably better-known disciples Muddy Waters and Robert Johnson.

Born in 1902, Skip James developed a style in Bentonia, Mississippi, that featured an unusual open D-minor guitar tuning, along with a repertoire of songs on themes such as hard times and the devil ("Devil Got My Woman" and "Hard Time Killin' Floor Blues"). Elements of James's lyric themes and guitar style occurred in the blues of other artists from Bentonia, suggesting the existence of a local blues tradition. James made commercial 78 rpm records in 1931 and was also rediscovered in 1964 by blues researchers, on the basis of his early recordings.

In the Carolina Piedmont, many of the early blues players were physically disabled and thus able to devote their time to music, which was their only means of making a living. There the guitarists developed a dense, more harmonically complex style with lighter, bouncier rhythms, usually adhering strictly to the twelve-bar and other standard patterns. In the 1920s, South Carolina–born Blind Gary Davis was a major influence on bluesman Blind Boy Fuller. Fuller often worked with blind harmonica player Sonny Terry, performing for tips outside the tobacco factories of Durham, North Carolina, as the workers changed shifts and playing house parties at night. When Fuller died in 1941, guitarist Brownie McGhee, who was crippled from childhood polio, adapted much of his style and began performing with Terry as Blind Boy Fuller No. 2. During the 1940s, Davis, McGhee, and Terry moved to New York, where they

became major figures on the folk scene for several decades. In recent years, blues guitarist John Cephas from Virginia and harmonica player Phil Wiggins from Washington, D.C., have carried on the McGhee-Terry duet sound. All of these artists influenced countless younger performers in the blues revival years.

New Orleans–born jazz guitarist Lonnie Johnson began recording as a blues singer in 1925 and had a successful career that lasted until his death in 1970. He sang with a smooth voice, composed sophisticated lyrics, and played guitar in a precise style that featured string bending and many passing notes and chords. Johnson became a model of the urbane blues artist that many southern performers would strive to emulate.

By 1928, solo pianists from southern honky-tonks and Chicago house parties were making records, following the success of "Pine Top's Boogie Woogie," by Clarence "Pine Top" Smith, a Birmingham pianist who resettled in Chicago. This piece gave its name to an influential piano style that featured riff patterns and walking figures in the bass. Boogie-woogie (or simply "boogie") riffs and rhythms would experience a revival in the late 1930s and 1940s, influencing big-band swing, country, gospel, and the guitar blues of artists such as John Lee Hooker. Among blues pianists, Jimmy Yancey also affected countless players in Chicago during the 1920s and 1930s with his boogie-woogie and walking-bass figures. Two of his disciples, Meade Lux Lewis and Albert Ammons, would popularize this sound in the 1940s in clubs and concert halls, as well as through the radio and recordings. From Helena, Arkansas, blues singer and pianist Roosevelt Sykes would help to create a style featuring deep, insistent left-hand bass notes and a freely roaming improvisational right hand that would later be heard in the music of many others, including Memphis Slim and Otis Spann, who would adapt the style to a small-combo format in Chicago and other urban centers.

West Tennessee musicians were among the leaders in transforming the harmonica from a solo instrument used to perform novelty tunes and train imitations into a lead voice in small blues combos. From the town of Henning, Noah Lewis played solo as well as with jug bands, developing a bluesy style with a piercing tone and many bent notes. Lewis disciple Hammie Nixon, from nearby Brownsville, performed strictly with guitarists and in small string-and-jug combos. The younger John Lee "Sonny Boy" Williamson of Jackson eventually took Nixon's regional harmonica style to Chicago and adapted it to a small-combo format, including guitar, bass, piano, and drums. One of Williamson's Chicago protégés, Little Walter played this style of

46

harmonica through an amplifier, blowing longer lines in the manner of a jazz soloist. Another harmonica player, Aleck "Rice" Miller from Mississippi, actually took over Sonny Boy Williamson's name and had a successful career into the 1960s.

Record companies not only recorded solo blues acts, but they also took an interest in small combos. Pianist/singer Leroy Carr and guitarist Scrapper Blackwell cut more than a hundred blues songs between 1928 and 1935, making the guitar-and-piano duet a popular format. A variant of this style, known as hokum blues, featured rapid dance tempos and humorous lyrics with plenty of sexual double-entendres. Pianist Georgia Tom Dorsey and guitarist Tampa Red pioneered hokum blues in 1928 with their hit record "It's Tight Like That." (Within a few years, Dorsey would undergo a religious conversion, apply his prodigious songwriting talent to gospel music, and become internationally famous as the father of that genre.) In the form of jug bands, juke bands, washboard bands, and skiffle bands, larger combinations of three to five instruments were also recorded, including Cannon's Jug Stompers and the Memphis Jug Band, both from Memphis, and Whistler's Jug Band from Louisville, Kentucky. They typically combined harmonica and guitar, sometimes with other stringed instruments, along with less orthodox instruments such as washboard, kazoo, jug, or washtub bass. Playing a mixture of blues, ragtime tunes, and popular songs, these groups created one prototype for the modern blues band.

In 1929, the effects of the Depression were first being felt throughout the record industry; by 1932, virtually all of the companies had gone bankrupt. As the industry slowly began to recover, its approach to blues recording changed. The vaudeville style of blues exemplified by the female blues artists popular in the Twenties all but vanished as most of the theaters closed or switched to screening movies. Without an entertainment circuit, the singers could not afford to mount their elaborate stage shows. Most of the women retired or were reduced to singing in clubs and cabarets, making occasional local appearances, or touring in tent shows. The record companies conducted fewer southern field sessions and focused most of their blues activities in Chicago. Only three companies — Decca, RCA Victor's Bluebird label, and American Record Company (later to become a part of Columbia Records) — accounted for almost all blues recordings from 1933 to 1942, and two Chicago producers and talent scouts, J. Mayo Williams and Lester Melrose, were performers' main gateways to the studios. The companies prized those artists who could sing, play an instrument in a distinctive style, and compose a never-ending stream of new blues songs.

Many of the Chicago stars guested on one another's records and shared their songs. Records were sold in large quantities for jukeboxes, which needed a new record by a popular artist every month or two. Many others were sold at discount chain stores, often on subsidiary budget labels with the artist listed under a pseudonym. Though recording paid the artists much less than it did in the 1920s, the records held the promise of national fame and the likelihood of steady work.

These recording sessions usually featured one or two guitars and piano; gradually, a string bass and washboard were added. In 1936, Chicago's Harlem Hamfats, who combined elements of Mississippi blues and New Orleans jazz, recorded with two guitars, piano, bass, drums, trumpet, and clarinet and, along with the groups that recorded in the wake of their success, established another of the foundations of modern blues bands. By the end of the 1930s, some of the leading blues stars had begun recording with an electric guitar; these musicians included Big Bill Broonzy, Tampa Red, Lonnie Johnson, and Memphis Minnie, who had settled in the North in the 1920s, and new Chicago arrival Arthur "Big Boy" Crudup, who would become an important influence on the young Elvis Presley and the emerging rock & roll sound of the 1950s. This electrification would give a whole new life to the guitar, as both a solo instrument and a lead sound in an ensemble, at a time when the acoustic guitar was becoming harder to hear in the ever louder bands.

Other important blues milestones of the late 1930s included two Carnegie Hall concerts titled From Spirituals to Swing, staged in 1938 and 1939 by impresario John Hammond. Presenting a broad range of current and historic black musical styles for a discerning, liberal, and predominantly white audience, the concerts helped open the door for the future acceptance of black music. The blues talent consisted of guitarist Big Bill Broonzy; Sonny Terry on harmonica; washboard player Bull City Red; boogie-woogie pianists Meade Lux Lewis, Albert Ammons, and Pete Johnson; and vaudeville-blues singers Ida Cox and Helen Humes — all of whom received major career boosts and gained new audiences.

Several of the folk-blues artists who recorded in the late 1920s and 1930s were among the bluesmen rediscovered in the 1950s and 1960s by researchers and amateur musicologists who were inspired by their old 78s. Among the most successful of those who began performing in coffeehouses, on college concert stages, and at folk festivals were Skip James, Son House, Furry Lewis, Sleepy John Estes, Bukka White, and Mississippi John Hurt, all of whom became leading figures in the folk revival movement. Memphis's Lewis impressed his new audiences with his lyric mixture of humor and pathos, his slide playing, and his guitar tricks. Estes, who lived in Brownsville, Tennessee, was known for his "crying" singing style and his repertoire describing people and events in his hometown. Having gone blind by the time of his rediscovery in 1962, Estes was accompanied during the next fifteen years by his longtime harmonica partner Hammie Nixon. Bukka White, originally from Mississippi but living in Memphis at the time of his 1963 rediscovery, played a hard-driving, percussive blues style on a steel-bodied guitar, featuring the slide technique, and sang lyrics about prison, hoboing, love, violence, and death. Mississippi John Hurt's second career in the 1960s was far bigger than his earlier one, which had been entirely confined to his hometown of Avalon; he left for only two forays, both in 1928, to Memphis and New York City to make the recordings that would lead to his rediscovery many years later. His delicate guitar picking, gentle personality, and large, varied repertoire of blues, ballads, ragtime songs, and spirituals won him many admirers and musical disciples everywhere. By the time they were rediscovered, several bluesmen — including Gary Davis, Ishman Bracey, Rube Lacy, and Robert Wilkins — had given up the blues to become preachers or gospel singers.

Many of the great early blues artists never made it to this new level of fame, as their lives were cut short, often by the hazards and excesses of the blues lifestyle. Pine Top Smith was killed by a stray bullet while performing in a Chicago saloon a few months after his record launched the boogie-woogie craze. In late 1929, Blind Lemon Jefferson froze to death in a Chicago blizzard, walking home from a house party after missing his ride. Leroy Carr died from the effects of acute alcoholism in 1935, and two years later Bessie Smith was the victim of an automobile wreck while touring Mississippi. Robert Johnson was murdered in 1938, with poisoned whiskey served at a Mississippi roadhouse by the jealous proprietor, whose wife Johnson was courting. In 1941, Blind Boy Fuller died of what was probably a treatable bladder infection, and in 1948 Sonny Boy Williamson fell victim to a fatal mugging in Chicago, while returning home from a late-night club appearance.

Thanks mainly to the efforts of folklorists, commercial record producers, and researchers and promoters working with veteran artists, many of the glory moments of early blues music have been preserved and remain available to future generations. The vaudeville singers have served as early models of independent women in the music business, inspiring such artists as Bonnie Raitt, who, early in her career, often performed with vaudeville veteran Sippie Wallace. The country bluesmen have influenced artists as diverse as Eric Clapton, Canned Heat, Taj Mahal, and John Hammond. In the 1990s, a number of younger black singer/guitarists emerged into prominence, such as Keb' Mo', Corey Harris, Guy Davis, and Alvin "Youngblood" Hart. Mostly from urban upbringings and college educated, they embraced country blues as their vehicle of personal and musical expression, often extending and modernizing it with elements of rhythm & blues. Performing at American concert halls and festivals and on international stages, they have assured a black presence in the future of the blues.

As the last of the early blues artists pass from the scene, they leave us a trove of music that continues to be imitated, adapted, and even synthesized into new sounds. The emotional power of the blues cuts across generations, races, cultures, and musical trends. It influences almost all new forms of popular music that appear and outlasts most. Through it all, however, the blues retains an identity, a dignity uniquely its own, and flows forever onward without any discernible beginning or end.

Rediscovered country-blues artists posing for a portrait at the 1964 Newport Folk Festival: Yank Rachell, Mississippi John Hurt, Skip James, Elizabeth Cotten, Doc Reese, Sleepy John Estes (from left)

W.C. HANDY:

One of the great popularizers of the blues, William Christopher Handy, was born in Florence, Alabama, in 1873, the son and grandson of Methodist ministers. He received a good education, including formal training in music, and decided to pursue a career in entertainment rather than the ministry. Handy learned guitar and cornet, and in the 1890s he led a vocal quartet and toured as the leader of a minstrel band that played popular music and light classics throughout the United States, Canada, Mexico, and Cuba. Between 1903 and 1905, he led a band based in Clarksdale, Mississippi, in the heart of the Delta, at a time when blues was in its earliest period of development. Handy had his first memorable encounter with the blues while he was dozing late at night at a Tutwiler, Mississippi, railroad station, waiting for a train to take him back to Clarksdale after a performance. He was approached by a young man playing a guitar in the slide style, by pressing a knife on the strings, and singing about traveling further down the line. Handy later wrote, "His clothes were rags; his feet peeped out of his shoes. His face had on it some of the sadness of the ages. . . . The singer repeated the line three times, accompanying himself on the guitar with the weirdest music I had ever heard. The tune stayed in my mind."

Soon after, Handy's band was performing at a white dance in the Delta town of Cleveland. During intermission, a local black trio consisting of a "battered guitar, a mandolin, and a worn-out bass" was allowed to play its "native music," performing what Handy described as "one of those over-and-over strains" with "a disturbing monotony, . . . a kind of stuff that has long been associated with cane rows and levee camps." Handy wrote, "A rain of silver dollars began to fall around the outlandish, stomping feet. The dancers went wild. Dollars, quarters, halves — the shower grew heavier and continued so long I strained my neck to get a better look. There before the boys lay more money than my nine musicians were being paid for the entire engagement. Then I saw the beauty of primitive music."

These encounters awakened in Handy an urge to become a composer and arranger of blues and folk music. His success with this new material led him to a position as a Memphis bandleader. In 1912, he published "The Memphis Blues," which became a popular nationwide hit, leading to his founding, with financial partner Harry Pace, the publishing company that in 1914 published "St. Louis Blues," one of the greatest hit songs of the Twentieth Century. He had further success over the next few years with "The Yellow Dog Blues," "The Hesitating Blues," "Joe Turner Blues," and "Beale Street Blues." In 1918, Handy moved his business to New York City, where he spent much of the rest of his career consolidating his reputation as "the Father of the Blues." He published a book-length anthology of his and other songwriters' blues in 1926 and his autobiography in 1941. Handy passed away in 1958, and a park and statue are dedicated to his honor in Memphis.

CLOCKWISE FROM OPPOSITE TOP LEFT: W.C. HANDY'S TURN-OF-THE-CENTURY BAND; HANDY AS A YOUNG CORNET PLAYER, CIRCA 1898; HANDY'S BAND PHOTOGRAPHED AT THE MANHATTAN CASINO IN NEW YORK CITY, 1919.

ROBERT JUNIOR LOCKWOOD:

The first music that we all heard was gospel. The next music that I really remember was Blind Lemon Jefferson and Blind Blake on the Victrola, playing the blues. The blues [originally came] from the plantation when we wasn't allowed to read and write, and the black people would communicate with each other [by singing]. I started playing a couple of things on the piano when I was eight. I had a couple of cousins who could play a couple of tunes and I learned that. I started playing the guitar at thirteen. So I got good enough with that to really understand the tim[ing] of music, and when [my stepfather] Robert Johnson came along I was not a greenhorn — I mean I was able to play them three changes and stuff. After [Johnson] had been teaching me for about four months, he didn't have to teach me no more, I'd just play. I learned so fast [I] scared him to death. Robert taught me to play "Sweet Home Chicago" and, really, he didn't have to really teach me nothing else. I watched him play and learned everything he was doing. He'd leave and when he come back, I'd be playing it.

I don't know where that special crossroads is that Robert Johnson was singing about. I mean, don't nobody know where any of it is. But standing at the crossroads [and] trying to flag a ride is just something that he wanted to sing about, that's all. And all that bullshit about him selling hisself to the devil, that's bullshit. 'Cause if he's sold to the devil, I'm sold to the devil. As far as you selling yourself to the devil, you already sold to the devil if you don't pray. [If] you don't put forth a good effort to redeem yourself, you already sold.

{ OPPOSITE: ROBERT JUNIOR LOCKWOOD AT THE CHICAGO BLUES FESTIVAL, 1985. ABOVE: LOCKWOOD (LEFT) WITH DRUMMER SAM LAY AND HOMESICK JAMES, 1998.

1867 Allen, Ware, and Garrison publish 'Slave Songs of the United States.' 1882 Harvard professor Francis James Child publishes the first volume of his masterwork, 'The English and Scottish Popular Ballads,' which will inspire American folksong collectors and scholars to identify "Child ballads" in different regions of the United States over the next decades. 1888 The American Folklore Society is organized in Cambridge, Massachusetts. 1890 Harvard University ethnologist Jesse Walter Fewkes makes the first ethnographic field recording on phonograph in Calais, Maine, where he documents Passamaquoddy Indian folk tales and songs. 1906 John Lomax records cowboy songs on phonograph; the following year he will publish 'Cowboy Songs and Other Frontier Ballads.' 1907 Immigration reaches an all-time high. By 1910 almost one out of every seven Americans will be a non-native. New York becomes the epicenter of this cultural melting pot. 1920 The women's suffrage amendment is passed. 1927 Poet Carl Sandburg compiles 'The American SongBag,' a collection of traditional songs, which will influence his own poetry. 1928 The Library of Congress's Music Division creates the Archive of American Folk Song, run by Robert W. Gordon; John Lomax will become its Honorary Curator in 1933. Bascom Lamar Lunsford establishes the Mountain Dance and Folk Festival in Asheville, North Carolina. 1933 Franklin D. Roosevelt signs fifteen major bills, combating the Great Depression with New Deal reform. John and Alan Lomax begin exploring the South with portable recording equipment, documenting white and black singers and musicians, as well as Tejano and Cajun ethnic traditions. 1934 John and Alan Lomax publish 'American Ballads and Folksongs.' 1935 Alan Lomax organizes a field expedition to Georgia, Florida, and the Bahamas with Zora Neale Hurston and Mary Elizabeth Barnicle. 1937 Oklahoma-born, nomadic folk icon Woody Guthrie develops his repertoire in Los Angeles, which includes "Dust Bowl Refugees," "Pretty Boy Floyd," "I Ain't Got No Home," "John Henry," and the American classic "This Land Is Your Land." 1938 Alan Lomax organizes a concert at the Library of Congress for the seventy-fifth anniversary of the Emancipation Proclamation; he will assist John Hammond in creating the From Spirituals to Swing concerts in New York, which feature some of the same musicians. 1939 Lead Belly puts a cap on five prolific years of touring and recording for the Library of Congress when he is incarcerated for assault. When he is released in 1940, he will host his own radio program, the groundbreaking Folksongs of America, on New York's WNYC. The Library of Congress receives a grant from the Carnegie Corporation, which facilitates a professional recording laboratory in which folk records are copied and recorded. Folklorist Herbert Halpert conducts an extensive field recording trip through several southern states for the WPA and the Library of Congress. 1940 Alan Lomax records hours of Guthrie's work for the Library of Congress. In New York, Pete Seeger and Guthrie form the Almanac Singers. 1941 Japan bombs Pearl Harbor, propelling the United States into war. New Deal agencies are closed down or shift to the war effort, and field recording becomes difficult because of rationing of key materials. 1942 The Library of Congress publishes its first six documentary folk albums. Benjamin A. Botkin becomes the head of the Archive of American Folk Song. 1943 Guthrie's socialist views and Communist sympathies result in the House Committee to Investigate Un-American Activities' ban of his music from all American radio networks. He publishes his acclaimed autobiographical novel, 'Bound for Glory.' 1944 Benjamin A. Botkin publishes 'Treasury of American Folklore'; he will leave the Library of Congress the following year. 1945 The U.S. drops the atomic bomb on Hiroshima, Japan, effectively pushing the world into the nuclear age. 1946 Lead Belly leaves New York and moves to the West Coast, where he will join People's Songs Inc., an organization seeking social reform through folk songs. The following year he will return to New York, where he will die on December 6 at age sixty. 1947 Tape recorders are first used in field recordings. 1948 The long-playing vinyl record, or LP, is debuted. Pete Seeger forms the Weavers with Lee Hays, Fred

Hellerman, and Ronnie Gilbert; the following year the group will play a six-month stand at the Village Vanguard. Moe Asch begins his Folkways label, which will release recordings by Guthrie, Lead Belly, and Seeger, among many others. Asch also begins to record and issue folk music from around the world. 1950 Wisconsin Senator Joseph McCarthy makes public charges that Communists had infiltrated the State Department, and the ensuing Red Scare affects many in the folk revival movement. The Weavers' version of Lead Belly's "Goodnight Irene" tops the chart for thirteen weeks, sells more than two million copies, and becomes one of the most enduring hits of the mid-Twentieth Century. 1952 Folkways Records releases the six-LP 'Anthology of American Folk Music,' compiled by Harry Smith. Smithsonian Folkways will reissue the set on CD in 1997. 1955 Rae Korson takes over the Archive of American Folk Song. The Weavers defy the blacklist and start releasing their own records; their first reunion concert is attended by members of Peter, Paul and Mary, who are inspired, along with others, to perform folk music. 1958 The Kingston Trio, formed in San Francisco in 1957, covers the traditional American folksong "Tom Dooley," which lands on the top of the pop chart. Club 47 opens in Cambridge, Massachusetts, and becomes the first regular venue for Joan Baez, Arlo Guthrie, Taj Mahal, and others. 1959 Sam Charters records Lightnin' Hopkins for Folkways. The Newport Folk Festival is inaugurated. 1960 Robert Allan Zimmerman, who in 1959 changed his name to Bob Dylan and began playing the college folk-rock circuit, drops out of college and goes to New York to visit Guthrie. 1961 'The Weavers at Carnegie Hall' hits Number Twenty-four on the pop chart. The Berlin Wall is erected. 1962 Joan Baez takes the album chart by storm; her self-titled debut, 'Joan Baez Vol. 2,' and 'Joan Baez in Concert' all go gold, spend more than one hundred weeks on the chart, and place in the Top Twenty. Peter, Paul and Mary cover the Weavers' "The Hammer Song," retitle it "If I Had a Hammer," and take it to Number Ten on the singles chart. 1963 Bob Dylan records "Blowin' in the Wind" and "Don't Think Twice, It's All Right," which Peter, Paul and Mary cover and turn into hits. The television program 'Hootenanny' becomes nationally popular. 1964 In San Francisco, Roger McGuinn forms the folk-rocking Byrds with Gene Clark, Chris Hillman, David Crosby, and Michael Clarke; future early hits include Dylan's "Mr. Tambourine Man" and "Turn! Turn! Turn!," a Bible passage that had been set to music by Pete Seeger. 1965 The Paul Butterfield Blues Band backs a plugged-in Bob Dylan at the Newport Folk Festival. The SNCC (Student Nonviolent Coordinating Committee) Freedom Singers also perform, inspiring college students to organize voter registration drives across the South. 1967 The Smithsonian Institution launches the Festival of American Folklife. On October 3, Woody Guthrie succumbs to Huntington's chorea at age fifty-five. 1972 Columbia releases two volumes of 'A Tribute to Woody Guthrie,' which feature Guthrie covers by Bob Dylan, Pete Seeger, Arlo Guthrie, Joan Baez, Odetta, and others. 1974 The National Endowment for the Arts launches its Folk Arts Program. 1976 The American Folklife Preservation Act becomes law, creating the American Folklife Center at the Library of Congress. 1979 The Weavers reunite for a concert at New York's Carnegie Hall; the concert is captured in the documentary film 'Wasn't That a Time!' 1988 The Smithsonian Institution, which has acquired Folkways Records and the Woody Guthrie archive, benefits from the film and accompanying album 'A Vision Shared: A Tribute to Woody Guthrie and Lead Belly,' a musical tribute featuring Dylan, Seeger, Willie Nelson, Taj Mahal, U2, and others and narrated by Robbie Robertson. 1989 The North American Folk Music and Dance Alliance holds its first meeting. 1993 Pete Seeger wins a Lifetime Achievement Award Grammy. 1997 Rounder Records releases the first in a hundred-plus-album series of the Alan Lomax recorded legacy. 1998 British folksinger Billy Bragg and U.S. roots-rock band Wilco introduce a new generation to Guthrie via their 'Mermaid Avenue,' featuring Guthrie lyrics and Wilco and Bragg's music. Two years later, the acclaimed album is followed by a second volume.

THE FLOWERING OF THE FOLK REVIVAL BY ALAN JABBOUR

One of the most striking features of Twentieth-Century America's cultural landscape was the flowering of the folk revival. *Folk music* is a general term for the roots music traditions of a country or region, songs learned not by formal instruction or through institutional sanction but through informal sharing within families and communities. It is person-to-person music in a participatory style. Every community has folk music, and in the multicultural swirl of America, it has been an especially important cultural asset. But it was little recognized and less honored in America during the Nineteenth Century. The great folk music revival of the Twentieth Century actively sought out,

documented, and celebrated folk music, so that what had once been taken for granted was elevated to a place of honor in the nation's larger fabric. The pioneers of "the revival," as it has come to be familiarly called, are now venerable or deceased, but each decade brings new developments in American music that display the revival's mark.

Many people associate the modern folk music revival with the 1950s and early 1960s, when it was inaugurated by such figures as Pete Seeger, the Weavers, the Kingston Trio, Joan Baez, and Peter, Paul and Mary and then swelled in a crescendo that resounded through the era's hootenannies and coffeehouses. Some are aware that the movement reaches back

into the 1940s and includes such visionaries as Woody Guthrie, Lead Belly, and Alan Lomax. But to understand it fully, we must reach back further still. As a cultural movement with a sense of its own history, the folk revival has roots in the 1930s. In its infancy, it was profoundly influenced by two powerful engines of cultural change in Twentieth-Century America: the surge of social and cultural activism during the New Deal era, with its epicenter in the federal agencies in Washington, D.C., and the emerging synergies between social progressivism and entrepreneurship in cultural communications, anchored in New York City.

{ OPPOSITE, FROM TOP: WOODY GUTHRIE IN CALIFORNIA, 1941; PETER, PAUL AND MARY, 1965.
ABOVE: FOLKLORIST/MANDOLINIST RALPH RINZLER OF THE GREENBRIAR BOYS, BOB DYLAN, AND GREENBRIAR
BOYS GUITARIST/LEAD VOCALIST JOHN HERALD (FROM LEFT) AT THE GASLIGHT CAFE, NEW YORK CITY, 1962.

One could argue that the folk revival began even earlier, or at least that it reflects a cultural process that can be traced well back into the Nineteenth Century. As the Civil War subsided, three abolitionists, William Francis Allen, Charles Pickard Ware, and Lucy McKim Garrison, published a volume of spirituals and other songs, *Slave Songs of the United States* (1867), collected and notated directly from African-Americans in the South. Just a few years later, in 1871, the Fisk Jubilee Singers began their bold touring campaign to raise funds for Fisk University by singing spirituals and other music. Soon college glee clubs began singing spirituals, which were eventually recycled back into African-American churches. Not unrelated events, these are the steps in the same cultural process that characterized the folk revival throughout the Twentieth Century: the documentation of grassroots musicians in the field; the presentation of their art to a wider public; the imitation of their songs, tunes, and styles by other Americans; and the feedback and stimulation to local cultural communities.

A key ingredient of the folk revival, as it gathered momentum in the Twentieth Century, was the invention of machines for sound recording. The machines made possible a new kind of cultural documentation that transmitted musical performances intact to faraway places and people. Edison invented the wax cylinder phonograph in 1877, and in 1890 Harvard University ethnologist Jesse Walter Fewkes took Edison's new device to Calais, Maine, to record Passamaquoddy Indian songs and tales. Fewkes published transcriptions from the recordings to show how the phonograph could assist in transcribing ethnological data garnered in fieldwork. Only gradually would it become clear that instantaneous field recordings had cultural powers far outweighing their practical uses for dictation and transcription.

Many early American collectors, often associated with the Smithsonian Institution's Bureau of American Ethnology, began using sound recordings to document American Indian music, lore, and ritual. Frances Densmore's documentary work was particularly broad and sustained, recording dozens of tribes' music over several decades. At the turn of the century, the recording machine was used for the first time to document non-Indian traditions. Charles F. Lummis recorded songs from Spanish California, and a young Texan, John A. Lomax, acquired a wax cylinder machine to record songs directly from cowboy tradition.

John Lomax (1867–1948), born in Mississippi and reared in Texas, developed an early interest in cowboy songs and wrote a paper on the subject for a class he was taking at the University of Texas. The professor responded with derogatory comments about the value of such songs, and as his family tells it, Lomax spent the rest of his life proving that professor wrong. His book *Cowboy Songs and Other Frontier Ballads* (1910) not only shared traditional cowboy songs with a wider audience but ultimately helped define and diffuse a repertoire known to and sung by millions of Americans. A generation later, Lomax returned to his earlier love of documenting folksong in the South and found a national base for his operations in the Library of Congress.

The Library of Congress came to be at the epicenter of folk music collecting in America after 1928, when its music division created the Archive of American Folk Song and brought in Robert Winslow Gordon as the Archive's first head. Gordon set the pattern for the Archive by immediately undertaking fieldwork in the North Carolina mountains and the Georgia Sea Islands. He began experimenting in 1931 with a portable disc cutter, which he foresaw would provide higher recording quality than wax cylinder recorders. But Gordon's diplomatic skills with the Library's administrators were lacking; his position was supported by private donations, and the Depression was taking its toll. The Archive fell into abeyance in 1932.

In 1933, John Lomax filled that breach, becoming honorary curator of the Archive of American Folk Song at a dollar a year. He thereby gained access to the Library's recording equipment and supplies as well as to its national reputation. Field expeditions in Texas and the Deep South began immediately, and at the end of many a disc one may hear his stentorian voice announcing, "Recorded for the Library of Congress in Washington, D.C."

Lomax soon acquired fresh recordings of not only cowboy singers and other British-American songs and tunes but also African-American songs from singers such as James "Ironhead" Baker, whom Lomax discovered in a Texas prison. Before the decade was out, Lomax had visited prisons in a dozen southern states, paying especially close attention to the rich black repertory of work songs used to organize and synchronize work teams for tasks like chopping wood.

For Lomax, fieldwork was a family affair, and from the outset he took along on field expeditions his son Alan, born in 1915. In 1935, Alan Lomax took command of an expedition himself, joined by pioneering African-American author Zora Neale Hurston and New York folklorist Mary Elizabeth Barnicle. They visited the Georgia Sea Islands, as Gordon had before them, then set up shop in Hurston's hometown, the historic African-American town of Eatonville, Florida. It was a dramatic begin-

OPPOSITE, CLOCKWISE FROM BOTTOM LEFT: JOHN LOMAX; RECORDING EQUIPMENT IN THE BACK OF JOHN LOMAX'S CAR, LATE 1930S; SON ALAN LOMAX, 1946.

ning for the career of one of America's most brilliant and devoted documentarians of roots music.

The New Deal bred an active cultural scene in Washington, D.C. Musicologist and eminent composer Charles Seeger came to the Resettlement Administration; folklorist and author Benjamin A. Botkin, who later succeeded Alan Lomax at the Library, joined the national office of the Federal Writers Project. In 1937, the Library of Congress obtained Congressional funding for a position in the Archive, and Alan Lomax became "assistant-in-charge," while his father continued to do fieldwork as honorary curator. In the later 1930s, the Archive began broadening its coverage, mindful of the dream of becoming a truly national repository of American folksong. Alan Lomax traveled to Kentucky, then farther afield to Vermont, Ohio, Indiana, and Michigan. Increasingly, he worked through contacts with regional collectors, and to complement the field efforts of the Lomaxes, the Archive began lending its recording equipment to other documentary projects around the country. Availability of the equipment helped the Archive become a national collection to which many collectors contributed.

In 1941–42, as America prepared to enter World War II, Alan Lomax returned to the South for a dramatically productive project, in cooperation with Fisk University, to record the whole range of African-American music in the Mississippi Delta. The expedition yielded wonderful sacred music, including recordings during church services, and amazing examples of oldtime black string-band music with Sid Hemphill and his band, featuring fiddle, fife, and "quills" (panpipes). But perhaps most striking were the benchmark blues sessions with Son House, by then already an older musician and mentor of Robert Johnson and other bluesmen, and with McKinley Morganfield, a budding young bluesman who was uncertain about pursuing a career in music. Perhaps the session helped persuade him to move to Chicago, plug in, and help invent modern blues under the name Muddy Waters.

Two public events in 1938 were auguries of things to come. Alan Lomax organized a special concert at the Library of Congress cel-

ebrating the seventy-fifth anniversary of the Emancipation Proclamation, featuring such folk musicians as bluesman Sonny Terry and gospel singers the Golden Gate Quartet. Later in 1938 and 1939, he worked with famed Columbia Records producer John Hammond to produce two similar programs in New York City, this time titled From Spirituals to Swing. The emphasis on collecting was beginning to shift toward finding ways to share the collecting effort with a wider public.

In the late 1930s and early 1940s, Alan Lomax began publicizing the Archive by hosting nationally syndicated radio programs of folk music. When the Works Progress Administration's cultural efforts wound down, much of the cultural documentation found its way to the Archive, which, in a real sense, had become a national treasury. In 1941, as the nation drifted toward war, a WPA-prepared checklist appeared of the Archive's recordings from this halcyon era, and in 1942 the first documentary record albums were released from the Archive for public sale and circulation. The collecting was far from over, but the Archive was now clearly immersed in the process of sharing its riches with the public — a process that fueled the folk music revival in the next generation.

In the grassroots folk music world, singers and musicians may be locally or regionally admired, but individual reputations are shaped by direct personal contacts and balanced by community knowledge of many similar artists. The folk revival, however, shared with American popular music a taste for stars and heroes, and the creation of a pantheon of publicly acclaimed folk performers began with the work of the Lomaxes in the 1930s. John Lomax was responsible for introducing Huddie Ledbetter to the world as Lead Belly. He discovered Ledbetter in a Louisiana prison in the early 1930s, had a hand in facilitating his release, and presented him in New York, Washington, D.C., and other cities as a visually and aurally commanding exemplar of grassroots authenticity.

The Lomaxes began comprehensively recording Lead Belly's capacious and diverse repertory, ranging from blues to dance tunes to religious music to sentimental songs. The recording sessions became the basis for *Negro Folk Songs as Sung by Lead Belly* (1936),

Opposite: The Lomaxes' recordings of Lead Belly were continuously released in different formats over the years; this album is from about 1940. Above: Lead Belly impressed audiences with his songcraft, his voice, and his twelve-string guitar. Here, with wife Martha, 1937.

and a generation later the recordings themselves would be issued on LP as grist for the revival mill. Lead Belly enjoyed the new window onto the world that his sponsors provided. But eventually disputes arose about their relationship, particularly regarding the legal rights to the folksinger's songs, and the Lomaxes and Lead Belly parted ways.

The Lead Belly sessions whetted Alan Lomax's appetite for recording projects that went beyond surveys and samplings of tradition. He began documenting the full repertoire of several key performers, including narrative interviews as well as songs – recording, in effect, artistic autobiographies. In addition to Lead Belly, there were long sessions with eastern Kentucky traditionalist and union radical Aunt Molly Jackson; legendary interviews exploring the origin and nature of jazz in New Orleans, as recounted and interpreted by Ferdinand "Jelly Roll" Morton; and equally famous sessions with Oklahoma author and singer Woodrow Wilson "Woody" Guthrie.

A child of the Southern Plains, Woody Guthrie was born in Okemah, Oklahoma, in 1912, grew up partly in the Texas Panhandle, then launched into a life of traveling, which is evoked in his autobiographical novel, *Bound for Glory* (1943). He spent time in his young adult years in California, then moved to New York City, where, as a writer, singer, and social advocate, he joined a growing network that included Pete Seeger, Alan Lomax, and others. He was a folksinger in the classic sense of having a large repertory of traditional songs learned from his family and community. But he also became a prototype of a "folksinger" in the emerging popular sense. A compulsive writer with a keen eye and a sharp wit, he began composing songs on contemporary issues, drawing on classic folk tunes and genres for his settings

Among Guthrie's many songs are "So Long, It's Been Good to

Know You," "Union Maid," "Tom Joad" (after the Okie hero of John Steinbeck's novel *The Grapes of Wrath*), and "This Land Is Your Land." He also popularized the "talking blues" genre of story song/social commentary. By the time of his death from Huntington's chorea in 1967, Guthrie had become a legendary model for singer/songwriters of the next generation – notably Bob Dylan, but also his own son, Arlo Guthrie. America has inherited from Woody Guthrie the image of folksinger as troubadour of the people, composing songs in a roots style that helps grassroots people reflect on their lives and lots.

Charles Seeger and his family were profound influences in many ways on the development of the folk revival in America. Seeger came to Washington, D.C., in the 1930s to work for the New Deal. His first position was with the Resettlement Administration, where he began cultivating ideas about using music as a tool in community development. He and his second wife, Ruth Crawford Seeger, became active participants in Washington's vibrant social and cultural life during the 1930s. A significant composer in her own right, Ruth Crawford Seeger labored intensively on meticulous transcriptions for the Lomaxes' folksong collection *Our Singing Country*. She managed to capture enough detail in her transcriptions to provide both the basic melody and some illumination of the actual style of musical rendition. Her transcription of "Bonaparte's Retreat," by Kentucky fiddler William Stepp, recorded by Alan Lomax for the Archive in 1937, became the source for Aaron Copland's "Hoedown" in *Rodeo*.

The whole Seeger family was seized with enthusiasm for folk music. Son Pete Seeger, by then a young man with a budding

OPPOSITE: WOODY GUTHRIE, 1943. ABOVE: THE SEEGER FAMILY, 1937: RUTH CRAWFORD, MIKE, CHARLES, AND PEGGY (FROM LEFT).

interest in the banjo, plunged into the holdings of the Archive of American Folk Song at the Library of Congress. And young siblings Mike and Peggy Seeger found an astonishing source of authentic folk music right in their own household. The Seegers' housecleaner, Elizabeth "Libba" Cotten, revealed herself to be a fine banjo and guitar player with an African-American repertoire and style she had learned growing up in Chapel Hill, North Carolina. Cotten taught Mike and Peggy Seeger, and she became a fixture on the festival stages of a later generation of the revival, playing her signature song "Freight Train" on guitar in her distinctive left-handed style (backward but tuned in the normal fashion).

After World War II, Washington entered a period of downsizing, and the cultural epicenter shifted to New York, with its growing concentration of communications media and its history as a home for left-wing political activism. Duncan Emrich, as the new head of the Archive of American Folk Song, encouraged regional archives, strengthened ties with the academic world, and broadened the Archive to include American Indian music,

world music, and verbal lore. But though the Archive struggled forward, it was slowed by the general downsizing of government in the late Forties and by the early-Fifties McCarthy hearings, which included investigations into the connections between the folksong revival and left-wing politics. By the later 1950s, Rae Korson, longtime assistant in the Archive and wife of the noted collector of miners' traditions, George Korson, became head of the Archive, nurturing it through an era of scarce resources.

A measure of the shift of energies to entrepreneurial New York was the emergence of Moses Asch's Folkways Records, a growing enterprise that can be seen as a private-sector response to the Library's documentary records. Among Folkways' important artists, which included Woody Guthrie and Lead Belly, was a new singing group that formed during the war, the Almanac Singers. The group included Pete Seeger and Woody Guthrie, as well as various other participants in the progressive movement. In 1948, after Guthrie's departure and with the addition of Lee Hays, Ronnie Gilbert, and Fred Hellerman, the group became known as the Weavers.

The budding folk revival movement also spawned a magazine, *People's Songs,* and it, too, was reconstituted in the 1950s, as *Sing Out!* After the war, Alan Lomax moved into private-sector work, producing folk music records on the Decca label. But with the acceleration of the McCarthy hearings as a national spectacle, the folk revival increasingly became targeted, defiance turned to discouragement, and the movement appeared doomed. But what seemed like the revival's death was only a period of absence from the limelight. Meanwhile, numerous scholars based in regional universities were energetically pursuing field documentation of folk music in their states and regions, publishing collections, starting festivals, and laying the foundation through their teaching for the next generation of the revival. The technological innovation of tape recordings revolutionized field recording in the 1950s by permitting inexpensive, high-quality documentation that greatly expanded the elapsed time. Eventually, everyone would gain ready access to the newer documentary media such as cassettes, digital audiotapes, and compact discs. Meanwhile, a new format for record-

OPPOSITE, FROM TOP: NEW YORK CITY'S WASHINGTON SQUARE PARK WAS THE GATHERING PLACE FOR EARLY FOLK MUSIC ENTHUSIASTS; THE ALMANAC SINGERS, 1941: WOODY GUTHRIE, MILLARD LAMPELL, BESS LOMAX HAWES, PETE SEEGER, ARTHUR STERN, AND SIS CUNNINGHAM (FROM LEFT); THE WEAVERS, 1950: PETE SEEGER, LEE HAYS, FRED HELLERMAN, AND RONNIE GILBERT (CLOCKWISE FROM LEFT). THIS PAGE, FROM TOP: THE KINGSTON TRIO IN SAN FRANCISCO, 1961: BOB SHANE, DAVE GUARD, AND NICK REYNOLDS (FROM LEFT); PETER, PAUL AND MARY, CIRCA 1964: PETER YARROW, MARY TRAVERS, AND PAUL STOOKEY (FROM LEFT).

ings, the long-playing record (LP), was immediately adopted as the favored medium for releasing folk recordings, and labels such as Riverside joined Folkways in producing records specializing in both the roots and the revival strands of folk music. The Library of Congress converted its older 78s to long-playing format and produced new LPs as well. A generation of students discovered the maroon-and-gray Library of Congress albums, often with red vinyl discs, in their university and city libraries.

The revival, as it turns out, was merely gathering its energies before bursting onto the public stage again in the late 1950s. Various revival songs such as "Rock Island Line" and the Weavers' version of Lead Belly's "Goodnight Irene" found their way into the pop market, keeping alive a sense of the revival as a movement. The Kingston Trio's 1957 recording of "Tom Dooley" was a particular benchmark event, not only because it became hugely popular but because it signaled the coming of age of a new generation of folk-revival performers. The group had modeled its singing to some extent on the Weavers, but its "Tom Dooley" had a vaguely Caribbean-style beat, despite being an Appalachian ballad recorded by song collector Frank Warner from mountain musician Frank Proffitt in western North Carolina. In the wake of the song's popularity, dozens of other singing groups sprang up in college dorms and urban folk gathering places like the legendary Washington Square Park in Manhattan's Greenwich Village. One of the most enduringly popular groups was Peter, Paul and Mary, whose 1962 recording of "If I Had a Hammer" reflected the revival movement's close ties with the civil rights movement, Vietnam War protests, and political activism throughout the 1960s.

New York City was unquestionably the center of the revival in the Fifties. Washington Square became a mecca that attracted not only New Yorkers but visitors from around the country. Izzy Young's Folklore Center, a Greenwich Village musical instruments and record shop and small performance space, provided another kind of convening place. In addition to Folkways and Riverside, many small labels specializing in folk music were based in the New York area, as were the major labels that periodically featured folk music in the wider national marketplace. Keeping the folk revival pulse alive on the airwaves were such WNYC radio segments as Henrietta Yurchenco's program and Oscar Brand's weekly show. New York was the perfect breeding ground for new talent such as Harry Belafonte, who, beginning in 1950, tapped his own Caribbean heritage and the folk music reservoir of the Library of Congress to launch a phenomenally successful career as a popular interpreter of Caribbean roots music.

"I DIDN'T KNOW WHERE BOB DYLAN HAD COME FROM, BUT I HEARD EVERYBODY TALKING ABOUT HIM. SAID, 'THIS GUY WRITES A GOOD SONG EVERY WEEK.' AND AT THE FOLKLORE CENTER THEY'D PUT UP COPIES OF IT ON THE BULLETIN BOARD — IT'D SAY, 'HERE'S BOB'S LATEST.' AND SO WE INVITED HIM TO A HOOTENANNY, AT CARNEGIE HALL, IT WAS. AND I REMEMBER MEETING WITH HIM AND SOME OF THE OTHER MUSICIANS — WE SAID, "LOOK, WE'RE ALL GONNA HAVE TO SING ONLY THREE SONGS, BECAUSE WE'VE ASKED TOO MANY PEOPLE TO BE ON THE PROGRAM. SO EACH OF US HAS ONLY TEN MINUTES." BOB KINDA SMILED, AND SAID, 'WHAT DO I DO? ONE OF MY SONGS IS TEN MINUTES LONG.' " —PETE SEEGER

One of New York's clubs and coffeehouses helped launch the television show *Hootenanny*, which captivated the country in 1963. In 1962, Ed McCurdy started a weekly evening at the Bitter End coffeehouse, when various singers could try out their new songs — what today would be called an "open mike" night. He called it Hootenanny, and when the idea became popular, the concept and name were sold to ABC-TV.

The word *hootenanny* for a singing party had already been adopted, but in limited circles. Pete Seeger and Woody Guthrie originally encountered the term when they visited a union social gathering in Seattle, and they imported it into the New York revival circle. From there, the word and concept spread across the country, particularly on college campuses. The network television show interjected the word *hootenanny* into common American parlance, but the show business values of the television program caused some anguish among the movement faithful, who always longed for a national audience but rarely found one on their own terms.

The most important artist to come out of the New York coffeehouse scene was Bob Dylan. Born Robert Zimmerman in 1941 in Duluth, Minnesota, Dylan grew up in nearby Hibbing. His career aspirations led him to adopt a new name and identity, shape his performance style around Woody Guthrie's model, and compose new songs, as Guthrie had, based on folk genres such as ballads and talking blues. Dylan embodied the revival's founders' dream for a new generation to carry the movement forward, and after Dylan arrived in New York City in 1960, Pete Seeger did much to foster his early career. Dylan's songs both tapped the folk reservoir and exhibited a creative knack for capturing the issues and spiritual rhythms of the times. Many, like "Blowin' in the Wind," were picked up by Seeger and Peter, Paul and Mary, as well as by other singers, and became the era's anthems. Today, they sound like musical posters of the 1960s. But if New York City was the hub for the revival during this period, the spokes stretched

THIS PAGE, CLOCKWISE FROM LEFT: THE FOLKLORE CENTER'S IZZY YOUNG: FOLKWAYS' MOSES ASCH:
MISSISSIPPI JOHN HURT WAS ONE OF SEVERAL BLUESMEN REDISCOVERED AT FOLK FESTIVALS IN THE 1960S:
THE PHILADELPHIA FOLK FESTIVAL, 1967. OPPOSITE, CLOCKWISE FROM TOP: THE NEW LOST CITY RAMBLERS:
TRACY SCHWARZ, JOHN COHEN, AND MIKE SEEGER (FROM LEFT); ELIZABETH COTTEN AT NEWPORT, 1963: A
FEATURE ON THE NEW LOST CITY RAMBLERS IN THE 1965 NEWPORT FOLK FESTIVAL PROGRAM.

throughout the nation. Clubs and coffeehouses provided bases for regional talent and venues for traveling acts. Club 47, for example, opened just off Harvard Square in Cambridge, Massachusetts, in 1958 and closed in 1968. It was the first regular venue for local singer Joan Baez, who was then invited to Rhode Island's prestigious Newport Folk Festival, where she quickly gained national fame. It also provided a regular venue for the Charles River Valley Boys, the Jim Kweskin Jug Band, Tom Rush, Arlo Guthrie, Taj Mahal, Phil Ochs, Dave Van Ronk, Ramblin' Jack Elliott, and many others.

A legacy of the 1930s, folk festivals reached as far back as 1928, when the Mountain Dance and Folk Festival was first organized in Asheville, North Carolina, by Bascom Lamar Lunsford, a local lawyer, folksinger, and folksong collector. Another important folk festival from 1931 onward, the Whitetop Folk Festival in southwestern Virginia was primarily organized by collector and scholar Annabel Morris Buchanan, and was once visited by Eleanor Roosevelt. Many other folk festivals sprang up over the next two decades, sometimes sponsored by regional university professors devoted to folksong.

The majority of the early festivals had a regional or ethnic focus, which could be loosely described as "mono-cultural." Perhaps the most important event for introducing a new multicultural model was the National Folk Festival, which began in 1934 in St. Louis, Missouri, and enlisted the support of a number of folk revival scholars and activists from around the nation. It had a track record of public visibility, often because of the support or sponsorship of local newspapers. Founded and long directed by Sarah Gertrude Knott, the National Folk Festival kept alive by traveling from city to city as a movable feast of folk music. Knott also helped share the model by developing state or regional folk festivals such as the Florida Folk Festival in White Springs. The National Folk Festival still flourishes today, directed by Joe Wilson under the aegis of the National Council for the Traditional Arts.

The inauguration of the Newport Folk Festival in 1959 gave the folk-festival movement enormous, fresh impetus. It brought together many movement leaders like Alan Lomax and Pete Seeger, and it was managed and directed by Ralph Rinzler, a young urban bluegrass performer and devotee of Library of Congress records. Rinzler was not only the festival organizer; he did field reconnaissance to locate new traditional musicians. The Balfa Brothers from the Cajun country of southwestern Louisiana and country-folk musician Doc Watson from the North Carolina Blue Ridge Mountains are among his famous musical discoveries.

Newport quickly became the national stage for a new generation of folk performers. Its organizers carefully interspersed grassroots musicians, like the Balfas or the Appalachians' Roscoe Holcomb and Clarence Ashley, with products of the burgeoning urban folksong circuit, like Baez, Dylan, and Peter, Paul and Mary. Newport became a proving ground for performers in a rapidly evolving national circuit of festivals, college shows, and clubs.

As a testimony to Newport's success, the Smithsonian Institution

brought in Rinzler to launch a new festival on the National Mall. The Festival of American Folklife in 1967 marked the return of the folk revival movement to Washington. The instantaneous success of the Smithsonian's festival led to legislation proposing a new folklife foundation to parallel the recently established National Endowments for the Arts and the Humanities. In 1974 this author joined the National Endowment for the Arts to create the Folk Arts Program, and the National Endowment for the Humanities increased its attention somewhat to folklore and folklife initiatives. In 1976 the American Folklife

Preservation Act was signed into law, transforming the grant-giving foundation into an operating organization, entitled the American Folklife Center at the Library of Congress. When this author moved to the American Folklife Center, Bess Lomax Hawes became the new head of the Arts Endowment's Folk Arts Program. Thus, the folk revival that began in Washington, D.C., in the 1930s returned in full force to its governmental base in the 1970s.

But just as the federal government seemed to be taking folklore

and folk music into account again, the folk revival movement was trapped in an identity crisis. Some argued that 1965 was really the turning point. The movement valued above all else the intimacy of personal expression, created by soloists and small ensembles; though the folk revival sometimes mobilized large crowds, its soul was found in intimate gatherings and informal sing-alongs. The roots music that the revival emulated seemed to stand for the same kind of personal interactions. Hence the revival always put a premium on acoustic instruments and defined itself as nonelectrified — not plugged in. Thus, by some accounts, the

revival ended when Dylan went electric. In a legendary appearance at Newport in 1965, Dylan, backed by the Paul Butterfield Blues Band, played his "Maggie's Farm" with shrieking electric guitar, harsh vocal delivery, and daunting volume, provoking anguish, confusion, and charges of betrayal from the revival community.

For the rising singer/songwriters of the revival stage, it was indeed a fork in the road. One path led to the national pop music scene, with its embrace of modernity, its countercultural tone, and its potential audience of millions. Many bands with folk-revival roots, like San Francisco's Grateful Dead, moved as if on cue onto this track. The other path led to the continuing evolution of the intimate singer/songwriter playing coffeehouses, bars, and clubs and recording on independent labels. This path could also lead to national fame in popular music, as Judy Collins, Bonnie Raitt, and Bruce Springsteen were to demonstrate, but it represented a different array of values and stylistic preferences. For the rest of the century these two paths continued to evolve, seeming to diverge but often crossfertilizing.

Meanwhile, the revival developed a third path devoted less to song and more to instrumental music and dance. The revival musicians of the 1950s and 1960s were for the most part singers whose instruments were employed primarily to accompany their songs. But the rise of the New Lost City Ramblers in the later 1950s and 1960s signaled a new kind of cultural chemistry. The band included Mike Seeger (Pete's younger brother), John Cohen, and Tom Paley, who was replaced by Tracy Schwarz in 1962. Their repertory and style drew heavily from old-timey and hillbilly records of the 1920s and 1930s, supplemented by pieces learned directly from rural southern musicians like Dock Boggs. The band carefully copied the tense, nasal vocal delivery, complete with the delicate vocal ornamentation, of their southern masters. Like other young revivalists, they were avid consumers of the pioneering Harry Smith six-LP compilation, *Anthology of American Folk Music*, an astonishing collection of early hillbilly, blues, and other 78 rpm records of roots music from the 1920s, which appeared on Folkways Records in 1952. Splendid instrumentalists all, wielding fiddle, banjo, guitar, and other instruments, the New Lost

OPPOSITE: YOUNG FOLK MUSIC ENTHUSIASTS AT THE NEWPORT FOLK FESTIVAL, 1968. ABOVE: TAJ MAHAL IN AN IMPROMPTU PERFORMANCE AT NEWPORT THE SAME YEAR.

City Ramblers imitated the old records in such impeccable detail that the hillbilly bands seemed resurrected, body and soul, for a new urbane audience.

Other instrumentalists joined this new wave of the revival. The Hollow Rock String Band, playing in the Durham–Chapel Hill, North Carolina, area in 1966–68, developed string-band versions of tunes learned by this author on fiddle, from such oldtime fiddlers as Henry Reed of Glen Lyn, Virginia. Others were drawn to bluegrass as a powerful new acoustic idiom of the Upper South. College students suddenly discovered fiddlers' conventions in the South and elsewhere, and some took the next step by visiting and apprenticing with musicians like Tommy Jarrell, whose home in Toast, North Carolina, became an oldtime music mecca. The square dance was rediscovered, too — always with live music rather than recordings — and young urban acolytes revived the dwindling New England tradition of contradancing and spread it from coast to coast. By the 1980s and 1990s, a national network of thousands of young people played "oldtime music," and dancing squares and contras became part of the cultural fare of the revival.

Southern white traditions were not the only object of the revival's attentions. Since the 1930s, documentarians like the Lomaxes had sought out spirituals, hollers, blues, and other veins of African-American music. In the 1940s and 1950s, the revival network incorporated blues singers like the Reverend Gary Davis and Josh White, and in the 1960s young enthusiasts rediscovered forgotten blues artists on the African-American "race" records of the 1920s and 1930s. Blues devotees in cities like Washington, D.C., and Berkeley, California, traveled through the South, sometimes steered by clues in blues lyrics from a half century earlier, to locate musicians whose voices they had discovered on old 78 rpm records. Thus Mississippi John Hurt, Skip James, Son House, Mance Lipscomb, and numerous other blues singers enjoyed a second artistic life in their old age and became palpable models for a generation of young blues players.

The revival's durable cultural pattern of documentation, presentation, imitation, and recycling spread in the 1970s to other ethnic and regional traditions. In the 1970s, for example, young urban musicians began learning Cajun and zydeco music from Louisiana masters, stimulating in the process a reawakening of interest in roots music throughout French Louisiana. Similarly, young urban musicians like New York's Henry Sapoznik, whose musical pilgrimages began with such oldtime southern musicians as Tommy Jarrell, proceeded to uncover and reintroduce the older Yiddish klezmer tradition as an active ingredient on the American music scene. Eventually the revival touched virtually every ethnic tradition resident in America.

After the civil rights era of the 1960s was superseded by the Vietnam War protests of the 1970s, the revival's taste for political advocacy gradually faded. The political agenda of the early revival movement — particularly the civil rights agenda — briefly reverberated once again in the 1960s, when "We Shall Overcome" was added to the national folk repertory. But in the long run, there was a contradiction between the movement's yearning for national political impact and its fidelity to a set of countercultural values. The next generation of the revival was more low-key about political agendas, while inveterate activist Pete Seeger found a new focus in environmental activism, showing with benefit concerts on the sloop Clearwater how community organizing could help clean up and save the polluted Hudson River.

Though political advocacy gradually dwindled or shifted ground, cultural advocacy was always inherent in the revival. Admiring and imitating the art of another cultural tradition grants that culture a voice and visibility. Thus the folk revival has always been inherently multicultural in its worldview. All the ethnic and regional revival movements of the later Twentieth Century reflect the revival's ingenious combination of scholarly research, cultural advocacy, and artistic immersion, and they have all had the larger effect of deepening the nation's sense of its multicultural fabric. The effect has been magnified by the academic fields of folklore and ethnomusicology, which have created a network of cultural specialists in the late Twentieth Century whose work in state and local arts councils, historical societies, and other cultural organizations identifies and fosters roots traditions around the country.

Today, particularly in rural and small-town regions where oldtimers' and newcomers' lives have gradually grown together, it is no longer easy to distinguish traditional musicians from revival musicians. The revival as a countercultural movement seems to be blending gradually with the older traditions it set out to revive. But in the meantime, the revival has added a new cultural process to the American cultural repertory. Working side by side with the classic process of ancient tradition, the newer cultural process of documentation, presentation, imitation, and recycling represents a powerful legacy that the American folk revival has bequeathed to the cultural future.

OPPOSITE: THE PROGRAM FOR THE NEWPORT FOLK FESTIVAL, 1965, THE YEAR DYLAN WENT ELECTRIC. THE COVER ART IS BY PAINTER BEN SHAHN'S SON JONATHAN.

Jonathan Shahn

**newport folk festival
july 22-25   1965**

ALAN LOMAX: *In 1933, my father, John Lomax, and I set out to record the unknown secular black music of the people of the country. And we went to the penitentiaries where the music was still being used to keep the hearts of the prisoners alive, under the terrible conditions in which they lived and worked in those dark old days. Lead Belly was one of the people we met. He was a champion among champions. He had work song traditions of both Texas and Louisiana, and he had the backwoods cowboy songs and square dance traditions of his own from growing up in Louisiana. He performed them all with an incredible fire that made him stand out. Even in a world where there were hundreds of other great singers, Lead Belly would be noticed, because he had a voice like a bugle. You could hear him a mile away when he got going. He felt himself to be the champion of the twelve-string guitar players of the world, because his hands moved like lightning.*

The thing that has impressed the world about Lead Belly was his fiery courage, the fact that, although he grew up in the environment which was really one of the most dangerous in the world — although he'd been in the penitentiary — it didn't really get to him. He came out of it feeling somehow more sure of himself. He said, "When I begin to blow my horn, the axes get to walkin' and the chips get to talkin'." That was the way he felt about himself. It was this note of triumph that echoed through Lead Belly's voice. He carried that sound right into his city performances, and he had standing ovations everywhere we presented him. And suddenly, Lead Belly and the Lomaxes were national figures.

I met Woody [Guthrie more than] fifty years ago. We were doing a benefit for the Spanish Loyalists fighting against Franco, and Woody was on the show. It was one of the first nights he was in New York. He stepped out on the stage, this little tiny guy, big bushy hair, with this great voice and his guitar, and just electrified us all. I remember the first song I heard him sing was a ballad about Pretty Boy Floyd. I realized, listening to this song, that I was meeting a guy who was a ballad maker, in the same sense as the people who made "Jesse James" and "Casey Jones" and all the ballads that I spent my life trying to find and preserve for the American people.

At that time I was doing a coast-to-coast radio show for CBS, and I wanted to have Woody on the show. So he went home with me back to Washington [D.C.] and spent about two weeks in my house. It was an amazing experience. It just happened that I had a record that he liked — "John Hardy" by the Carter Family. He played that record, and before the two weeks were over, he wore it completely slap-dab out. That was the tune he used for "Tom Joad." He wouldn't sleep in a bed. He said he didn't want to get soft, because he was on the road at that time, and he didn't want to get used to sleeping in beds. And he wouldn't eat from the table; he ate out of the sink. He said he didn't want to get softened up by civilization.

When I met Woody and Lead Belly, I was in charge of the collecting work at the Archive of American Folk Song that my father and I helped to found at the Library of Congress. I was traveling all over the country, handing out recording gear, opening up new areas of America that hadn't been recorded before, and finding all kinds of people. The thing that I always tried to do with important singers when I met them was to sit down and record everything they knew. Give them a first real run-through of their art. They heard it all back, they listened to it, they rejoiced in it with someone who appreciated it, maybe, as much as they did. And this was a tremendous experience for people who may have been isolated in their own communities. It's a process I call TLC, and I think that's the most important thing that folklorists and people interested in people's art do in their work. They give music, musicians, talent an audience that maybe they lost in their own community because times have changed. Commercial music has come in and taken the place of what they had. So they get a chance to understand how great they are in that process of listening, recording, and recapitulating their whole artistic heritage.

BELOW, FROM LEFT: ALAN LOMAX (CENTER) JAMMING WITH BLUES AND FOLK MUSICIANS, INCLUDING PETE SEEGER (RIGHT), 1962; LOMAX (FAR RIGHT) AT NEWPORT WITH A GATHERING OF ROOTS ARTISTS AND FRIENDS, INCLUDING HOWLIN' WOLF (IN CHAIR NEXT TO LOMAX) AND BUKKA WHITE (CENTER, WITHOUT GUITAR). OPPOSITE: LOMAX IN 1941.

PETE SEEGER: *When my father [Charles Seeger] first played me a record of "Pretty Polly," it was totally strange to me. Where did this kind of music come from? My father explained, "Well, people in the southern mountains still play this way." In 1935, he took me down to a local festival, a mountain song and dance festival run by a country lawyer in Asheville, North Carolina, for local people. Not many people came from very far. It was held in the local baseball field. There must have been a thousand or two thousand people there. One of the singers was a woman probably in her forties or fifties, leaning back in a rocking chair and strumming a banjo and singing and having so much fun. She had decorated her banjo with butterflies and flowers. She'd painted on the drum of the banjo. Her name was Samantha Bumgarner, and I was completely intrigued and got [festival promoter] Bascom [Lamar Lunsford] to show me one or two ideas about how you would play the [five-string banjo]. He says, "Well, you don't fret it, you just play it with your thumb. You call it the thumb beat." So you get both the harmony and the little high ring. When I traveled around hitchhiking in 1940 that's when I really learned [to play the banjo] because up until that time I only could just pick at it. But by the end of 1940, I'd known there were numerous ways you could pick a banjo.*

When I was young, I wanted to be a journalist. I figured if I could be a reporter on some newspaper, I could live a happy life. . . . But I failed utterly to get a job. It was 1938 when I dropped out of college, and I had an aunt who taught school, and she said, "Peter, come sing some of your songs for my class. I can get five dollars for you." It seemed like stealing to do what [I'd] done all my life for the fun of it, but I went and took the money and quit looking for a regular job. And pretty soon I was singing at another school for three dollars, and another one for two dollars. And then I had a relative who had fallen in love with the Soviet Union. She was [a] well-to-do woman and she was in her sixties at that time. And she said, "I'm coming back with some lantern slides to show and raise money for the magazine 'Soviet Russia Today.' Will you come sing some of your songs?" I said, "They don't have anything to do with Soviet Russia." She said, "That's all right. You'll get the people singing. That's the important thing." Well, she paid me ten dollars—can you imagine? I said, "Cousin Susan, this is ridiculous to pay me ten dollars. These people have to work all week to make ten dollars." She said, "Well, you deserve it." She had the money. She didn't want me to starve to death and I think she wanted to encourage me as a musician.

In '39, I was the first intern at the Library of Congress. Alan [Lomax] paid me fifteen dollars a week to help him. He had stacks of hundreds of records to go through and didn't have time to do it all himself, so he had me listen to 'em first and try and pick out some which were more useful for him to listen to. So that's where I heard Uncle Dave Macon for the first time, and I heard Dock Boggs and Gid Tanner and His Skillet Lickers. All sorts of country songs. Record companies sold a hillbilly catalogue in the South, and they also had what they call a "race" catalogue, which had in it blues and also gospel music and some preaching, too.

Well, I never expected, really, to do much more than sing in occasional schools and summer camps. But after World War II, in 1946, I saw Lead Belly and Josh White singing at a little place called the Village Vanguard. I don't know whether it was my wife or Alan Lomax or somebody suggested [I sing there], but I got all of two hundred dollars a week singing—that's like two thousand a week [today]. And [I] got a nice review in 'The New

Yorker': "Pete Seeger singing of far-off places like Tennessee." I think they were all amused to see this relatively innocent, skinny New Englander singing songs of strange places [where I'd] never been—"bloodshed in Kentucky" and so on. I really [didn't] like singing in nightclubs, [though]. I'm a cheap drunk—give me a couple beers and I fall asleep—and I don't smoke and I hate to smell all the smoke in a nightclub. So I didn't look for any more jobs like this. However, three years later, Lee Hays and I said, "Why don't we get a group together like the Almanac [Singers], and let's rehearse." Woody [Guthrie] used to say the Almanacs were a group that rehearsed on the stage. So the Weavers started in. Roy Ashley first sang at a hootenanny on Thanksgiving 1948. And by February 1949, we had given ourselves a name, the Weavers. Well, we were about to break up come fall because we had tried to make a living at little parties, but there weren't enough little parties. The so-called left wing was being blacklisted into oblivion. And I wanted to sing with a group. You can't sing "When the Saints Go Marching In" by yourself unless you've got a great voice like Mahalia Jackson's. And I just felt my own limitations too much as a musician and as a singer, and I wanted to sing with a group. So I went back to this nightclub. And Max Gordon, the man who ran it, says, "Pete, I'd hire you again for two hundred dollars a week, but I don't want this group." I said, "If the whole group would work for two hundred dollars a week, would you take 'em?" He had to laugh. He said, "Well, I guess I can't turn you down. Try it." And then he must have been intrigued by us because we were a good gang. We needed a little rehearsing, but he literally gave us free rehearsal time for six months. Well, four months later, we were attracting pretty big crowds. But in February, I can remember one night, there were four people in the whole nightclub. We didn't bother singing from the mike. We went around and sat around the table with them and said, "What would you like to sing?" And he raised our pay. Originally we were supposed to get two hundred dollars a week and free hamburgs. And he came in one night to the kitchen and saw the size of the hamburgs I was makin' several times a night. And he said, "Let's raise your pay. Two hundred fifty dollars a week, but no more free hamburgs."

[Later on] I taught banjo to half a dozen young people, and one of them was such a good banjo picker, he was playing rings around me in three months. Eric Weissberg. He became famous later on [through] a movie called 'Deliverance.' Teaching some students taught me enough so I thought I could write a book and I put out a fifty-nine page book, 'How to Play the Five String Banjo,' mimeographed it and sold it for $1.59. Had someone run off five hundred copies and sold them in four years. But one of those five hundred copies was sold to a student at Stanford University named Dave Guard. And he sends me a letter, says, "Pete, I've been putting that book to hard use. I and two others have a group we call the Kingston Trio." The third edition in 1962 has sold a few thousand copies every year. That book put my kids through school.

"PETE SEEGER WAS A HERO AND MENTOR, NOT JUST IN TERMS OF WHAT HE DID WITH HIS MUSIC, BUT THE WAY IN WHICH HE INCORPORATED HIS OWN VALUES AND DREAMS, AND HIS ACTIVISM, INTO A MUSICAL SETTING." —PETER YARROW

OPPOSITE, CLOCKWISE FROM TOP: PETE SEEGER WITH HIS FAMILY AT THEIR HOUSE IN BEACON, NEW YORK, 1958; SEEGER WRITING AT HOME; THE WEAVERS AT THE TIME OF THEIR 1979 REUNION, RE-CREATING THEIR 1950 PUBLICITY PHOTO: PETE SEEGER, LEE HAYS, RONNIE GILBERT, AND FRED HELLERMAN (FROM LEFT).

DOC WATSON:

I loved the guitar when I didn't know what it was. I heard the guitar on early [folk] recordings, and I wondered what kind of instrument it was. What did it look like? I'd heard the guitar played by a local blind lady when I was just a little boy. It was the sweetest sound I thought I'd ever heard.

When I was thirteen, my brother borrowed a guitar. What Dad didn't know was, an old boy I went to school with, named Paul Montgomery, taught me three or four chords. And when my brother borrowed that guitar, I was foolin' with it one morning, and Dad said, "Son, learn to play me a song on that thing by the time I get back from work and I'll get you a guitar Saturday." Well, it didn't take me but fifteen or twenty minutes after Dad got going before I figured out the chords to "When the Roses Bloom in Dixieland." I got my guitar.

The first thing I did playing outside the home was playing on the street. It was tough, hard work in hot weather. But I felt I had to get along, you know. And in those days a show had to be flashy, and a fellow with a handicap couldn't do much on the stage in the way of acting to go with his pickin'. So I didn't get into that until they began to do fiddlers' conventions, which had contests for guitar players. I got into that, and began to win a few prizes, and I thought that maybe I was doin' pretty good.

I first met [banjoist] Clarence Ashley in the late Forties. . . . Somebody told Clarence Ashley that I was a pretty good guitar player and knew a lot of the old-timey things, and that was his thing, the good oldtime tunes. So, he came and asked me if I'd play music with him. We sat down and did four or five songs. He said, "Son, you'll do. I do believe I'll take you along."

8

[In the early Sixties], Ralph Rinzler came down looking for Clarence Ashley, and Clarence told him about me. He heard me play, and in the fall of '60 he came back with his friend Eugene Earle, and they recorded me for Folkways. He decided I had something to offer in the form of entertainment in the folk revival. So, I went along. He was a member of the Greenbrier [Boys], the folk-bluegrass group that was popular in those days. And he decided, as the old saying goes, [to] take me under his wing and help me get used to being out on the road and doing things on my own. The first thing he said to me was when we were discussing programming: "Now Doc, play the good oldtime traditional music until you get your foot in the door in coffeehouses and clubs, and then you can expand your repertoire a little bit there and delve into the other things you like in music and play a few of those." And that's exactly what I did.

By the time I'd played a few engagements at coffeehouses and college folk festivals, I began to earn enough money to kinda realize that I didn't need charity from the Commission for the Blind in the state, and I went and canceled it. My little daughter went with me, bless her heart, to file my first income tax. She was more excited about it than I was, and she was just a child: "I'm so proud of you, Daddy." Well I meant, if it was possible, to earn enough that I'd never have to go back [there] again. A man's got some pride, you know. There's more to it than playing music for a livin' — there is a whole lot more that goes with it. You have a family to love and look after.

OPPOSITE: DOC WATSON AND HIS SON MERLE WATSON, 1964.
BELOW: A LIBRARY OF CONGRESS PHOTO OF RURAL AMERICA IN THE 1930S.

1638 Colonial communities begin to convert African-born slaves to Christianity. **1650** Work songs, spirituals, and jubilee songs, as well as clapping and the playing of homemade instruments, become common on southern plantations. **1734** The Great Awakening, a series of religious revivals sweeping the American colonies, revolutionizes worship, and many slaves convert to Christianity. At the end of the century, James McGready leads the Second Awakening, attended by both blacks and whites. **1801** After years of unfair treatment in white churches, African-Americans begin a movement toward separate congregations. Richard Allen compiles a collection of hymns for use only in all-black congregations. **1861** The Civil War begins when the South secedes from the Union and becomes the Confederate States of America. **1865** The war ends with the Confederate surrender. **1871** The Fisk Jubilee Singers, a group of African-American students, tour for the first time, raising funds for Fisk University. They will perform for white audiences, publish 'Jubilee Songs,' and share their spirituals with the world. **1900** The Johnson Brothers, Baptists from Jacksonville, Florida, write the Negro national anthem, "Lift Every Voice and Sing," for a presentation in celebration of Abraham Lincoln's birthday. **1920s** The recording of black gospel singers and black sermons becomes more popular. Toward the decade's end and throughout the 1930s, African-Americans stray from their a cappella style and bring musical accompaniment into the church. **1920** Commercial radio helps gospel music reach audiences beyond the local crowd. **1921** 'Gospel Pearls,' a songbook for the National Baptist Convention, is published in Nashville. **1928** The Silver Leaf Quartet travels from Norfolk, Virginia, to New York to record for Okeh Records. **1931** Thomas Dorsey and Theodore Frye establish the National Convention of Gospel Choirs and Choruses, the first black gospel chorus. Dorsey would later become known as "the Father of Gospel Music." **1932** Dorsey opens the first black gospel-music publishing company, the Dorsey House of Music. Philadelphia's Tindley Quaker City Gospel Singers record. **1938** Rosetta Tharpe records "Rock Me" (Decca), the first gospel recording to sell one million copies. She also takes gospel music into a secular setting for the first time when she sings at New York's Cotton Club. **1944** Robert H. Harris forms the National Quartet Convention. **1950** Becoming gospel's first heart-throb, Sam Cooke joins the Soul Stirrers as lead vocalist. Mahalia Jackson performs at Carnegie Hall. **1955** The Montgomery bus boycott furthers African-Americans' fight for equality when blacks refuse to ride segregated buses. **1957** Sam Cooke becomes the first major gospel star to cross over to secular music when he leaves the Soul Stirrers to record pop hits. The Southern Christian Leadership Conference (SCLC) is formed and led by the Reverend Dr. Martin Luther King Jr. **1959** The music of the black church enters the pop charts with hits such as the Isley Brothers' "Shout" (Number Forty-seven) and Ray Charles's "What'd I Say" (Number Six). **1960** SNCC is formed to speed desegregation in the South. **1961** The National Academy of Recording Arts and Sciences introduces a Grammy category for Best Gospel or Other Religious Recording. Mahalia Jackson wins for her single "Everytime I Feel the Spirit." **1962** The James Cleveland Singers, organized by Reverend James Cleveland in 1960, release their debut album, 'Peace Be Still.' **1963** Mahalia Jackson, Marion Anderson, and the SNCC Freedom Singers are present at the March on Washington, where Dr. King delivers his famous "I Have a Dream" speech. **1964** Congress passes the Civil Rights Act, ending the Jim Crow laws. **1968** Dr. King is assassinated in Memphis. James Cleveland helps found the Gospel Music Workshop of America in Detroit. **1969** Unadulterated gospel music reaches the pop chart with the Edwin Hawkins Singers' "Oh Happy Day," which hits Number Four in the U.S. and becomes the world's biggest-selling gospel record to date. **1972** Aretha Franklin wins a Grammy for Best Soul Gospel Performance with her single "Amazing Grace," from the album of the same name (Atlantic), which hits Number Seven on the pop chart and Number Two on the R&B chart. **1980** Al Green begins recording strictly gospel albums, rather than pop, signing to the gospel label Myrrh. 'Gospel According to Al Green,' a documentary by Robert Mugge, is released four years later. **1987** The Winans, a gospel quartet of siblings from Detroit, release 'Decisions' (Qwest), which reaches Number Thirty on the R&B chart. **1991** BeBe and CeCe Winans's 'Different Lifestyles' (Capitol) goes to Number Seventy-four on the pop chart and is a Number One hit on the R&B chart. **1994** Kirk Franklin's debut, 'Kirk Franklin and the Family' (GospoCentric), becomes a Number Six R&B hit and reaches Number Fifty-eight on the pop chart. **1995** David Gough, president and CEO of DoJohn Records, establishes the Gospel Music Hall of Fame and Museum in Detroit. Its purpose is to archive gospel materials and induct individuals who have furthered gospel music.

THE
JUBILEE SINGERS,
EX-SLAVE STUDENTS
OF
FISK UNIVERSITY, NASHVILLE, TENNESSEE,
WILL GIVE A
SERVICE OF SONG
UNDER DISTINGUISHED PATRONAGE,
IN THE
FREE TRADE HALL, MANCHESTER,
ON TUESDAY, JANUARY 13TH.
CHAIR WILL BE TAKEN AT 7.30.

The Jubilee Singers have appeared and sung their Slave Melodies before many illustrious persons, the following names being among the number:—

HER MAJESTY THE QUEEN, at Argyll Lodge.
THEIR ROYAL HIGHNESSES THE PRINCE AND PRINCESS OF WALES, at Carlton House Terrace.
THE DUKE AND DUCHESS OF ARGYLL, on three different occasions.
REV. C. H. SPURGEON, at his residence; also at Metropolitan Tabernacle.
IN SCOTLAND—JOHN BURNS, ESQ.; SIR PETER COATS; CHARLES DALRYMPLE, ESQ., M.P.; CAPTAIN SULIVEN; ARCHDEACON PREST; THE LORD PROVOST OF GLASGOW; LORD PROVOST OF EDINBURGH; LORD PROVOST OF PERTH; COUNTESS OF KINTORE, &c., &c.

Seats, Numbered and Reserved, 3s.; Balcony and Second Seats, 2s.; Third Class, 1s.

Plan of Hall and Tickets for sale on Saturday, Jan. 3rd, at Mr. JOHNSON'S, 104, Market Street, Manchester. Persons can be supplied with Tickets by sending P.O.O. to Mr. Johnson.

STATEMENT.

THE Jubilee Singers are a company of eleven students of Fisk University, one of the chartered institutions established by the American Missionary Association for the education of freedmen, in Nashville, Tennessee, U.S.A.

They appear, not as professional singers, but as a company of students desirous of using their musical ability to help the University of which they are members, in the time of its necessity. They have undertaken to earn fourteen thousand pounds, which will pay for the new site of twenty-five acres, and build Jubilee Hall, the first of the series of permanent college buildings necessary to the success of the University.

Eight thousand pounds have already been earned in America. They come to Great Britain by the advice of many friends, hoping to secure the six thousand pounds required to complete the building.

The Services of Song are given under the management of the Rev. G. D. PIKE, District Secretary of the American Missionary Association, and GEORGE L. WHITE, Treasurer of Fisk University.

ADDRESS—18, Adam Street, Strand, London; and 1, Acomb Street, Oxford Road, Manchester.

HALLELUJAH: THE SACRED MUSIC OF BLACK AMERICA BY
CLAUDIA PERRY

Black American gospel music has its roots in every aspect of culture that matters – commerce, ardor, and self-determination. On the most basic level, gospel music forged together in the fire of slavery two seemingly irreconcilable musical traditions: the timeless, indigenous music of Africa and Eighteenth-Century European Christian hymns. Slave owners – like Christian imperialists the world over – viewed but the first African-Americans Christianity as a "civilizing" force, owners could not have foreseen. found in the faith something their tures, families, and homes, the Brutally cut off from their cul- figure of the martyred Christ and earliest African slaves found in the ance and redemption an iconogra- the religion's promises of deliver- their own plight. phy and a worldview that spoke to

When sung by slaves, the very same hymns the slaves' white overseers sang in their churches could take on an entirely different, though not entirely unrelated, meaning. For example, when slaves sang "Steal Away to Jesus," it was often a way to communicate plans for escape or rebellion: "Steal away, steal away, steal away to Jesus! Steal away, steal away home, I ain't got long to stay here," they sang before they "board- ed" the Underground Railroad to freedom. Today, gospel music remains a vibrant part of African- American church life, offering spiritual uplift in the face of modern trials and tribulations.

{ OPPOSITE: AN EARLY FISK JUBILEE SINGERS HANDBILL FOR A BRITISH PERFORMANCE. ABOVE: THE FISK MEMORIAL CHAPEL.

"THE SPIRITUAL WAS A MULTIFACETED FORM OF STATEMENT [FOR THE SLAVES]. YOU'RE TALKING ABOUT PEOPLE WHO HAD NO OTHER WAY OF COMMUNICATING WITHOUT SUFFERING SOME SORT OF PUNISHMENT. THEY USED THE SONGS AS A MEANS OF COMMUNICATING TO EACH OTHER, EXPRESSING THEIR SORROW, EXPRESS- ING THEIR JOY, EVEN LEARNING THE BIBLE. AND IT WAS VERY IMPORTANT THAT IT BE TRANSMITTED TO WHOEVER THE LISTENERS WERE, IN A WAY THAT WAS MEANINGFUL AND REALLY PROVIDED THE SAME DEGREE OF RESPECT AND REVERENCE TO THE LISTENER." —ERSKINE LYTLE, FORMER MEMBER OF THE FISK JUBILEE SINGERS

Because they arose from the early spiritual songs sung in white churches, black spirituals are inextricably linked to the European song tradition. The seven thousand hymns written by Eighteenth-Century Methodist pioneer the Reverend Charles Wesley were especially popular, and songs such as "O for a Thousand Tongues to Sing" relied on old hymn tunes that traveled from Europe with the first settlers. One of the best-known spirituals was "Amazing Grace," written by John Newton, an Englishman who once captained a slave ship and wished to atone for such deeds.

The canon of European religious songs began evolving from spirituals into what we recognize as gospel with the addition of African rhythms and some vocal syncopation and alternate harmonies. First heard on this continent in the work chants of the fields and, later, the factories, these rhythms and call-and-response vocal patterns came from the song styles of West Africa. Initially, black gospel was more of a stylistic interpretation of the European spirituals. Later, blacks wrote their own songs, and gospel started to draw on such popular contemporary genres as ragtime and blues in addition to the traditional hymn tunes. No doubt much of gospel's power derives from the tension between its pious lyrics and the sometimes "worldly ways" of the music, instrumentation, and vocal delivery that accompanied them.

Gospel blossomed after the Civil War, when what we would term the black church rose as the center of African-American civic, political, and social life. In truth, however, there was no one black church but an ever growing array of churches, each with its own deeply held views on all matters pertaining to faith. Not surprisingly, the type of music considered appropriate for church services varied widely, not only between denominations but even between churches within a denomination. Where some Pentecostal sects saw the road to heaven in their ecstatic, high-energy dancing, tambourine shaking, and shouting, other, more restrained brethren (most notably Methodists and conservative Baptists) saw the road to hell. The debate about what is proper musically for gospel continues to this day.

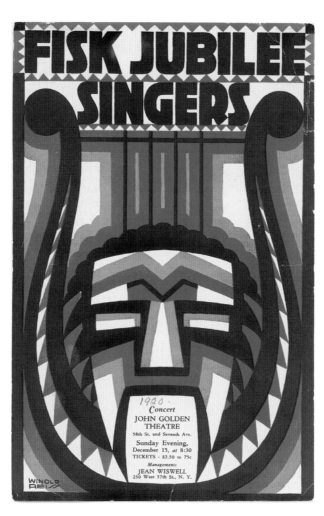

Black gospel began exerting an influence outside the walls of black churches early on, as black gospel performers found white audiences. The Fisk Jubilee Singers were the most influential performers of the time and pioneers on several frontiers. First, the Fisk Jubilee Singers were a commercial enterprise, formed in 1871 as a means of raising twenty thousand dollars to enable the American Missionary Association to maintain and expand the all-black Fisk University. The group (an incarnation of which exists today) found international fame with a repertoire of slave songs — including "Steal Away," "Couldn't Hear Nobody Pray," and "Swing Low Sweet Chariot" — that their white audiences had never heard before. But they also suffered from the racist stereotyping of the time. The *New York Journal* wrote of their performances in December 1871, "They are all natural musicians and doubtless have sung from childbirth, likely because they could not help it."

In spite of such prejudices, the Fisk Jubilee Singers broke the color barrier here (they were the first African-American entertainers to perform in Cincinnati's Mozart Hall) and abroad (they toured Europe for three years) and were the first to "commercialize" gospel music.

This commercialization was explained by the Reverend Gustavus D. Pike of the American Missionary Association, who said, "We were out to promote the cause of [our] mission; [we were] not like an organ grinder, [playing] to gain a livelihood." Nonetheless, group members were not volunteers; the Jubilee Singers were paid as much as five hundred dollars for a season of performances. Financially, the Fisk Jubilee Singers were an unqualified success: In the first two years of its existence, the popular ensemble achieved its original financial goal, and by 1878, the group had raised about $150,000 for the school. (Several other colleges — most successfully Hampton Institute, a historically black school in Virginia now known as Hampton University — also had gospel singing groups, but none had the longevity of Fisk's.)

ABOVE: A 1920 HANDBILL FOR A NEW YORK CITY APPEARANCE. OPPOSITE, FROM TOP: THE FISK JUBILEE SINGERS, CIRCA 1881; THE FISK CAMPUS, 1909.

Their most enduring contribution, however, was the music itself. With simple harmonies and jaunty melodies unlike white church hymns, the Fisk Jubilee Singers' oeuvre "developed a new repertoire of concert music and a new genre of black sacred music, because when they [sang] they actually used the ecstatic system of western choral music," observes gospel authority Bernice Johnson Reagon, herself a singer. "Sacred music moved into this particular category of a commodity that is sacred, and [yet] it was also put on the marketplace for sale, and it exploded as a movement when we turn the corner into the Twentieth Century."

The beginning of the century found the first black gospel composers publishing their own work, and using the medium of sheet music to spread it throughout the country and the world. In 1901, the Reverend Charles A. Tindley, a Methodist minister who left the South and settled in Philadelphia, published "The Lord Will Make a Way." Four years later, he added "The Storm Is Passing Over," "I'll Overcome Someday," and "Stand by Me" to his catalogue of nine hymns. With its stately cadences, "I'll Overcome Someday" evolved, with a different structure, into the civil rights anthem "We Shall Overcome." Perhaps not surprisingly, Tindley was a civil rights activist in his own time. He was injured in a demonstration protesting the racist black stereotypes in D.W. Griffith's *Birth of a Nation.* He also spoke out against vaudeville entertainers who performed in blackface.

In its gospel music, the Pentecostal tradition made room for secular instruments such as guitars, harmonicas, washboards, drums, trumpets, and trombones. The Pentecostal church also refined the old field shouts and hollers to produce a rough-voiced, wide-open singing style, and two Pentecostal ministers, Charles Harrison Mason and Charles Price Jones, created early compositions that continued to further the music's evolution. Mason's two watershed songs, "I'm a Soldier in the Army of the Lord" and "Yes Lord," both featured a rhythmic complexity that earlier gospel songs didn't possess. Jones's 1906 hymn "His Fullness Songs" also exemplified some black Christians' contention that the Pentecostal worship service was too rich with the secular temptations of rhythm and instrumentation found in nightclubs and bawdyhouses, not to mention the emotional catharsis congregants displayed.

After World War I, gospel — along with other heretofore "regional" musics such as blues and jazz — was disseminated throughout America and the world through phonograph recordings and radio broadcasts. Several singers and ministers recorded in the early Twenties, but little is known of their work. Between 1926 and 1928, Arizona Dranes cut more than thirty songs for Okeh Records. Dranes, who was blind and lived in Dallas, was one of the label's biggest commercial successes with such songs as "By and By We're Going to See the King," "I Shall Wear a Crown," and "He Is My Story." Her down-home style suited the audience for Okeh's "race" records.

Improvements in recording technology helped gospel-group recordings come into their own in the early Thirties. Inspired by the Fisk Jubilee Singers, gospel quartets had sprouted up in every black neighborhood and town. By this time, however, the same quartets who had thrilled congregations in churches and at tent revivals were beginning to make records and gain reputations far beyond their local communities. Groups such as the Famous Blue Jay Singers, the Tindley Quaker City Gospel Singers (who sang Reverend Tindley's songs), and the Silver Leaf Quartet were some of the first quartets to record. The Dixie Jubilee Singers performed "Swing Low Sweet Chariot" and "Carry Me to the Water" in the 1929 King Vidor film *Hallelujah,* which contrasted the blues life with the sacred.

At the heart of gospel's evolution in the Depression era was Thomas Dorsey, a former blues piano player who had been known as Georgia Tom in those days. Dorsey was the cowriter of "It's Tight Like That," a suggestive blues loaded with double-entendres. According to gospel authority Bishop Kenneth Moales, the young Dorsey "would steal away with other friends and relatives and go to the juke joints . . . when Ma Rainey would come through Atlanta. When he came of age, he wanted to pursue his own dream, which was to become musical director of Rainey's band. After that, while going back to his roots [as the son of a minister], he heard a woman by the name of Magnolia Lewis Butts in Chicago singing a song that touched his heart."

Moved by the spirit of Butts's song, Dorsey joined the Pilgrim Baptist Church in Chicago, where he wrote such enduring gospel classics as "Peace in the Valley" and "Precious Lord Take My Hand." One of Dorsey's most famous songs, "Precious Lord" was inspired by the death of his wife and child. Given its inspiration, it is interesting to note that because of the song's pure emotionalism, many deemed "Precious Lord" too secular when it was

OPPOSITE: A COUNTRY CHURCH IN MISSISSIPPI. ABOVE: THE FATHER OF GOSPEL MUSIC, THOMAS DORSEY.

published in 1932. Dorsey was accused of bringing the sounds of the speak-easy into houses of worship. Over time, however, the personal, emotional element would become a hallmark of both gospel and the pop-music genres it influenced. Singers were freed to improvise, ad-lib, and use the music as a means of personal expression. Indeed, the ability to move a congregation emotionally as well as spiritually became the very definition of great gospel singing.

For his music alone, Dorsey would come to be called "the Father of Gospel Music," but he did even more. His Thomas A. Dorsey Gospel Songs Music Publishing Company was the first publishing house devoted to the promotion of black gospel. He organized the National Convention of Gospel Choirs and Choruses, which debuted in 1932 and is still held annually today. (The 1983 event was captured in the documentary *Say Amen Somebody.*) In addition, many important local stars in gospel music passed through his church at one time or another, including Mahalia Jackson and Roberta Martin.

Although Dorsey drew from many sources of musical inspiration, some gospel performers were careful not to blur the line between the sacred and the secular. Josh White recorded spiritual music as "the Singing Christian" and secular music as "Pinewood Tom" in 1935. He appeared at blues clubs with Billie Holiday in the Forties and had pretty much abandoned his gospel singing by then. White, who would become a fixture at civil rights rallies and marches during the Sixties, saw his career destroyed by McCarthyism in the Fifties and found peace in Europe for a while. He wasn't the first performer who drew inspiration from gospel to distance his — as biographer Elijah Wald described it — "somewhat raucous personal life" from his spiritual output. Years later, popular singers from Little Richard to Al Green would draw upon gospel (and Christianity) as a corrective, stabilizing force in personal lives gone astray.

During the years following the Second World War, sacred messages were increasingly wed to popular rhythms and cadences. The effects of this style continue to be felt today. The Golden Gate Quartet, with its percussive and energetic vocals, changed

quartet singing the way Charlie Parker revolutionized jazz. Golden Gate vocalist Willie Johnson has said his group tried to add jazz syncopation and rhythm to traditional plantation and gospel songs. The Quartet's version of "Swing Down Chariot," a variation on "Swing Low Sweet Chariot," starts with smoothly blended harmonies, then bursts into a hard-swinging explosion of spiky syncopation with some of the vocal flourishes that would be associated with doo-wop.

"What we tried to create was what I used to call 'vocal percussion,'" Johnson told music historian Doug Seroff in 1980. "It was just like a drum, but it had notes to it, it had lyrics to it, you see. And you had different beats, you had different accents. Like a bunch of guys beating a tom-tom somewhere, and that's what it had to sound like. It all had to be done sharply and together, along with the harmony. And we sang simple chords. We were trying to sing chords that sounded good to the ear." "No Restricted Signs" — an indictment of Jim Crow — shows that the Quartet had a social conscience as well. You can hear the group's sound in just about every rhythm & blues singer who has followed, especially Sam Cooke and Curtis Mayfield. Even today, the Golden Gate Quartet sounds unmistakably modern.

One of gospel's lasting contributions to male pop vocal groups was the rumbling sound of the bass singer. It would be hard to imagine vocal pop without those low, commanding tones. The important gospel groups, including the Soul Stirrers, the Swan Silvertones, the Dixie Hummingbirds, and the Sensational Nightingales, influenced many rhythm & blues legends who heard them, including David Ruffin of the Temptations, Sam Cooke (who joined the Soul Stirrers before embarking on a pop-music career), Curtis Mayfield, and Al Green.

Although vocal groups were important in gospel, the genre never lacked for charismatic solo stars. Sister Rosetta Tharpe achieved national stardom in the Forties, singing and playing guitar with bluesy energy and sacred fervor. Tharpe had a big voice and a melody-plucking style resembling that of the popular blues singer Memphis Minnie. She recorded one of Dorsey's songs, "Hide Me

{ Opposite: The original Golden Gate Quartet. Above: The Quartet in the late Sixties.

in Thy Bosom," under the title "Rock Me." The Dorsey track was one of four she recorded with Lucius "Lucky" Millinder's jazz orchestra for the decidedly secular Decca Records. The titles included "That's All," "My Man and I," and "Lonesome Road."

Working with jazz orchestras and playing guitar made Tharpe the object of derision by the deeply sanctified. Southern congregations denounced her, and Tharpe responded to the criticism by asking Decca if she could record with her solo guitar. The label compromised, and Tharpe recorded with piano, bass, and drums, with boogie-woogie stylist Samuel "Sammie" Blythe Price often serving as her pianist. Tharpe would play a church one night and with jazz bandleader Cab Calloway the next. Despite criticism from some quarters, she was the most popular gospel performer of her era.

The next big star — and arguably the greatest — in the gospel firmament was Mahalia Jackson. Jackson followed in Tharpe's footsteps by recording for Columbia Records, a mainstream pop label. Jackson had toured and recorded extensively with Dorsey, combining the loose, direct manners of jazz and blues with fervent passion. "The blues are fine for listening, but I would never sing them. I was saved," Jackson once said. She recorded her first big hit for the Apollo label in 1947. Released a year and a half later, "Move On Up a Little Higher" eventually sold more than a million copies, which was unheard of in the gospel realm.

By the Fifties, Jackson's name was nearly synonymous with gospel music as she toured the world. When she sang "Silent Night" on Denmark's national radio, twenty thousand requests for copies flooded the station. Some conservative black churches, however, viewed her as a rebellious upstart. Why play Carnegie Hall when she could be saving the flock? Jackson didn't pay much attention to the criticism. She sang gospel with Duke Ellington and for four presidents — Truman, Eisenhower, Kennedy, and Johnson.

In the Sixties, Jackson explored other interests. She was a leader in the field of black education; she owned a chain of restaurants. She also used her music to support the civil rights movement. Jackson sang Dorsey's "Precious Lord Take My Hand" at Martin Luther King Jr.'s funeral in 1968. Four years later, Aretha Franklin sang the same song at Jackson's funeral.

As rhythm & blues, and then rock & roll, took hold of pop passions in the Fifties, some of the era's better gospel singers were torn between their spiritual and worldly sides. Sam Cooke, who had become the Soul Stirrers' lead singer, left the group to pursue stardom in 1956. In secular songs such as "You Send Me" and "A Change Is Going to Come," he was still singing with the same satin-smooth tenor with which he had captivated gospel fans in the Soul Stirrers. Cooke was not the first gospel performer to pursue pop success, nor would he be the last.

Beginning in the Fifties, the black church and gospel influence on pop was so pervasive that it would be easier to list the black rhythm & blues and pop stars who were not touched by it or did not sing in church than the hundreds whose work bore the gospel tinge. From Clyde McPhatter and Ben E. King, Solomon Burke and James Brown, the Temptations' David Ruffin and the O'Jays' Eddie Levert — the sound of soul was the sound of gospel. Everything from the emotional singing style and harmony parts to the rhythm in rhythm & blues came from Sunday morning services. As rhythm & blues became the underpinning of rock & roll, singers such as Bobby Womack left the church for secular stages. Womack recorded gospel music with the Womack Brothers in the early Sixties before becoming a rhythm & blues star with hits such as "That's the Way I Feel About Cha" and "More Than I Can Stand" from the Sixties through the Eighties.

Although Womack found his expression in secular pop, there were some dynamic performers who saw no need to leave the gospel world. Dorothy "Dot" Love Coates — known for skipping across the stage during performances – and the Gospel Harmonettes emerged as some of the best performers in this genre. Coates and the Harmonettes sang in a traditional call-and-response style backed by rousing piano. Aretha Franklin has cited Coates as an influence, and country, blues, and rock singers have tried to imitate Coates's distinctive singing style. She was also a prolific songwriter; her compositions have been recorded by Johnny Cash, Etta James, and Ray Charles.

Among Coates's powerful musical testimonies were songs about southern segregation. And, indeed, the civil rights movement of the Sixties both drew inspiration from and inspired gospel music. The SNCC Freedom Singers, which included Bernice Johnson Reagon (who later founded the all-woman a cappella group Sweet Honey in the Rock), sang at various protests and marches, including the March on Washington in August 1963. "We Shall Overcome" and "We Shall Not Be Moved" became movement anthems.

The sweeping social changes of the time also made it possible for gospel performers to reach new listeners. Gospel performers appeared at the Newport Folk Festival, on rock and soul concert bills, and at other festivals. This meant that younger, white audiences were introduced to performers such as Clara Ward and the Ward Singers. Ward was known for her flashy jewelry, towering wigs, and penchant for playing secular sin pits such as Las Vegas. Her versions of "How I Got Over" and "Surely" showed her strength as an arranger. Ward gave the extraordinary vocalist Marion Williams a chance to perform with the Singers, and Williams later left the group to form her own ensemble, Stars of Faith. She then went on to a successful solo career, playing on college campuses and touring Europe until her death in 1994. Before she died, she was honored with a MacArthur Foundation "genius grant" and, in 1993, was a Kennedy Center Honors recipient.

The most important and prolific composer of the contemporary

gospel era was the Reverend James Cleveland. His James Cleveland Singers made a number of successful records, the first being *Peace Be Still* in 1962. Cleveland, who was born in Chicago and died in 1972 in Los Angeles, also composed more than five hundred songs. He had a foghorn baritone voice and sang with Thomas Dorsey when he was young. He taught Aretha Franklin how to play the piano, wrote for the Roberta Martin Singers, and was important as an arranger for choirs. "With leveland the choirs became the professional presenters of the new gospel music, and they led the way to what we call contemporary gospel," says Bernice Johnson Reagon.

Fittingly perhaps, one of our most esteemed gospel singers is also the Queen of Soul. Few could claim to have grown up as steeped in the church as Aretha Franklin, whose father, the Reverend C.L. Franklin, recorded numerous popular sermons and was renowned for his flamboyant, highly charged preaching that incorporated singing. Virtually every future Motown artist grew up listening to Reverend Franklin's radio broadcasts, which also featured the top gospel artists of the day, among them the aforementioned Clara Ward, Dorothy Coates, Sam Cooke, and James Cleveland — all of whom personally influenced Aretha. After touring with her father, Aretha signed to Columbia Records in 1960 as a jazz singer. Six years later, she moved to Atlantic Records – and throughout her career has made some of the most passionate secular and spiritual music the world has ever heard.

For some of her recordings, Franklin was backed by the vocal trio the Sweet Inspirations. One of those Inspirations was acclaimed gospel vocalist Cissy Houston, cousin of Dionne Warwick and mother of Whitney Houston. Houston was part of her family's

OPPOSITE: ROSETTA THARPE, EARLY 1940S.
ABOVE: THE SOUL STIRRERS: SAM COOKE, J.J. FARLEY,
T.L. BRUSTER, R.B. ROBINSON, S.R. CRAIN, AND PAUL
FOSTER (CLOCKWISE FROM FRONT LEFT).

gospel group, the Drinkard Singers, before recording with Franklin. (Houston and the Sweet Inspirations later performed with Elvis Presley on gospel numbers in the 1970s, when his repertoire included a riveting version of "How Great Thou Art.")

In 1969, gospel hit the pop charts with the Edwin Hawkins Singers' "Oh Happy Day." Hawkins led an Oakland, California, choir, and his music found its way onto the radio across the bay in San Francisco. Hawkins had been recording since 1957, but "Oh Happy Day" was his only breakthrough to mainstream success. Before Hawkins's hit, gospel was sung in the church or at

"THE STYLE OF GOSPEL SINGING EXEMPLIFIED BY CLARA WARD BECAME THE GREAT MUSICAL INFLUENCE OF MY EARLY CHILDHOOD. LATER I LEARNED THAT THE FIFTIES, THE MAIN DECADE OF MY CHILDHOOD, WAS CONSIDERED THE GOLDEN AGE OF GOSPEL. ALL THE GREAT GOSPEL LUMINARIES CAME TO DETROIT, AND MANY TO MY DAD'S CHURCH. I HAD NEVER HEARD A VOICE LIKE CLARA WARD'S — AND STILL HAVEN'T. I WAS ONLY A SMALL CHILD, BUT AFTER HEARING CLARA — AND LATER REVEREND JAMES CLEVELAND — THERE WAS NO QUESTION IN MY MIND THAT ONE DAY I WOULD BE A SINGER." —ARETHA FRANKLIN

rarefied gatherings such as the Smithsonian Folklife Festival or the Newport Folk Festival. After the song's success, various pop, rock, and soul groups essayed gospel or religious material — among them Pacific, Gas, and Electric ("Wade in the Water") — and numerous recordings were made of "Amazing Grace." In addition, through the Sixties and Seventies, more socially conscious black R&B bore a distinctly gospel feel: Harold Melvin and the Blue Notes' "Wake Up Everybody" and Curtis Mayfield and the Impressions' "People Get Ready" and "Amen," to name a few.

Gospel went not only into nightclubs but onto the stage. The first important gospel play was Langston Hughes's *Black Nativity*, featuring the Reverend Alex Bradford and Marion Williams. The play ran on Broadway and toured Europe in the Sixties. In 1976, the Vinnette Carroll gospel play *Your Arms Too Short to Box With God* debuted off-Broadway and traveled to cities with large black populations, such as Washington, D.C., and Detroit. (The show has been revived several times, including once in 1982 with Al Green and Patti LaBelle. For the twentieth-anniversary revival in 1996, Carroll wrote a new part especially for Teddy Pendergrass, who had been rendered quadriplegic in a 1982 car accident and who brought to the production his own gospel composition "Truly Blessed.")

No other hitmaking group had so pure a gospel lineage as the Staple Singers, who were recently inducted into the Rock and Roll Hall of Fame. This family hailed from Chicago, where, beginning in 1953, the late Roebuck "Pops" Staples sang with his daughters Mavis and Cleotha and (until the early Seventies) a son, Pervis. Pops played guitar and would also record blues; however, the family was best known for a string of stellar, undeniably gospel pop and soul hits between 1971 and 1973: "Respect Yourself," "I'll Take You There," and "If You're Ready (Come Go With Me)."

"MAHALIA JACKSON WAS ABLE TO SING AND REACH THE PEOPLE. I DON'T CARE IF YOU WERE WHITE OR BLACK — THERE WAS NOBODY THAT MAHALIA COULDN'T TOUCH." —GENEVA GENTRY, MEMBER OF THE NATIONAL CONVENTION OF GOSPEL CHOIRS AND CHORUSES

OPPOSITE: MAHALIA JACKSON, 1961.
LEFT: ARETHA FRANKLIN, 1968.
BELOW: CLARA WARD, CIRCA 1956.

Al Green, one of the most magnetic rhythm & blues singers ever, performed soul hits such as "Let's Stay Together" and "Love and Happiness" in the Seventies. In 1977, he recorded *The Belle Album,* which was his first foray into gospel. Green left pop music in 1980 to make gospel albums for Myrrh and became the pastor at a Memphis church, the Full Gospel Tabernacle. Since then, he occasionally has performed his pop hits in concert, while continuing primarily to record gospel.

In the Seventies and Eighties, prolific gospel songwriter Andraé Crouch found a home on black radio next to soul performers such as the Gap Band and Parliament/Funkadelic. His "Soon and Very Soon," "Jesus Is the Answer," and "Just Like He Said He Would" became very popular and influential recordings. Among those purveying Crouch's blend of pop-soul production and spiritual messages in the Eighties were various members of the Winans family. Four of the brothers recorded as the Winans, while brother and sister BeBe and CeCe made several records together. Some felt that the Winans family members had obscured gospel's message of Christian salvation because the words *Jesus* and *God* appeared infrequently in their songs. The

Winans used rhythm & blues–style instrumentation with electronic keyboards, drums, bass, and guitar along funky grooves and sophisticated vocal harmonies.

Starting in 1983, Black Entertainment Television gave a home to gospel music with *The Bobby Jones Gospel Hour.* A syndicated awards show for black gospel, the Stellar Awards, continues to be broadcast around the country.

The latest gospel upheaval concerned Kirk Franklin of Dallas. The diminutive choir director incorporated rap rhythms and testimony into his work, to the delight of radio programmers but to the horror of gospel traditionalists. Franklin collaborated with rapper Salt of Salt-n-Pepa and sex-drenched soul singer R. Kelly, and tongues set to wagging. His work with the groups the Family and God's Property yielded soulful ballads such as "The Reason Why I Sing," a traditional call-and-response number. Franklin also sampled Parliament/Funkadelic's "One Nation Under a Groove" on the 1997 track "Stomp," on *God's Property.*

Franklin has not been the only gospel artist embracing more

{ OPPOSITE: AL GREEN PREACHING AT HIS
FULL GOSPEL TABERNACLE, IN MEMPHIS.
ABOVE: THE EDWIN HAWKINS SINGERS (WITH
HAWKINS AT THE PIANO), CIRCA 1971.
BELOW: THE STAPLES FAMILY.

"MY DADDY SANG, AND MY MAMA SANG, AND SO DID MY GRANDPARENTS ON BOTH SIDES. MY BROTHERS
AND SISTERS SANG, AND WHEN IT CAME TO BE MY TURN, I SANG, TOO. CHURCH WAS WHERE WE CAME
TOGETHER, AN EXTENDED FAMILY, EACH ONE WITH A NATURAL-BORN GIFT FOR PRAISING GOD. BUT
SINGING WAS AN EVERYDAY THING, TOO. IT JUST SEEMED TO FLOW OUT OF THE STREAM OF OUR LIVES,
MAKING THE CHORES AND ROUTINES MOVE BY A LITTLE FASTER
AND GIVING THE SPECIAL OCCASIONS AN EXTRA MEASURE OF
CELEBRATION. WHEN ONE OF MY BROTHERS WOULD BREAK OUT
A GUITAR ON THE FRONT STOOP OR SIT DOWN AT THE CHURCH
PIANO BEFORE THE SERVICE, WE'D ALL GATHER AROUND LIKE
FLIES TO HONEY. MOST OF MY EARLY MEMORIES, GOOD AND
BAD, HAVE MUSIC IN THERE SOME-
WHERE. MUSIC HAS ALWAYS BEEN MY
CLEAREST CHANNEL TO GOD, MY WAY
OF TOUCHING THE HEM OF HIS GAR-
MENT AND FEELING THE STRENGTH OF
HIS LOVE." —AL GREEN

contemporary sounds. Fred Hammond made several records, most notably 1998's two-CD set *Pages of Life*, that blended funky grooves with an unmistakably Christian message and rich choral arrangements. Yolanda Adams of Houston, who often pointed out in interviews that she thought of her music as a ministry, signed to Elektra Records in 1999 and released *Mountain High Valley Low*. Also during this period, rapper Run of Run-D.M.C. started making gospel records and signed several artists to his gospel label, Rev. Run Records. Choir leaders such as Hezekiah Walker and soloist Donnie McClurkin also combine sanctified ardor with secular sounds.

As gospel music moves into the Twenty-First Century, there are still those who fret when it embraces more contemporary forms of musical expression. At the same time, many of the traditions and sounds that fueled gospel more than one hundred years ago remain the heartbeat of the music. As the tree's branches grow, its roots are as strong as ever.

"GOSPEL MUSIC IS SO POWERFUL
BECAUSE OF THE CONNECTION IT HAS
TO THE HEART STRINGS. IT IS POWERFUL
BECAUSE IT GIVES YOU HOPE."
—MARABETH GENTRY, MEMBER OF THE
NATIONAL CONVENTION OF GOSPEL
CHOIRS AND CHORUSES

{ MARION WILLIAMS LIFTING UP
THE CROWD IN BRYANT PARK,
NEW YORK CITY, 1973

MATTHEW KENNEDY, DIRECTOR, FISK JUBILEE SINGERS:

I remember [when I was in the Fisk Jubilee Singers], we were in the state of Kansas and passing through some little town. We had gone several hours without really having a decent meal, and [our director] decided to go into this hotel and inquire about the possibilities for this group of young people who were traveling and needed a meal. And they agreed to let us come in and be served. We went in and were pressured into a semiprivate area, table all set, and we were ready to take our seats, looking forward to this meal. And something happened — we don't know what, but we think some of the other guests, when they saw this group of Negroes coming in, must have complained, because the opportunity was withdrawn and we were told, rather politely, that they couldn't serve us, and [they asked] for us to leave. I think one of the young men had requested a glass of water, and as we were leaving, we could hear his glass being broken behind the counter, showing us that they were not going to let anyone else use this same glass that this black person had used.

I don't know whether experiences [like these] influenced our performance to any great degree, beyond the fact that we could empathize so much with the former groups and the slave experiences that gave birth to those songs. And we had heard the stories of how the spiritual "Steal Away" was actually a signal to the slaves that there might be a religious meeting that evening going on in some distant part of the plantation. This was the signal for them to steal away quietly and take part in this religious experience that was prohibited. And also we were told that this might have meant that some of the slaves would attempt a dash to freedom, steal away, that the Underground Railroad might have been available to them. Those things were in our subconscious as we sang these songs.

CISSY HOUSTON: *The first music I remember hearing as a child was sanctified music. At that time, I was a small child; I started singing when I was five years old. So you can take it from there what that meant to me: not a great deal. But as life went on, I found out what it was all about. I met Christ for myself when I was fourteen years old and became a born-again Christian. Then the light shone bright in my life. There was a wonderful feeling when I sang now — fire, burning. I couldn't wait to take my solo, close my eyes and praise him.*

My sisters and brothers and I were a group called the Drinkard Singers. We were booked on a lot of gospel concerts. We appeared with all the big gospel quartets of the day. We were flattered to be included on the same program with these groups, but we never did get any stars in our eyes. Singing was, first and foremost, still a ministry for us.

I learned harmonies when I was in school. But, really, it's just God-given. [Singing backup for Aretha Franklin] was great, because we came from the same church and musical background. She could feel me, and I could feel her. Mostly I knew what she was gonna do next and did something to enhance that. And it was great. Whether it be the blues, gospel, or whatever it might be, you can depend on Aretha to bring it out of that song.

LEFT: THE FISK JUBILEE SINGERS IN 1898.
TOP: GOSPEL VETERAN CISSY HOUSTON.
OPPOSITE: THE SWEET INSPIRATIONS: CISSY
HOUSTON, MYRNA SMITH, ESTELLE BROWN, AND
SYLVIA SHEMWELL (FROM LEFT), 1968.

2

1682 Sieur de La Salle lands at the mouth of the Mississippi; he claims the surrounding land for Louis XIV and names it the Louisiana Territory. **1716** African slaves begin arriving in Louisiana to work in fields around Natchitoches. **1755** Great Britain seizes the Acadian peninsula in French Canada; King George II deports six thousand Acadians, who end up in France, Santo Domingo (present-day Haiti), and all along the East Coast of the United States. **1763** The Treaty of Paris is signed, ending the Seven Years' War in Europe; the treaty states that land east of the Mississippi River belongs to Britain and the territories west of the river belong to Spain. **1760s** The first Acadians arrive in Louisiana from Nova Scotia and Acadians continue to immigrate there for the next thirty years. **1791** Blacks and mulattoes in Santo Domingo revolt against French colonists, demanding the freedom granted to them by France's National Assembly. Many black and white residents flee to Louisiana. **1800** As a result of the classified Treaty of San Ildefonso (1796), Spain returns the Louisiana Territory to France. **1803** The United States purchases the Louisiana Territory from France for eighty million francs (fifteen million dollars). **1854** The button accordion arrives in Louisiana with German immigrants. **1882** Construction of the Southern Pacific Railroad — the first to connect New Orleans and Lafayette — is completed. **1908–1930** Cajun musicians such as Amédé Breaux, Joe Falcon, and Amédé Ardoin rise in popularity. **1925** The Buegeleisen & Jacobson Co. of New York begins importing Monarch and Sterling model accordions tuned in the fiddle-compatible keys of C and D. **1928** At the behest of local merchants, Cajun musicians travel to New Orleans to audition for record label scouts. Joe and Cleoma Falcon record "Allons à Lafayette," the first Cajun record. Fiddler Leo Soileau and accordionist Mayeus LaFleur record "Hé, Mom" under the title "Mama, Where You At." Nine days after the recording session, LaFleur is shot and killed in a barroom brawl. The song soon becomes a Cajun classic. **1929** Fiddle player Dennis McGee and accordionist Amédé Ardoin collaborate on some tunes for Brunswick. Douglas Bellard, the first black French recording artist, records an early version of the dancehall favorite "The Flames of Hell." **1930** Fiddler Luderin Darbone and guitarists Floyd Rainwater, Lonnie Rainwater, and Lennis Sonnier form the Hackberry Ramblers. **1932** John Lomax begins documenting Cajun music and culture. **1934** Leo Soileau organizes the Three Aces, whose repertoire includes Cajunized versions of American pop songs and string-swing standards. **1936** Lawrence Walker, Aldus Broussard, and Evelyn Broussard perform with an all-star lineup of Louisiana Acadian musicians at the National Folk Festival in Dallas. **1940–1944** In search of oil-refinery and shipyard jobs vacated by departed soldiers, many young musicians cross the border into Texas towns such as Port Arthur and are exposed to fiddle music by such artists as Bob Wills, Roy Acuff, and Cliff Bruner. The accordion supply from East Germany to the U.S. is cut off. 1946 Fais Do Do, south Louisiana's first regional record label, is created. The postwar recording boom begins. 1948 Iry LeJeune and the Oklahoma Tornadoes cut their landmark recordings for Opera; the following year, LeJeune records twenty-four songs for Lake Charles music-store owner Eddie Shuler. Shreveport-based radio show the Louisiana Hayride plays the music of Hank Williams and other country artists. 1949 Accordionist Clifton Chenier and his brother Cleveland Chenier begin performing at Freeman Fontenot's club in Basile. 1950 Clarence Garlow's "Bon Ton Roula" peaks at Number Seven on the R&B chart. 1952 Melodically derived from the Cajun song "Grand Texas," Hank Williams's hit "Jambalaya (on the Bayou)" peaks at Number One on the C&W chart. 1954 Boozoo Chavis records the hit "Paper in My Shoe" for Folk-Star. Clifton Chenier cuts his first recording at radio station KAOK in Lake Charles. 1958 Floyd Soileau of Ville Platte opens his Cajun record company, Swallow Records. 1960 Cleveland Crochet has a national hit record with the song "Sugar Bee," which goes to Number Eighty on the pop chart. 1962 Aldus Roger plays the National Folk Festival in Washington, D.C. 1964 Talent scout Ralph Rinzler enlists Wallace Lafleur, Vinus Lejeune, Gladney Thibodeaux, and Cyprien Landreneau for the Newport Folk Festival. 1967 The Balfa Brothers play the Newport Folk Festival and make their first recording of traditional Cajun music for Swallow. 1968 The Council of the Development of French in Louisiana (CODOFIL) is formed. 1969 The first New Orleans Jazz and Heritage Festival is held. 1970–1971 Chris Strachwitz of Arhoolie Records reissues important Cajun 78s in a series called 'Louisiana Cajun Music' on the Old Timey label. 1972 Revon Reed's live radio broadcast from Mamou and Jim Olivier's Cajun-French morning television show 'Passe Partout' promote Cajun culture. 1974 CODOFIL cosponsors the inaugural Festivals Acadiens at Lafayette's Blackham Coliseum. 1982 Queen Ida's 'Queen Ida and the Bon Temps Zydeco Band on Tour' wins a Grammy for Best Ethnic or Traditional Folk Recording. Clifton Chenier's 'I'm Here' will win the same award the following year. 1985 At his father's request, C.J. Chenier takes over as lead accordionist for Clifton Chenier's Red Hot Louisiana Band. 1980s–1990s The Balfas, Beausoleil, Savoy Doucet, and D.L. Menard play presidential inaugurations in Washington, D.C. 1987 Buckwheat Zydeco's 'On a Night Like This' receives critical acclaim and spends five weeks on the pop chart. 1996 Beausoleil plays the half-time show at Super Bowl XXXI. 1997 Beausoleil's 'L'amour ou la Folie' wins a Grammy for Best Traditional Folk Album.

CAJUN AND ZYDECO: THE MUSICS OF FRENCH SOUTHWEST LOUISIANA

BY ANN ALLEN SAVOY Few American states can claim a culture as varied, vibrant, and distinctive as Louisiana's. From the moment in 1682 when French explorer Sieur de La Salle claimed the valley he found at the mouth of the Mississippi River and named it for his king, Louisiana has been shaped by French, Spanish, and American traditions. In 1714, France established its first permanent settlement, Natchitoches, on the border of Spanish territory, and Spain remained a presence in and had possession of the area before the Louisiana Purchase. Though technically Louisiana has belonged to America since 1803, the fierce pride of its people has created a way of life impervious to the cultural homogenization seen elsewhere. Instead, Louisiana has had a huge impact on the shaping of America, and among the state's greatest contributions have been Cajun and zydeco music.

Amid Louisiana's disparate influences, the French has long dominated – in language, law, music, cuisine, and lifestyle. But even what we refer to as "French" actually encompasses a spectrum of different attitudes and values, ranging from those of early French aristocrats who owned vast sugar-cane plantations, to those of refugees from Santo Domingo, to those of Canadian Acadians. Ultimately the Acadian, or Cajun, culture became the dominant French culture in the state. Though today's Cajuns are no longer of purely Acadian stock, due to intermingling with numerous cultures during their three centuries in North America, their Gallic tendencies continue to reign on the southwest prairies.

The Acadians emigrated from another New World French stronghold on the east coast of Canada and Nova Scotia. These were the descendants of settlers who had come to present-day Nova Scotia and Prince Edward Island from the French regions of Poitou, Normandy, and Brittany. After

Britain usurped this area from France, many of the Acadians were expelled in the mid-1700s after they refused to defend the British against their cultural brethren, the invading French. Scattered, they landed in various places along the eastern seaboard and on the Caribbean island of Santo Domingo (half of which is known in French as Saint Domingue and which later became Haiti), and some even returned to France.

Dimanche matin le 12 Août 1883

Mon cher,

Eh, ha! ma vié zami — à la papa, à la papa; Mazire A. Pancho, Simon Bélar, Simon Grillot, mangeur de poules routies si yen na, si yen na pas, toi t'en passeras; mon content apprendre toi nivelle

Toi va rire; quette; — — toi connais été capitaine, [...] tous les Kimps
chanter, [...] monde
dans Ki [...] his [...] après
chanter [...]
bois [...]
ta [...] tété,
heu [...]
to [...]
après [...] toujour
li non à force li fé ien, ien, ien, après
toi, tété obligé aller boire avec li et tous lé zote
aussi; et pis à force li fé toi et nou zote bois et
chanter et danser jusqu'à minuit ou deu zeures,
tout monde été Sou. Li grand capitaine pas

The Hackberry Ramblers

"OURS WAS THE FIRST CAJUN GROUP TO HAVE A NAME. BEFORE THAT PEOPLE JUST WENT BY THEIR NAMES, LIKE LAWRENCE WALKER OR JOE FALCON. EDWIN DUHON AND I CAME UP WITH THE NAME THE HACKBERRY RAMBLERS IN 1933. WE WANTED A NAME THAT WAS CATCHY AND COULD BE ANNOUNCED ON THE RADIO. WE WERE ALSO THE FIRST BAND TO USE AMPLIFICATION. WHEN WE PLAYED IN THESE DANCEHALLS, WE'D GET BIG CROWDS, AND A FIDDLE WITH TWO GUITARS AND NO AMPLIFIERS — YOU CAN IMAGINE HOW IT SOUNDED IF YOU HAD A HUNDRED COUPLES DANCING. THEY COULDN'T HEAR US ON THE OTHER END." —LUDERIN DARBONE

Though Acadians can be found throughout the eastern United States and Canada, nowhere have they so doggedly preserved their native folk culture as in Louisiana. There, over time, families started reassembling, particularly in the state's western region, where they raised wild cattle and later farmed rice, cotton, sugar cane, and corn. They continued to practice Catholicism and speak French. For the next three hundred years, the French-speaking Acadians, a reticent people, maintained this geographically isolated stronghold where their way of life thrived, undiluted and uncompromised.

Not a literary people in the typical sense, the Acadians in the past did not keep many written accounts of their lives and interests. As is the case in most folk cultures, the Acadians didn't write down their early music, so the most primitive example we have of Acadian music is ballad singing. When the Acadians settled along Bayou LaFourche in the latter part of the Eighteenth Century, many French sugar-cane planters were already situated along the river. There was surely an exchange of music between these two cultures, both in ballads and in fiddle-music melodies. Today, in isolated prairie towns, you can still find ballad singers whose repertoire sounds amazingly similar to the original Seventeenth-Century French versions of the same songs — even though early folklorists and scholars did not document the music until the early 1930s and 1940s. Examples are the lyrically pure French ballads "Sept Ans Sur Mer" and "Sur le Bord de l'Eau."

Developing at the same time, in a similar manner to the Acadians, were the black French, ranging from the light-skinned Creole of color to the African-American. Each of these black groups had its own unique music and culture, which were also shaped by a blend of several influences: African, Native American, French aristocratic, and Caribbean, each with its own religious culinary leanings and musical traits. From 1790 to 1803, the revolution in Santo Domingo sent huge numbers of black and white French citizens pouring into Louisiana for refuge. With them came their

Caribbean rhythms, religious practices, and spicy cuisine, as well as the Creole language. Creole French had been created by African slaves as they worked to communicate with French planters, and the dialect emerged on American soil at the same time it was developing in the French West Indies.

Not surprisingly, singing was also an integral part of black Creole culture. A cappella singing was the first form of musical expression among various groups in America and remains an extremely important and rich element today. For the early slaves, instruments were hard to come by, so to accompany singers they clapped their hands and stamped their feet; they also employed primitive "found" percussion instruments, such as jawbones, sticks, and homemade drums. Because the vocals bore not only the melody but the rhythm and also functioned as the "instrumental" accompaniment, a rich and sophisticated a cappella tradition developed that is still heard in churches and on the streets of New Orleans. The Creole repertoire included French lullabies, ballads, religious songs learned on plantations or from Creoles of color descended from aristocracy, and the field chants and songs of early black settlers. The latter eventually found their way, via dancehalls, into Cajun and zydeco music.

Both Cajun and black Creole culture shared another tradition: fiddle music, which contained a wide range of dance rhythms, such as polkas, mazurkas, quadrilles, and contradances. The French Louisianians have always loved to dance, and at early house dances, or "fais do-dos," fiddlers would play a round of seven dance styles, then start the round again. Usually two fiddlers performed together — one taking the high melody and the other handling the melody or chord accompaniment on the low strings.

"DEWEY BALFA PLAYED A BIG PART IN MAKING PEOPLE [IN LOUISIANA] REALIZE HOW SPECIAL AND HOW BEAUTIFUL THE [CAJUN] CULTURE AND THE MUSIC IS. HE WENT UP AND PLAYED THE NEWPORT FOLK FESTIVAL IN THE SIXTIES, AND JUST THE ECHO OF APPLAUSE THAT HE GOT UP THERE CAME BACK TO LOUISIANA. I MEAN, PEOPLE IN THE PAPERS WERE WRITING ABOUT HOW THE MUSIC SHOULDN'T BE TAKEN UP THERE — PEOPLE SHOULDN'T SEE THIS CAJUN MUSIC, IT'S JUST NOT GOOD.... AND THE ECHO OF [THE REACTION THEY GOT AT NEWPORT] CAME DOWN [AND] JUST STARTED THIS WHOLE REVOLUTIONARY THING DOWN HERE, WHERE PEOPLE BEGAN TO REALIZE THAT WHAT THEY HAD WAS BEAUTIFUL." —STEVE RILEY

OPPOSITE: CAJUN FIDDLER WILL BOLFA (A.K.A. BALFA), 1935. ABOVE: THE MUSICAL BROTHERS, WILL, DEWEY, AND RODNEY BALFA (FROM LEFT) WITH ACCORDIONIST HADLEY FONTENOT, IN 1948.

The late 1920s would prove a turning point in the preservation and dissemination of native Louisiana folk music. Through the recordings of Dennis McGee, a fiddler who was born in the Bayou Marron region of the Louisiana prairies, we can hear the music as it was played in the 1800s. McGee had dabbled in sharecropping, barbering, and cooking, but his passion was playing his fiddle whenever possible. Because McGee learned much of his repertoire from a hundred-year-old man, his jigs, reels, polkas, contradances, and mazurkas (which comprise a wider variety of tempos than the waltzes and two-steps in the regional music of today) document the old music. Were it not for the daring trip he made to New Orleans in 1929 to record for Brunswick, these tunes might easily have been lost forever. McGee's early tracks have a haunting quality, possibly due to the open drones of the fiddles or to his high-lonesome singing style. Later recorded by folklorists and students, McGee left behind hundreds of taped performances and a treasure trove of early Acadian music.

Interestingly, 1929 was also the year of the first recording by a black French fiddler, Douglas Bellard. Renowned as a tough bully, Bellard worked in a solo blues style and recorded four sides. Only two of these were issued, one of which was the first recorded version of the dancehall favorite "The Flames of Hell." Accompanying Bellard's lone fiddle on the recording was a very simple accordion backup.

In 1882, when a railroad was laid through the eighty uninviting miles of swamp separating New Orleans and Lafayette, Acadians were suddenly able to leave the bayou banks and go farther west to rice-growing territory, and free people of color could depart from the confines of New Orleans and travel west to set up small homesteads. These vast prairies were already inhabited by Germans, Spaniards, French, Irish, and other nationalities, all of whom had settled in the vicinities of the Opelousas and Postes des Attakapas to pursue various enterprises mostly connected to the raising of sugar, indigo, and rice.

It may have been this move to the prairies that introduced the Acadians to the diatonic (or single-row) accordion, another important ingredient in the Cajun musical mix. Invented in Vienna in 1829, the accordion quickly found its way into regional musics the world over. By the mid-1800s, Acadians, too, were enamored of the loud little box, finding its volume an asset in noisy dancehalls and its lack of strings a convenient feature on the isolated prairies, where strings were very hard to come by. Though we do not know exactly how the accordion made its way to the Cajuns, the strong German presence in the area near the Opelousas Post no doubt played a role in its appearance and immense popularity.

The earliest accordions did not find immediate favor with Cajun musicians, however, since they were in keys that Cajun fiddlers found very difficult to accompany, such as A, B, and G. At that time, rural fiddlers, being self-taught musicians, thought they had to tune their instruments to the accordion. Frustrated, the fiddlers broke many precious strings and had to travel miles to replace them. Around 1908, when accordions in fiddle-compatible keys (such as C and D) came to the prairie, the accordion caught on like wildfire among the Cajuns and the Creoles. Soon fiddle duets were a thing of the past, and the relatively indestructible accordion was the instrument of choice for dances and parties.

From this era (1908-1930) came many outstanding Cajun musicians, among them Amédé Breaux, Joe Falcon, and Amédé Ardoin. Ardoin was a black accordionist who recorded numerous songs that later became the core of traditional Cajun standards, and he often recorded and played in dancehalls with white fiddler Dennis McGee — a surprising combination in the segregated South of the 1920s and 1930s. It was locally acceptable for McGee and Ardoin to perform together because of Ardoin's gentility and popularity with the neighboring white farmers. Even so, Ardoin was never truly safe, and McGee had to protect him in difficult situations, such as the time when drunken farmers threatened the black musician and he had to escape out a window. Nevertheless, the two artists traveled and recorded together extensively. Today, in any Cajun dance, you will hear the songs of Amédé Ardoin, though his words have been slightly changed.

In the 1920s, record company talent scouts traveled to New Orleans looking for Cajun musicians to sign, after the nationally successful

Creole Folk Songs

LIKE CA... ...Creole dialect group
lack that ... often short. Like
them they re... ...llant perhaps, but
probably right ... girl as a pig loves
m...d... thinks of her
in conne... ...house,[3] he gets
rope into ma... ...mother, and he asks
hi... g... ...with h... to his home like
wretches.

Possibly, however, the... ...ly found in songs
of this group ... ...extent in members of the other
groups are ... ...mockery, a sort of crude, suggestive vulgarity ... ...mention of food. The negro ridi-
cules ... in allusi... a po... Frenchmen, a girl jilted by
h... ...riders of lean
horses,[11] and well-dressed or over-dressed negroes, poorly
g... ...H... e... jambala... ...rice dressing,[14] pota-
to...

[footnotes, left column]
... Cf.: Croissel Crabisset
... ...phine.
... ...pes jambes fines.
[10] Cf.: La Peau ... peau! La peau et des os!
... ...Renard Rchani
... Madame ... ...ric... Cribisse
... Cf.: Suzette ... ...enfant
... Cf.: Jambala... gât
[15] Cf.: Quand mo te pili.
[16] Cf.: Ol Caïlanne.

Creole Folk Songs

Since much has already been written about this Creole
dialect, I shall not discuss it further than to say that it is the
language of the Negroes of Louisiana who were formerly
owned by French masters and who evolved this dialect from
the French of their owners. It is still spoken in several sec-
tions of the state not only by Negroes but also by Creoles who
use it in addition to their French.

Complete studies of this Creole dialect have been made by
the Department of Romance Languages of the Louisiana
State University, a... ...ses submitted for
the master's degree.

MO L'AIMÉ TOI, CHÈRE

Mo l'ai-mé ... chère, ...
mo l... mé ... m5 ... ...

robe de laine ... ...bandi... tout pour toi, ...
rɔb də lɛ̃... ... tu pu twa

Translation:

Je t'aime, chère, de tout mon ...
Ma... ... de laine... mon "Grecian ...
C'est tout pour toi, chère.

Seconde Version

... main toi, chère, to tout pou' mon, chère, mon
m... ... tu tu pu m5 ʃe m5

[17] "Noël ...

America's Fin

FEATURES

- Big Easy-to-read Airplane
- Natural Tone 5" P.M. Spe
- Automatic Volume Contro
- Tunes Police Calls
- Uses Economical 1.4 Volt
- Batteries Enclosed in Cab

Here's A Beauty

Knight 6-Tube 2-Band Supe

A gay little beauty you'll be proud to ow
luxuriously styled of molded plastic — meas
only 10⅞" x 7¼" x 5½". Has built-in anter
Just plug into any 110 volt AC or DC outlet
delightful reproduction of all programs. Ex
tionally sensitive and powerful — covers A
ican broadcasts and the 5.7 to 18.3 MC b
for foreign news and entertainment. Availe
in Walnut or Ivory. Shipping wt., 8 lbs.

B10596. Walnut finish.
Complete with tubes.
NET...................................... **$9**

B10598. Ivory finish.
Complete with tubes.
NET...................................... **$10**

Use This Coupon When You Order
Check box indicating radio desired

t Low-Priced Radios
For Farm and Town

Knight 4-Tube
Superhet

USES ECONOMICAL 1.4 VOLT BATTERY

Here's the radio that has everything — covers standard American and Canadian broadcasts and the popular 1712 K.C. police channel. Provides thrilling, natural tone — long distance performance — amazing economy of operation.

Low-drain 1.4 volt tubes permit 350-400 hours of service from "AB" battery pack. Richly styled cabinet of mahogany plastic measures 12" long, 8" high, 7" deep, with space inside for battery pack.

ONLY
10⁴⁵

B10541. Complete with tubes, but less "AB" battery pack. Shpg. wt., 10 lbs. NET **$10⁴⁵**

B10546. As above, but complete with battery pack which fits inside cabinet. Shpg. wt., 19 lbs. NET **$13⁰⁵**

For 110 Volt AC-DC Use

ONLY
$9⁹⁵

"race" and "hillbilly" recordings had suggested that the regional music market might be larger and more profitable than expected. Scouts would contact local businessmen, who would recommend the best area musicians. Such searches resulted in large-scale accordion and fiddle contests, the winners of which would journey to New Orleans to audition for the scouts.

On April 27, 1928, husband-and-wife team Joe and Cleoma Falcon recorded the first Cajun disc, "Allons à Lafayette," which featured accordion, bare-bones guitar, and Joe Falcon singing a clever two-step: "Let's go to Lafayette, to change your name . . . you're too cute to act so naughty." The Falcons were groundbreaking in that Cleoma played guitar on the record, and both the idea of a woman playing in a Cajun band and the use of a guitar on a recording were revolutionary.

The Falcons' success among the general population had a profound, positive effect on the self-esteem of the stigmatized, French-speaking Acadians, who, despite the high regard in which they are held today, were considered a lower class by their fellow Louisianians during the early part of the Twentieth Century. (The word *Cajun*, in fact, was once a pejorative, connoting an uneducated underdog.) This stigmatizing of the Cajun culture was at its worst from 1910 to 1930, when speaking French became a punishable offense at public schools, and children began dropping out in droves and working full time on family farms. Their lack of conventional education and the Acadians' "Old World" agrarian

OPPOSITE, FROM TOP: AN UNIDENTIFIED CREOLE FAMILY, CIRCA 1928; CAJUN PARTY, 1927. ABOVE: IN THE 1950S, CAJUN MUSIC WAS POPULARIZED BY SUCH GROUPS AS LAWRENCE WALKER AND THE WANDERING ACES: ORSAY VANICOR, LAWRENCE WALKER, JUNIOR BENOIT, MITCH DAVEY, AND DUB HIGGENBOTHAM (FROM LEFT), 1954.

lifestyle were factors in the discrimination against them and their culture. Acadians of higher social standing, therefore, listened primarily to mainstream brass bands and string quartets and thought of accordion music as country or "old folks' " music. With this recording, however, the tables began to turn, and, subsequently, other Americans began to respect the Cajuns' music and language.

In 1932, just after the national record companies began making regional recordings, folklorist John Lomax traveled through Louisiana to record Cajun music for the Library of Congress. Lomax encouraged young people to document Cajun culture while he recorded music as it was played and enjoyed in the home, in the fields, in the church, and elsewhere. Documenting folklore in its natural environs, he left a record of the true music of the people, as opposed to the popular dancehall music most often heard on records. Without these recordings, we would no longer have any idea of the variety of Louisiana music in the 1930s, or of what was actually being sung, played, and enjoyed by Acadians as intimate social music.

One of the young people Lomax inspired was Irene Therese Whitfield. In 1939, she published the first book of notated French Louisiana songs, *Louisiana French Folk Songs*, initially as a masters thesis for Louisiana State University. Divided into French, Cajun, and Creole songs, it is a rare collection, without which many of the songs would be lost.

The 1930s were significant years in Louisiana folklore, not only because of the commercial and scholarly recording going on but also because, perhaps for the first time, a Louisiana Acadian group was featured at Dallas's National Folk Festival. In 1936, Lauren Post, who was gathering material for his important book *Cajun Sketches,* organized an excellent group of six musicians to play the festival, among them Lawrence Walker, Aldus Broussard, and Aldus's sister Evelyn Broussard.

The documentation of Acadian music marks a significant point in the music's history. But, as always, the music moved on, influencing and being influenced by other musics and styles. As early as 1910, the oil fields of southwest Louisiana attracted outsiders from Texas and the rest of the United States. In the 1920s, radio came to the prairies of southwest Louisiana, the airwaves carrying new musical influences, such as blues and hillbilly. The border radio station XET in Monterrey, Mexico, was probably heard on the prairies, and the Cajuns delighted in the recordings of such early country greats as the Carter Family and Jimmie Rodgers. Cleoma Falcon was one of the first artists to translate country and jazz songs into French, including Fats Waller's "Lulu's Back in Town" and "It's a Sin to Tell a Lie."

Other Cajuns proved no less susceptible to the new sounds, and some young bands began emulating country & western big-band hybrids such as Bob Wills and His Texas Playboys. The Hackberry Ramblers were Cajun pioneers on many fronts: They were the first to play music standing (contrary to the seated position of the accordion band), the first to use amplification in dancehalls (utilizing a generator in their Model T), and the first to remove the accordion as a key instrument in a Cajun band. Much of their repertoire was country music translated into French. In 1933, they began broadcasting on KFDM, a radio station in Beaumont, Texas, that had a hookup in Lake Charles. This was one of the first Cajun live radio connections, and these appearances became an important force in the marketing of Cajun bands. The Ramblers played all kinds of music, and when they sang or recorded in English they called themselves the Riverside Ramblers because the weekly radio show was sponsored in part by Montgomery Ward's Riverside tires. Many other local bands who saw the national trend toward string bands followed suit, and the accordion was pushed to the background for the next ten or fifteen years. The Cajun recording artists of this time were very prolific, and artists such as Leo Soileau, Harry Choates, and Chuck Guillory recorded hundreds of string-swing standards in French and English.

While the Cajuns were turning west to Texas for inspiration, black French musicians were playing all styles, creating popular string orchestras to perform at the more elite, upper-class venues as well

OPPOSITE: HUSBAND AND WIFE JOE AND CLEOMA FALCON, WHO CUT THE FIRST CAJUN DISC IN 1928

as taking up accordions and fiddles at country dances. The radio brought urban blues to the prairies, and black musicians started to put aside the single-row (of buttons on the treble side) accordions favored by Cajuns and play double- and triple-row accordions. Because these accordions had the halftones and chromatic scales lacking in single-row diatonic accordions, musicians could play blue notes and the blues' more complex melodies. The earliest form of this French urban blues was called French La La. There are few recorded examples of the style, though Sidney Babineaux and Peter King, both early La La musicians, have been documented on such compilations as Arhoolie's *Zydeco — Volume 1: The Early Years 1949-1962* and Folkways' *Louisiana Creole Music.* The late Boozoo Chavis, of Lake Charles, played this rhythmic old style on a single-row accordion. His recording of "Paper in My Shoe" in 1954 was a regional success and became a dancehall standard in both the La La and Cajun scenes.

This era brought another important change in how the music was created, performed, and heard, as dances began to move out of the home and into the dancehalls. Dances had been friendly, informal social affairs including young and old. Friends and neighbors pushed back furniture and shared their humble good times with all generations of their family, including children. The early dancehalls did not sell alcohol, had a room where children could sleep, supplied abundant chaperones, and maintained an air of respectability. As the times changed, however, so did the dancehalls. The shift from the home to the honky-tonk redefined the dance in Cajun culture. With the selling of liquor on the premis-

es, dancehalls developed a bad reputation, viewed as no place for children, nor for respectable women. Because the dancehalls began attracting a louder, drinking clientele, amplification became very popular, which transformed the music, too.

World War II arrived, taking many men away from home but also making jobs for those left behind. The shipbuilding and petroleum industries experienced a wartime boom and offered much higher wages than farming. Many civilians went to work in the oil refineries and shipyards of Port Arthur, Texas. While there, they were exposed to even more Texas-style music, and many copied the fiddling techniques used in the bands of such popular country & western performers as Bob Wills, Roy Acuff, and Ernest Tubb.

In the 1940s, black Louisiana artists such as Clifton Chenier were influenced by the music they heard in urban centers in Texas. Clifton had been playing the accordion in his hometown of Opelousas, but the rhythm & blues bands he heard in Houston helped him fine-tune his style. When he returned home, he mixed the blues with the French language in a powerful and inimitable way, creating the style later called zydeco. Houston became a center for early zydeco because many French Creoles moved there for work.

Radio was another powerful influence. Not only did it help introduce and disseminate new sounds but it also provided a means through which local bands could be promoted, thus widening their market. Leo Soileau, one of the top fiddlers in Louisiana

from the 1920s to the mid-1940s, gave daily radio broadcasts from KPLC in Lake Charles during and after World War II. There he worked with another future Cajun radio personality, Happy Fats (born Leroy LeBlanc). Though he began his career as a traditional Cajun artist, Happy Fats became the MC of the popular television show *Mariné* after a long bout of serving as Governor Jimmie Davis's musical sidekick.

Once the war ended, veterans returned home hungry for the familiar comforts they had left behind. As a result, the accordion and more traditional accordion music enjoyed a resurgence and revival. Cajun artist Iry LeJeune, a partially blind son of a sharecropper, recorded the first of his rare and extraordinary recordings on Houston's Opera label in 1948, with the Oklahoma Tornadoes. In 1949, he cut twenty-four songs for Lake Charles music-store owner Eddie Shuler. These recordings comprised the beginning and the best of the Folkstar/Goldband label. Many of LeJeune's recordings were songs he had learned from 78 rpm discs by legendary black French artist Amédé Ardoin.

At the same time, George Khoury, another Lake Charles record-store owner, financed Virgil Bozeman's O.T. label and then set up his own Khoury and Lyric labels. Khoury recorded some important early classic Cajun musicians, including the beloved accordionist Nathan Abshire and dancehall favorite Lawrence Walker. Soon small, independently owned record companies began to crop up everywhere.

Pre-zydeco recordings started to appear after the war. Lead Belly recorded a couple of French songs with his "windjammer" (accordion), bluesman Lightnin' Hopkins imitated an accordion with an organ on one of his recordings, "Zologo," and Clarence Garlow recorded the classic "Bon Ton Roula" in 1950. Garlow, born in Welsh, Louisiana, referred to himself as a black Cajun, since he grew up attending black French house dances. His pre-zydeco recording made the national charts, going to Number Seven on the R&B singles chart.

The Louisiana Hayride, a down-home country radio show from Shreveport, started in 1948 and was very popular among the Cajuns in southwest Louisiana. Hank Williams got his start on the show, and he loved the Cajuns' music as much as they liked his. Williams borrowed the melody of the Cajun tune "Grand Texas" for his hit "Jambalaya (on the Bayou)." In turn, Cajuns used several Williams tunes in their repertoire. Cajun artist D.L. Menard was so heavily influenced by Williams, in both his singing and his personal style, that he became known as the Cajun Hank Williams.

The accordion was back to stay, and the dancehalls gained a little respectability with smooth, tasteful bands such as those led by Aldus Roger and Lawrence Walker. These musicians were perfectionists who played Cajun music with a fine dancing rhythm, a little less

OPPOSITE: BOOZOO CHAVIS WORKS HIS ACCORDION, 1999. ABOVE: DENNIS MCGEE (LEFT) SHOWS CENTURY-OLD FIDDLE TUNES TO MICHAEL DOUCET, 1983.

rough, perhaps, than the frenetic LeJeune or the bluesy Abshire. KFLY Channel 10, a Lafayette television station, began to feature Aldus Roger every Saturday afternoon, and French blacks and whites tuned in weekly, impressed with Roger's skill on the accordion and his musicians' immaculate Western dress style.

In the mid-1950s, zydeco music saw a surge in its popularity when Chavis's "Paper in My Shoe" became a surprise hit. Featuring

ABOVE: D.L. MENARD, "THE CAJUN HANK WILLIAMS," CIRCA 1980. OPPOSITE: QUEEN IDA TAKES A BREAK BEFORE PLAYING ZYDECO SONGS ON HER ACCORDION AT THE NEW ORLEANS JAZZ AND HERITAGE FESTIVAL, 1999.

"HANK WILLIAMS'S MUSIC SOMEHOW OR OTHER FIT RIGHT WITH OUR CAJUN MUSIC. HANK WILLIAMS WAS IN HIS PRIME IN THOSE DAYS. EVERY TIME HE'D COME OUT WITH A SONG, OUR CAJUN BAND WOULD PLAY IT BECAUSE HE WAS POPULAR. AND WE PLAYED A FEW LEFTY FRIZZELL NUMBERS, TOO, WHEN HE BECAME VERY POPULAR. WE PLAYED A LOTTA ENGLISH SONGS, BECAUSE IN THOSE DAYS, IF YOU COULDN'T PLAY A LOT OF COUNTRY & WESTERN SONGS, YOU WERE ALMOST NOT CONSIDERED A BAND. YOU WOULDN'T A HAD NO JOB IF YOU PLAYED STRICTLY CAJUN MUSIC." —D.L. MENARD

accordion and saxophone accompaniment, Chavis's recording had a wonderful rhythmic quality and a rawness that was irresistible. The second big success of the newly forming zydeco scene was the rise of Clifton Chenier. Clifton and his brother Cleveland had by this time perfected their blend of urban rhythm & blues and French accordion roots and were driving dancers wild. Besides Clifton's mastery of the piano-key accordion, the group boasted his brother Cleveland on the rubboard (a percussive "washboard" attached to the chest and strummed with the fingers), which he had honed into a high art, even inventing the design of the rubboard with shoulder hooks. In addition, the Cheniers' group incorporated a heavy electric bass, a strong drum beat, and, at times, a rocking piano into its sound. Their music was soon called zydeco, but just who coined the term is controversial. Some say the word came from Clifton's hit song "Zydeco Sont Pas Salé" ("Snap Beans Aren't Salty"). There is also the African phrase *a zaré,* which means "I dance." Clifton, who died in 1987, once explained that the old people had called the French dances "zydeco," saying, for example, *"Allons au zydeco"* ("Let's go to the dance"). This term has become synonymous with the music of Clifton Chenier and those who have followed in his footsteps.

Although the Louisiana music scene was exploding with innovation, it remained traditional in the sense that it was largely male dominated. Female musicians and singers had made great strides in other genres, particularly country, folk, and rhythm & blues, but in Louisiana, with very few exceptions, women played and sang mostly in the home, primarily because of dancehalls' ill repute. Nonetheless, in addition to Cleoma Falcon, there were a few women who also recorded in the 1930s and 1940s, such as Cleoma's niece Marie Falcon, and Therese Falcon, whom Joe Falcon married after Cleoma's death. Country singer Dottie Vincent recorded a Cajun song in the 1960s. In the 1970s, Sheryl Cormier led her own band, and this author and accordionist Marc Savoy re-created the type of husband-and-wife team that had slipped out of sight since the Falcons. Eva Touchet played bass and sang with her brothers. In addition, zydeco's high-spirited Queen Ida drew on her Lake Charles, Louisiana, roots and emerged from the Northern California Creole community to introduce the music to a West Coast audience, while Ann Goodly and Rosie Ledet formed bands in their native Louisiana, playing single-row accordions and singing primarily in English.

The 1960s brought an influx of music lovers and folklorists to Louisiana in search of roots music for a variety of reasons: to find representatives of American regional musics to perform at folk festivals; for academic research projects; or simply to find something they had heard about and wanted to understand. Arhoolie's Chris Strachwitz came from California, looking for artists to record; Harry Oster made important field recordings; Gerard Dole traveled from Paris to study and collect Acadian folklore; Les Blank made several documentary films; Dick Spottswood, Bob Jones, and Ralph Rinzler scouted for the National Folk Festival. In 1964, when Rinzler arrived on his talent search, he found as guides two local cultural saviors, Revon Reed and Paul Tate, both from Mamou. Reed and Tate had been trying, on a local level, to preserve what was left of the traditional Cajun culture. They guided Rinzler in the right direction, and as a result, a small, choice group of authentic, French-speaking roots musicians that included Wallace Lafleur, Vinus Lejeune, Gladney Thibodeaux, and Cyprien Landreneau, went to

the prestigious Newport Folk Festival in Rhode Island. When the musicians came back and reported that they'd played alongside such stars as Peter, Paul and Mary, Bob Dylan, and Joan Baez, the younger generation was sufficiently impressed to give its Cajun roots a second listen. Many Cajun musicians began to play their traditional music for a national audience. Clifton Chenier toured the world, while a young Doug Kershaw made Cajun music famous with his 1961 hit "Louisiana Man." In 1971, popular folk revivalist Mike Seeger took accordionist Marc Savoy and fiddler Dennis McGee on the road. The Balfa Brothers, from Bayou Grand Louis, near Mamou, made a considerable impact on the national folk scene with their acoustic, soulful sound. Dewey Balfa was a great spokesman for the preservation of the Cajun culture, and with his brothers and accordionist Nathan Abshire, he traveled the globe. D.L. Menard toured with his band, the Louisiana Aces.

In the late 1960s, a movement began to raise awareness about French heritage in general and French language in particular. The Council of the Development of French in Louisiana (CODOFIL) was founded in 1968 to try to revive the French language within the state and to counteract the stigma against speaking French. Two young music lovers in New Orleans, Quint Davis and Allison Kaslow, started the New Orleans Jazz and Heritage Festival to preserve all the traditional musics of Louisiana. Others who helped to popularize Cajun music included Michael Doucet, a young musician from Lafayette who later formed the progressive Cajun band Beausoleil and cofounded the traditionally oriented Cajun group Savoy Doucet with this author and Marc Savoy. In 1965, Marc Savoy started the Savoy Music Center, which holds large weekly Cajun jam sessions, built traditional Cajun accordions at his shop, and strove to enlist younger Cajun generations in his effort to preserve their culture. He traveled as an accordion player with the Balfa Brothers, the Louisiana Aces, and the Savoy Doucet Cajun Band. Zachary Richard also played a part in the music's popularization, becoming a renowned Cajun rock artist in France and Canada. In 1974, with the guidance of the National Endowment for the Arts, the Smithsonian Folklife Program, and dedicated local folklorists, CODOFIL sponsored the first Festivals Acadiens at Blackham Coliseum in Lafayette.

On the zydeco front, many bands blossomed during the 1970s and 1980s. Due to the strong commitment to zydeco that is passed down from generation to generation, musical fathers inspired their sons to preserve family traditions while adding their own music. For example, Rockin' Dopsie's son has his band, Rockin' Dopsie Jr.; John Delafose's son Geno has French Rockin' Boogie; Preston Frank's son Keith has the Keith Frank Band; Clifton Chenier produced C.J. Chenier, and so on. In zydeco tradition, children often perform in bands from a very young age, and so the music and the dancehall lifestyle become a part of their lives.

Today, Louisiana's zydeco and Cajun cultures are very healthy. Zydeco bands have become prominent on a national level, with Terrance Simien, Nathan Williams and the Zydeco Cha Chas, Geno Delafose, Keith Frank, Rockin' Dopsie Jr., Buckwheat Zydeco, C.J. Chenier, and the late Beau Jocque drawing praise throughout the world. Their music is so popular because it grows and absorbs other influences while maintaining a sound and style uniquely its own. Despite a louder, almost rock-style rhythm section, these bands remain more a product of their roots than of mainstream American pop music.

Le Rendez Vous des Cajuns, a weekly live-music radio show present-ed in French, airs Saturdays from Eunice, Louisiana. Along with Beausoleil, Marc Savoy, and Zachary Richard, many excellent young groups are touring and recording, playing traditional Cajun music: Filé, Coteau, Jambalaya, Steve Riley and the Mamou Playboys, Balfa Toujours (which includes Dewey Balfa's daughter Christine), the Magnolia Sisters, and Bruce Daigrepont among them. Various venues in Lafayette are bringing the music back to the community at large. Families flock to restaurants where children can hear music the way their great-grandparents did — among family and friends. Louisiana hosts several large festivals celebrating its music, food, and culture, which bring in millions of tourists from around the world.

If history is any indication, Louisiana music will continue to change and grow. Proud and independent, Louisianians are more dedicated than ever not only to the preservation of their traditions and culture but to sharing them with the world. Through their music, their food, and their basic attitudes toward life, they have made far greater cultural inroads into the world around them than the world has made into them. And therein lies the endur-ing strength and resilience that makes their music both uniquely their own and distinctly American.

OPPOSITE: NATHAN WILLIAMS AND THE ZYDECO CHA CHAS

CLIFTON CHENIER: *[I started playing the accordion in] 1947. A fellow I know used to play accordion; he gave me that accordion. It was a piano key.*

[When I was about eight or nine,] I listened to Claude and the Reynolds a lot. They had an old Model A Ford with a rumble seat in the back. When they'd pass by my daddy's house to go play at a dance, I'd jump in that back seat, that little rumble seat. And when they'd get where they'd gone to play at, I'd get out the car. They couldn't do nothing [to stop me]; it was too far for me to walk back. I'd stay there with 'em and listen to 'em. And I used to follow my daddy, too, when he was playing places. I was about five then. I got a lot of experience watching people dancing.

I've been recording since '54. Me, a guitar and a drum. And we recorded in Lake Charles [Louisiana's] KAOK station. They took it from there, and they took that record on to California. And that's where Specialty Recording Company was. . . . I went on in there. The man talked to me — we talked, we talked. So we recorded that record about "Ay-Tete-Fee" and "Boppin' the Rock." And that made a hit.

In 1955, when I started playing big dances, nobody around here was playing the accordion anymore. They'd gave it up. Claude had stopped, Sidney Babineaux and the Reynolds, they had to stop. So now when I come up and made a hit . . . see, black people, they don't even wanna hear talk of accordions. They don't want to even listen to you. But I kept it going, kept it going, now everybody wanna' play accordion. Fellows call 'em at my house wanting me to show them how to play. I tell 'em, "I can't show you nothing. I learnt my own way. I did what I liked, and I learnt my own style."

In Europe, they had an accordion contest, and they had about five hundred accordion players. They couldn't capture my style, but I could play their style. So that's how I walk out with the crown — I been havin' it ever since. I tell you what: To get that crown, you have to roll me.

OPPOSITE, FROM TOP: CLIFTON CHENIER AT HOME IN LAFAYETTE, 1983; CLEVELAND (LEFT) AND CLIFTON CHENIER, CIRCA 1950. ABOVE, FROM TOP: THE CHENIER BROTHERS, IN THE EARLY FIFTIES; A NEIGHBORHOOD NIGHTSPOT ADVERTISING CHENIER'S MUSIC IN THE WINDOW.

"I BROUGHT FRENCH MUSIC FURTHER THAN ANYBODY DOWN HERE. AND EVERY-WHERE I WENT WITH IT, THEY RECEIVED IT, YOU KNOW. I WENT ALL OVER EUROPE, ALL THE WAY TO ISRAEL. PEOPLE DOWN HERE, THEY NEVER BEEN THERE."
—CLIFTON CHENIER

MARC SAVOY: *[When] I grew up, I never rebelled against what my parents [were doing]. Especially when I started school, when I saw what my peers were pursuing. Actually, I tried as a young kid to get into football and sports, but I thought that it was so mundane and trivial compared to what my grandparents or my parents were doing. My mother used to tell me, "Why do you want to pursue what all these old people [are doing]? You know, learn their stories, learn their music, learn how to speak French — why do you want to do that?" "Mom," I said, "this stuff is so fantastic. It's just a matter of time when the rest of the world finds out about this; this is gonna explode like a nuclear bomb."*

When I started school, I thought that all my peers would've been French-speaking people who loved Cajun music and all of this. And let me tell you, I didn't let it be known that I was Cajun when I saw the reaction that these kids had toward Cajuns. It was almost like you were talking about a very dirty subject, or a dirty word, when you mentioned the word 'Cajun' with them. I mean, they, like, cringed in their skin over 'Cajun.'

I was immersed in this all-American lifestyle in school. And I had this other side of my life that I was immersed [in] with these old wonderful, gentle, French-speaking, charismatic people who had all this music — who had all this earthiness about 'em. And they would come to my father and mother's and visit. . . . And it was all these stories they told each other, you know. They just showed their whole soul. That's why I wanted to play music as a kid — it's because I loved the people. It wasn't just the music I loved, but I loved the people. They were such characters. If it would have been anybody else, I might not have been attracted to the music as much. But it was the people that I fell in love with. And that's what I wanted to be.

As a child playing in the yard in the late afternoon, I'd hear this music that would come across the fields, just faint faint faint. But it sounded so good. You ever heard an accordion far, far away? It sounds so pretty. The distance has something to do with it; it makes it so sweet. I grew up with my grandpa playing fiddle — he detested accordions. But I had never seen an accordion before. I saw people playing fiddles and all this, but they had never really had that much of an impact on me. I'd hear

this [accordion] music, and I'd ask my dad, "So, what is that? What is that sound?" And he'd say, "That's old man Hiram playing his accordion." Hiram Courville was a little guy that weighed about ninety-eight pounds soaking wet. Skinny skinny skinny skinny. He lived probably about a half a mile away from our home. Way across the field there was a Catalba grove, a little tiny house — that's where his family lived. So he'd come over and talk to my daddy. So I'd ask him, I'd say, "Next time you come talk to Dad, why don't you bring your accordion, your box?" — he'd call it a box. "Ah, no," he'd say, "I don't wanna do that." He was very modest and very shy.

One year, my father invited old man Hiram to come play his accordion at our Christmas party. I guess I was about ten years old. That was my first big exposure to accordions. That was the first time that I'd really seen somebody play the accordion up in my face, and it was a revelation. It was just like a bright light. I knew there was something I had to do.

The minute I picked up my accordion, when I pulled it out of the box, I put it in my hands and I played it. Because I'd heard the tunes all my life and I had the tunes in my head. My mother would tell me, "I knew you'd learn 'cause I'd hear you outside whistling, and you hit every note of the tunes." So when I picked up this accordion, I had watched Hiram Courville for so many years, and it was like playback. When I put my hand on that thumb strap, I just ran my hand over the buttons to get each one's voices, and I sat down and said, "Okay, I'm gonna play it. Here we go."

RIGHT: MARC SAVOY, 2000. OPPOSITE, CLOCKWISE FROM TOP LEFT: SAVOY AND D.L. MENARD, 1976; SAVOY IN HIS ACCORDION WORKSHOP IN EUNICE, LOUISIANA, CIRCA 1988; SAVOY AND FELLOW CAJUN MUSICIANS AT THE WEEKLY SATURDAY MORNING JAM SESSION HELD AT THE SAVOY MUSIC CENTER, CIRCA 1993.

1821 Mexico declares its independence from Spain. 1830 Mexico proclaims that U.S. citizens may no longer colonize its Texas Territory. 1836 On March 6, Mexican general Antonio López de Santa Anna defeats U.S. troops at the Alamo. Sam Houston defeats Santa Anna at the Battle of San Jacinto on April 21. The new republic of Texas claims all land between the Rio Grande and the Neuces River. 1845 Despite protest from the Mexican government, the U.S. annexes Texas. In December, Texas joins the Union as the twenty-eighth state. 1848 After two years of bloodshed, the Mexican American War ends. Mexico gives up 35 percent of its territory, including its claim on the land north of the Rio Grande. 1860 The button accordion is introduced to the tejanos and norteños. 1901 The story of Mexican rancher Gregorio Cortez becomes the subject of one of the most famous of the heroic corridos — songs challenging Anglo authority and calling for Mexican American self-empowerment. 1928 Eduardo Martínez's group records two sides for the Vocalion label, becoming the first tejano orquesta to record for a major label. Weeks later, the Orquesta del Norte begins its recording career with Victor. Bruno Villarreal becomes the first tejano accordionist to record commercially (for Okeh Records). 1930 Roca y Amador record the canción "Radios y Chicanos," a critique of capitalism and commercialism. Los Rancheros, the first modern-style orquesta, form in Houston. Los Rancheros model themselves after American big bands and play jazzy orquesta for cosmopolitan tejanos. 1934 Lydia Mendoza's hit "Mal Hombre" ("Evil Man") breaks the canción tradition of stigmatizing women as traitorous and avaricious. 1936 Narciso Martínez cuts his first record for Bluebird. Santiago Jiménez introduces the contrabass to conjunto on his first recording. 1947 Armando Marroquín launches Ideal in the living room of his house in Alice, Texas. Narcisco Martínez, Lydia Mendoza, and Beto Villa cut their first postwar recordings. Beto Villa, one of the orquesta tejana forefathers, cuts his first recordings for the Ideal label. 1948 Conjunto artists start performing at commercial dancehalls in areas ranging from Sacramento, California, and south Texas to Nebraska and Illinois. 1954 Paulino and Eloy Bernal form El Conjunto Bernal, an experimental group that becomes known for its innovative experiments in conjunto music. 1955 Accordionist Tony de la Rosa and his ensemble incorporate the electric bajo sexto and electric bass into their performances. 1957 The newly organized David Coronado and the Latinaires open for Isidro

López in Victoria, Texas. **1958** El Conjunto Bernal release "Mi Único Camino," one of the first conjunto recordings to feature three-part harmonies. Strongly influenced by the rock & roll craze in America, Little Joe and the Latinaires record "Safari, Part I & II" – one of the first tejano-rock crossover tunes. **1963** Sunny and the Sunliners' hit "Talk to Me" hits Number Eleven on the pop chart; the record eventually goes gold. **1964** Bajo sexto player Cornelio Reyna and accordionist Ramón Ayala form Los Relámpagos del Norte, one of the only conjunto groups to achieve followings on both sides of the border. **Mid-1960s** Little Joe Hernández and his Latinaires record the popular 'Por un Amor' for Zarape. **1965** César Chávez incites a faction of farm workers to strike in the vineyards of Delano, California. The strike helps spawn the Chicano movement. Chromatic accordion virtuoso Oscar Hernández joins El Conjunto Bernal and helps the group reach its highest level of technical sophistication. **1967** The corrido "Los Rinches de Texas," composed in the aftermath of a melon-worker strike in Starr County, Texas, becomes a rallying cry for United Farm Workers organizing union members in south Texas. The following year, the Independent Party of Starr County, whose platform favors local farm workers, is voted into office. **1972** Little Joe y la Familia release the anthemic song "Las Nubes." A musical hybrid of ranchero and swing elements, "Las Nubes" eventually becomes the rallying cry for Mexican Americans involved in the Chicano movement. **1982** Lydia Mendoza becomes the first tejano artist to be awarded the National Endowment for the Arts' National Heritage Award, for her outstanding contributions to America's roots music. Narciso Martínez, Santiago Jiménez, his son Flaco Jiménez, Valerios Longoria, and Tony de la Rosa will each receive the award in subsequent years. **1986** Selena y Los Dinos sign with Manny Guerra's GP Records and record their first hit, "Dame un Beso." **1989** Former Sir Douglas Quintet members Doug Sahm and Augie Meyers hook up with Freddy Fender and legendary accordionist Flaco Jiménez to form the Texas Tornados. **1992** The success of Emilio Navaira's 'Unsung Highways' (EMI Latin) solidifies Navaira as the most popular male tejano performer of the Nineties. **1994** As a result of the North American Free Trade Agreement, Mexico lifts its ban on Tex-Mex groups going south of the border. **1995** Selena's final recording, 'Dreaming of You,' debuts at the top of the pop chart, selling 331,000 copies in its first week of release.

MÚSICA TEJANA: THE MUSIC OF MEXICAN TEXAS
BY MANUEL PEÑA

Historically, Texas-Mexicans, or *tejanos*, as they sometimes call them-selves, are among the most musically productive regional groups in the Americas, having created several influential styles. Collectively referred to as Tex-Mex, or *música tejana*, these styles of music include the immensely popular accordion-based group known as *conjunto*, as well as the multistyled brass-and-reed ensemble known as *orquesta tejana*. Texas-Mexicans forged yet another highly popular music known as Tejano, a hipper, synthesizer-driven offshoot of conjunto that also borrows ele-ments from the orquesta tejana. The tejanos have also been involved in the development of the Mexican narrative ballad known as *corrido*, a folk genre with far-reaching impact.

The Texas-Mexicans descend from the Spanish-Mexican colonists who settled the provinces of Tejas (1718) and Nuevo Santander (1746); thus they have deep roots in the American Southwest. They came into conflictive contact with the Americans in the 1820s, and they became a subordinate minority when Texas was annexed by the United States in 1845. Tejanos were eventually integrated into the dominant "Anglo" society, but their integration did not come about smoothly. Their antago-nistic relations with the *americanos* persisted well into the Twentieth Century, and their eventual assimilation was uneven, if inevitable. Given the frequent hostil-ity between the two groups, tejanos were forced to adapt culturally in ways that worked both to facilitate their acculturation *and* to promote ethnic resistance.

'El Capitan," Highest Peak in Texas   99

64238

TOP: A YOUNG PARTICIPANT AT THE CHARRO DAYS FIES-TA, BROWNSVILLE, TEXAS, 1942. OPPOSITE: AN ENGRAVED MAP OF TEXAS AND MEXICO, CIRCA 1849.

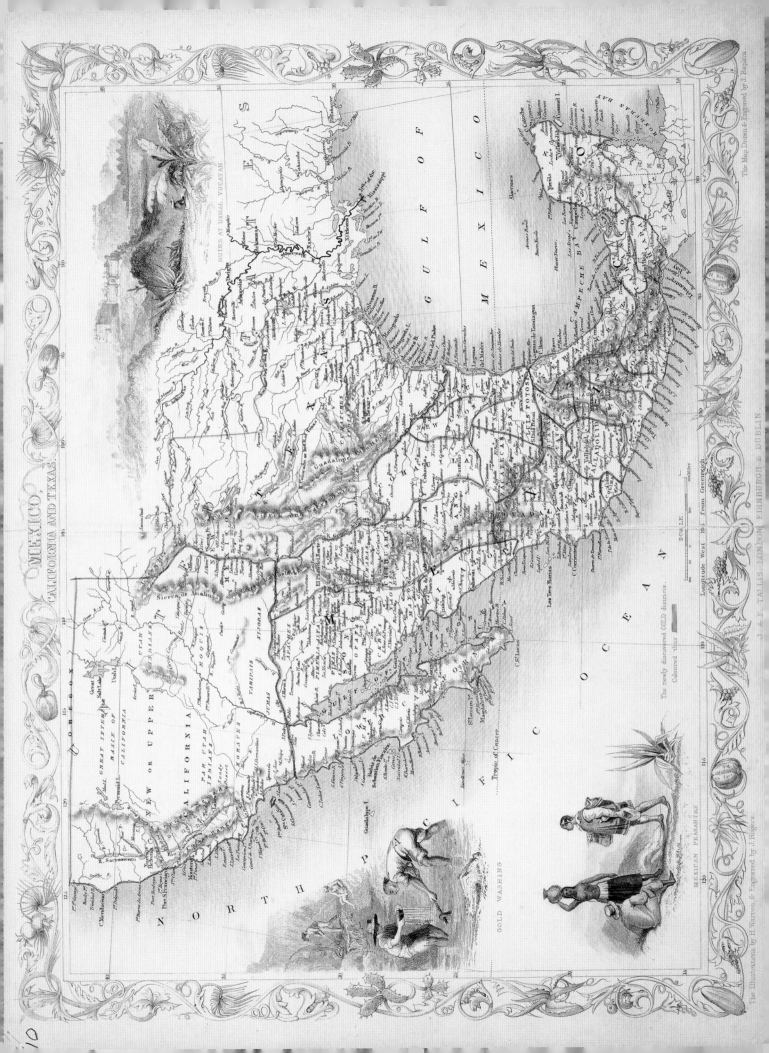

MEXICO,
CALIFORNIA AND TEXAS.

RUINS AT UXMAL, YUCATAN.

GULF OF MEXICO

NORTH PACIFIC OCEAN

GOLD WASHING

MEXICAN PEASANTRY

The newly discovered GOLD districts.
Coloured thus

SCALE
200 Miles

Longitude West 105 From Greenwich

The Map Drawn & Engraved by J. Rapkin.
The Illustrations by H. Warren, & Engraved by J. Rogers.

J. & F. TALLIS, LONDON, EDINBURGH & DUBLIN.

In this climate of conflict, accommodation, and adaptation, the corrido, conjunto, orquesta, and Tejano emerged and flourished. Partaking of both American and Mexican musical elements (for example, American jazz and Mexican-styled "country," or *ranchero*), the conjunto, orquesta, and Tejano, in particular, form part of the bedrock texture of what may justifiably be called an American roots music.

CONJUNTO/TEJANO The accordion conjunto (literally, ensemble), known more generally as *música norteña*, emerged in the latter part of the Nineteenth Century along the Texas-Mexico border. Of humble folk, rural origins, this ensemble became a powerful Hispanic style during the Twentieth Century thanks to commercialization, which carried it far beyond its original folk base. However, the conjunto always remained at its core a working-class dance music — first as an expression of rural workers in south Texas and northern Mexico and later as the musical voice of an urban working class — no matter where it migrated: to California, to the Midwest, and to interior Mexican states such as Michoacán and Durango.

The modern conjunto was invented primarily by the Texas-Mexicans, with some help from their *norteño* neighbors across the border. The ensemble's development can be divided into four distinct stages (or eras), the first of which may be labeled the "diffuse," indicating a time when no firm style yet existed. The second stage is the "formative," when the conjunto began to take on a unique regional flavor, due to the introduction of the Mexican twelve-string guitar known as *bajo sexto*. The "classic" era arrives with the final evolution of the ensemble, when all the now standard instruments were included — the button accordion (usually the three-row melody-button model), bajo sexto, drums, and electric bass — and various other musical innovations occurred. Finally, there is an era of "consolidation," when the pace of innovation slowed, the conjunto became more bound to the "classic" style, and "progressive" conjuntos emerged, crossing over into and borrowing from other types of music.

The diffuse stage began when the button accordion was first introduced to the tejanos and norteños, sometime after 1860. During this period, the tejanos did not change the playing style of the main instrument, the accordion. Imitating the accordion style of Germans and other European immigrants, tejanos and norteños played those groups' polkas, redowas, schottisches, and waltzes — and, like the Europeans, used the right-hand keyboard for melody and the left for bass and harmonic accompaniment. By the turn of the century, however, the accordion and bajo sexto had become a common pairing, creating a different sound from the Europeans'. The tejanos and norteños even introduced one unique type of music: the *huapango*, a bouncy regional genre originally from the Mexican gulf coast region known as the Huasteca.

The formative stage began in the late 1920s, when the American recording companies — RCA Victor, Brunswick, Decca — turned their sights toward the rich musical bounty of the Hispanic Southwest. Beginning in 1926, the major labels established operations in such cities as San Antonio, El Paso, and Los Angeles and commercially exploited every type of music present among Mexicans, from singers such as the legendary Lydia Mendoza to string orquestas. A unique tejano accordion ensemble emerged, characterized by the interplay between the accordion and the bajo sexto. The "father" of the modern conjunto, Narciso Martínez, cemented the singularity of the tejano polka style when he began relying exclusively on the treble side of the accordion, leaving the bass and harmonic accompaniment to his bajo sexto player, Santiago Almeida. Santiago Jiménez, another innovator, further advanced the conjunto style when he introduced the contrabass (or bass fiddle, later replaced by the electric bass) to the fledgling ensemble.

The classic era (1940s–1970s) ushered in the most productive stage in the history of the conjunto. Among its prominent innovators was Valerio Longoria, who introduced the trap-drum set,

ABOVE: AD HOC FOLK ORQUESTA, 1912.
OPPOSITE: NARCISO MARTÍNEZ AND
SANTIAGO ALMEIDA, 1936.

radically altering the music's style. Longoria was also the first to add vocals to the music, in the form of the *canción ranchera,* as well as the bolero, an urban and more sophisticated genre previously missing from the conjunto. Another major player, Tony de la Rosa, developed the *tacuachito*-styled polka, performed at a much slower tempo in response to a new south Texas dance style, *el tacuachito* (the possum) — a deliberate, swaying glide reminiscent of a pregnant possum. The group El Conjunto Bernal expanded the conjunto in multiple directions, adding complex three-part harmonies, dual chromatic accordions, and Afro-Hispanic song types such as the Colombian *cumbia.* By 1960, the mature conjunto ensemble had taken final shape, anchored by the three-row button accordion, bajo sexto, drums, and electric bass. It became a highly recognizable tejano musical expression, its popularity ensured through the development of an extensive dancehall network that provided steady work for conjuntos, and through commercial recordings, which brought fame and small fortunes to the best-known groups.

Commercial recording had landed in the hands of local entrepreneurs when major labels abandoned música tejana with the advent of World War II (not to return until the 1980s). Chiefly responsible for the regional marketing of the conjunto from the 1940s to the 1970s were companies such as Ideal, Falcon, Corona, and Sombrero, whose limited regional reach kept the conjunto (and other tejano music) grounded to its roots audience. Particularly influential was Ideal, the first of the regional labels to fill the vacuum left by the majors. Its founder, Armando Marroquín, started the label in 1947, in his Alice, Texas, living room. There conjunto stylist Narciso Martínez, singer Lydia Mendoza, and Beto Villa, the founder of the orquesta tejana, cut their first postwar recordings.

The classic era also witnessed the resurgence in Mexico of *norteño,* as conjunto was called in that country. Initially, norteño groups had shunned the innovations introduced by their neighbors across the border — such as Martínez's emphasis on the treble end and tacuachito polkas — but in the 1960s, they began to adopt much of the style of the tejano groups. In the Sixties and Seventies, a number of norteño ensembles rose to prominence, but three dominate the entire period until the beginning of the Twenty-First Century. Los Relámpagos del Norte were organized in about 1964 by bajo sexto player Cornelio Reyna and accordionist Ramón Ayala. Los Relámpagos played the canción

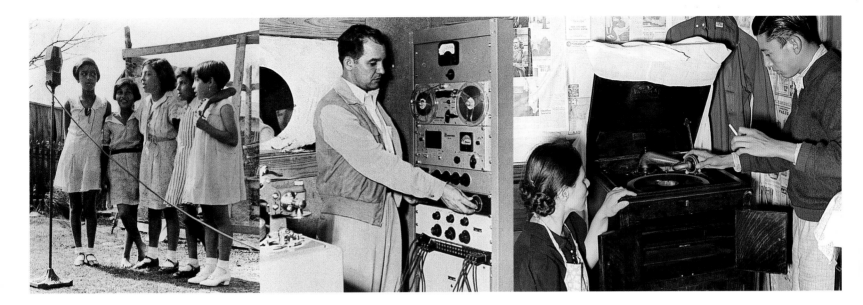

OPPOSITE: VALERIO LONGORIA AND HIS SON, AT HOME. THIS PAGE, CLOCKWISE FROM TOP LEFT: MEXICAN GIRLS SINGING FOR FOLKLORIST ALAN LOMAX IN SAN ANTONIO, TEXAS, 1934; ARMANDO MARROQUÍN, CIRCA 1950; MEXICAN MUSIC FANS TRYING OUT THEIR NEW PHONOGRAPH, 1939; EL CONJUNTO BERNAL, 1965.

ranchera in the tacuachito vein of the tejano conjuntos, and Reyna and Ayala's heavily nasalized duet-singing style, long popular in northern Mexico, had enormous appeal on both sides of the border. Los Relámpagos exerted great influence on every group that came after it, particularly in Mexico. In the early Seventies, Reyna and Ayala parted ways, with the latter forming Los Bravos del Norte, a group that dominated the market for many years. Another iconic música norteña group, Los Tigres del Norte, debuted in the Seventies and still remains popular.

In Texas, the period from the 1980s to the end of the century marked the era of consolidation, when the classic style became a fixed norm. Yet it was also an era of experimentation, with extensive cross-fertilization between conjunto and American music, particularly country & western. Diversification took place as well, with the conjunto now divided into two camps, the "traditional" and the "progressive." Considered a throwback to the classic era, the traditional group was represented by figures such as accordionists David Lee Garza, whose sound had been influenced by El Conjunto Bernal, and the young Michael Salgado, who cultivated the style of Los Relámpagos. The progressive wing was most prominently represented by such accordionists as Mingo Saldívar, Flaco Jiménez, and a carry-over from the classic era, Esteban Jordán. The progressive conjuntos were much more susceptible to "crossover," or the process of intercultural musical borrowing, whereby performers such as Jiménez interlaced their songs with English lyrics and the twangy lilt of country & western, while others such as Jordán added extensive jazz riffs to the tejano polka.

Critical to the conjunto's split was the intervention of CBS/Sony and EMI Latin, which reentered the música tejana market in 1985. The labels played a pivotal role in extending the reach of both the conjunto and Tejano beyond the Texas borders — into other parts of the United States, Mexico, and Latin America. Among those who benefited most from major-label promotion was Flaco Jiménez, whose uncanny ability to switch between traditional conjunto style, country & western, and rock & roll epit-

omized the whole crossover process. Descending from a long line of accordionists, Flaco is the son of early tejano innovator Santiago Jiménez. Flaco followed in his father's footsteps, and by the time he was a teenager, he was an active player in the conjunto scene. Flaco's fame began to spread when he appeared in the well-received Les Blank and Chris Strachwitz documentary *Chulas Fronteras* and then signed to Strachwitz's Arhoolie Records, which had a wider distribution base than the tejano labels. Eventually, Flaco became a virtual ambassador of conjunto music in the larger national (and international) market, particularly through his participation in the popular Texas Tornados (with Freddy Fender, Doug Sahm, and Augie Meyers), but also through his collaborations with Ry Cooder, the Rolling Stones, and other rock artists.

Meanwhile, some of the progressive conjuntos morphed into the synthesized Tejano groups. By the late Eighties, these new "turbo conjuntos" had splintered into a spectrum of sounds, merging at one end with both country and pop rock, and at the other with various rhythmically complex Afro-Hispanic styles collectively known as *música tropical,* primarily characterized by the complex rhythms and percussion of the Colombian cumbia. EMI Latin artist Emilio Navaira was the best-known exponent of the country-cumbia combination, while the immensely popular singer Selena, who recorded for EMI Latin until her untimely death, best represented the pop rock–cumbia mix.

Indeed, the conjunto has evolved from a rural, small-scale folk music into a globally reaching modern ensemble. Throughout, the conjunto has retained as its core the voice of a tejano and, later, a more generalized *mexicano* working class. Perhaps this is why one of the pioneer singers associated with the conjunto, Lydia Mendoza, known as *la cancionera de los pobres* (the singer of the poor), has remained one of its icons. A true norteña artist, Mendoza, who began singing in 1928 and whose career coin-

ABOVE: DANCING AT THE LERMAS CLUB, SAN ANTONIO, TEXAS, 1989. OPPOSITE: THE TEXAS TORNADOS, 1996: FLACO JIMÉNEZ, DOUG SAHM, FREDDY FENDER, AUGIE MEYERS (FROM LEFT).

cided with much of the conjunto's development, represents historically both the artistic and political values of the working class. These values had such staying power that even at the end of the Twentieth Century, despite extensive crossover and the attempts to convert the music into a profitable, transnational commodity, the conjunto stubbornly clung to its working-class roots, providing its supporters with a strong sense of shared identity and a generalized feeling of community.

THE ORQUESTA TEJANA Dating from Nineteenth-Century Mexican Texas, the orquesta tejana, like the conjunto, was primarily a dance-music ensemble. Initially, orquestas were ad hoc groups built around the violin, though in the latter part of the Nineteenth Century, military-styled brass bands began to appear with increasing frequency. From its inception, the orquesta strove to represent the musical tastes of an emerging middle class, made up of professionals and small merchants. The orquesta repertoire, however, was indistinguishable from that of the early conjunto, consisting of waltzes, polkas, redowas, and the like. Due to their improvisational nature, early orquestas also tended, like the conjunto, to have folk characteristics and to play for a rural audience. As in Mexico, these ensembles were sometimes known as *orquestas típicas* (traditional orchestras).

In the 1890s, the first truly organized string orquestas appeared in San Antonio, El Paso, and other cities. By the 1930s, a more modernized wind ensemble, patterned after the American big bands, had evolved among the upwardly mobile, urbanized tejanos. Heavily influenced by Thirties American swing music, modern wind orquestas such as Houston's Los Rancheros (possibly the first of its kind) were unabashed imitators of American big bands. The orquestas' fan base consisted of a growing segment of urban Mexican Americans who were undergoing rapid acculturation and who, despite their roots in Texas-Mexican culture, wished to become more fully "American." Most of these were small merchants and white-collar workers, although the new orquestas received some support from the more stable working class, and craftsmen in particular.

In 1947, saxophonist Beto Villa approached Armando Marroquín with the proposal that his Ideal label record a dif-ferent kind of music from conjunto. He offered a more ranchero (country), or folk-styled, version of the wind orquesta, which he was putting together. Villa reasoned that this kind of orquesta would enjoy a much wider audience than the big-band imitations, given the persisting ethnic, rural, and ranchero outlook of most tejanos.

After some hesitation, Marroquín agreed with Villa, and the first recording of what came to be known as orquesta tejana was produced: a 78 rpm disc with a *polca ranchera* (country-styled polka), "Las Delicias," on one side and a *vals ranchero* (country-styled waltz), "Porque Te Ríes," on the other. The record quickly captured the enthusiasm of Mexican Americans throughout the Southwest, who packed the dancehalls wherever Villa played. At this time, Villa's orquesta was minimal, featuring the bandleader on saxophone in addition to a trumpet, piano-accordion, contrabass, guitar, and drums. The ensemble played a "country" style long associated with the conjunto: simple harmonies and an unpolished, wide-vibrato sound on the horns. Villa's accessible style rapidly blossomed into a culturally powerful music, adopted by many tejanos as their musical signature.

Villa had received his musical training at Alice High School, where he was exposed to the big-band style of Duke Ellington and Benny Goodman. But he had also been introduced to the string orquesta by his father, a musician. When the string orquesta was replaced in Mexico by the modern, Latin-styled big bands, he developed a taste for their Afro-Hispanic style as well. Villa was thus among the first orquesta musicians to receive bimusical training — that is, an education in both Mexican and American traditions — and by 1949, after the initial success of his more ranchero offerings, he had decided to put this training into practice. He extended his repertoire to include more sophisticated Afro-Hispanic music such as the bolero, mambo, and cha-cha-cha on the one hand, and big-band swing and fox trot on the other. The result was a unique bimusical style of orquesta tejana, which alternated between the ranchero to which tejanos had become accustomed, and a more sophisticat-

ed sound, called *jaitón* (from the English *high-toned*). Reminiscent of the complex sounds of urban big bands like those of Benny Goodman, Glenn Miller, and, in Mexico, Luis Arcaraz, jaitón music fulfilled the middle-class aspirations of upwardly mobile Texas-Mexicans. Now considered "the Father of Tex-Mex," Villa spawned many imitators, the most innovative of which were vocalist/saxophonist Isidro López, whose band went one step beyond Villa by incorporating rock & roll into its canciones rancheras, and Balde González, whose group cultivated a more sophisticated, urban style of fox trots and boleros.

The next generation of orquestas was eventually dominated by two vocalist/bandleaders: Sunny Ozuna and his Sunliners, and Little Joe Hernández and his Latinaires. Both Ozuna and Hernández began their careers in the late 1950s, in search of fame and fortune in the burgeoning rock & roll market. Sunny achieved a Top Forty hit, "Talk to Me," in 1963, but his moment of glory in that market was brief, and for the remainder of his career he made his mark exclusively on the orquesta tejana circuit. Meanwhile, Little Joe also started his commercial career with a rock & roll instrumental he recorded, "Safari, Part I & II,"

but the venture was unsuccessful. Thereafter, he dedicated himself to the música tejana market, where his success began to mushroom in the mid-Sixties, when he recorded an enormously popular LP for the Zarape label, *Por un Amor*.

In the early 1970s, Little Joe and the renamed *la Familia* (the Family) began synthesizing a broad range of styles that included both Mexican-Latino and American. On the Mexican-Latino side, the gamut ranged from ranchero to jaitón; on the American, it drew from country & western, rhythm & blues, and swing jazz. Orquestas had been doing this since Beto Villa, of course, but Little Joe's experiments went well beyond what Villa and López had attempted twenty years earlier: He juxtaposed folk-ranchero and swing-jazz elements *within* the same musical piece (usually a polca ranchera) to create a wholly new and arresting form of bimusical "code switching" — that is, the continuous alternation between ranchero and jaitón, as well as between Mexican and American. Strongly resonant with the musical tastes and ideological bent of the "Chicano Generation," Little Joe's powerful new synthesis was soon christened *la Onda Chicana,* a name inspired by the Chicano political movement surging in Texas and the Southwest at that time.

The first of Little Joe y la Familia's bimusical innovations, in 1972, was heard on a landmark album titled *Para la Gente* (*For the People*), which included the song "Las Nubes." Written about the hopes and disappointments of a common workingman, "Las Nubes" deftly synthesized ranchero and swing-jazz elements to create a truly hybrid sound — based, again, on the juxtaposition of ranchero (Mexican, folk) and jaitón (American, sophisticated) — and became a virtual anthem for the 1970s Chicano movement. Little Joe's chief rivals in la Onda Chicana, Sunny and the Sunliners, followed his lead, creating their own highly popular style, which also consisted of the musical code switching that Little Joe had invented. A number of other groups with similar approaches emerged, such as the Latin Breed and Jimmy Edward, all of whom followed the pattern set by Little Joe y la Familia.

La Onda Chicana orquestas, with their heavy brass-and-reed instrumentation, declined rapidly after 1980. Several factors, including a new, "post-Chicano" generation much more influenced by MTV and especially the hard recession of the early Eighties, forced orquestas to change direction and to drastically downsize. Innovation rapidly came to a standstill as the bimusical efforts of the 1970s were abandoned in favor of a simpler, more strictly ranchero approach. Despite their downsizing efforts, la Onda Chicana orquestas were replaced by the new Tejano groups and their synthesized keyboards, which owed much of their style to the conjunto but which co-opted some of the orquestas' elements as well.

Throughout its development, the orquesta tejana always retained a splintered character. Particularly with its emphasis on the jaitón, it aimed, on the one hand, to appeal to a more Americanized, better-educated constituency that considered the conjunto to be beneath its artistic tastes. Yet due to the enduring discrimination even upwardly mobile tejanos often experienced from Anglos, the orquesta tejana was unable to completely sever ties with its folk-Mexican roots — hence its attachment to the ranchero. Becoming inescapably more Americanized, yet seeking to maintain a sense of ethnic solidarity, these middle-class tejanos opted in the end for a bicultural, bimusical orientation. Intimately connected with its constituents, the orquesta necessarily engaged in its own balancing act, moving between various extremes: Mexican and American, folk and modern, working and middle class, all bound up in the stylistic terms of ranchero and jaitón. Beginning with Villa's initial efforts to strike a balance between the two stylistic extremes, the movement culminated with the bimusical innovations of Little Joe y la Familia.

The musical legacy of the tejanos has few parallels in the Americas. Not only are their musical creations genuinely home-grown, they represent a unique synthesis of the many cross-cultural currents that historically sweep through the Hispanic Southwest in the form of diverse musical styles: Mexican/Latino on the one hand (the canción ranchera, the bolero, the cumbia), American on the other (swing jazz, country & western). It is not surprising, then, that música tejana has spread far beyond its homeland and gained popularity not only in the Hispanic Southwest but in Mexico and many other parts of the United States. Among the various tejano musics, the corrido alone has remained insulated from American influence, though occasionally American artists have borrowed its narrative structure with good results (as Marty Robbins did in his popular 1959 ballad "El Paso"). The corrido continues to function historically as a folk narrative that documents a broad range of topics, from major disasters to love tragedies, and, most important, the intermittent conflict between the Anglo-Americans and Texas-Mexicans (as in the classic ballad "El Corrido de Gregorio Cortez").

Meanwhile, the conjunto, orquesta, and Tejano have all been

OPPOSITE: LITTLE JOE AND THE LATINAIRES, 1965. ABOVE: THE LATE SELENA, CONTEMPORARY TEJANO'S BIGGEST STAR.

influenced in one way or another by the give-and-take of interethnic relations. In cultivating a folk, ranchero style, these musical forms have helped to stake out a distinctive "roots" tejano identity; in crossing over into other musics, they have not only created strong hybrid forms but helped accelerate the process of acculturation. Most important, in its astonishing fusion of so many diverse styles, música tejana has in turn influenced genres such as country and zydeco, in this way contributing to the rich cross-cultural exchanges that have occurred within America's roots music.

"I THINK [THE MIX OF] COUNTRY & WESTERN MUSIC AND CONJUNTO [IS] TEJANO MUSIC – THEIR SONGS ARE OUR SONGS. THEY BOTH RELATE TO EVERYDAY LIVING." —MINGO SALDÍVAR

BELOW: LITTLE JOE'S BAND, LA FAMILIA, HELPED HIM TO CREATE A NEW HYBRID OF MEXICAN AMERICAN MUSIC, LA ONDA CHICANA, IN THE EARLY 1970S. OPPOSITE: NARCISO AND IDUVINA MARTÍNEZ, AT HOME.

FLACO JIMÉNEZ: *I come from a musical background. A lot of people consider my dad a pioneer of Tex-Mex, or conjunto music. He bought an accordion in San Antonio, where they were very scarce. He started copying the oompah beat of the waltzes and polka from the Germans and the Polish who settled around New Braunfels. He used to come to their dances to check out how they play.*

I started playing the accordion when I was about five years old. When I was seven, I [would] observe my father teaching young kids from the barrio. I caught on real fast — whenever the student went home, I picked up their accordion and I knew the tune.

My first professional job was when I sat in with my dad, at this place he used to play on Fridays, Saturdays, and Sundays. I was about nine years old. . . . I played about two or three polkas, and then the bass player, Ismail Gonzales, took me in to the public with a big cup for them to put some money in — their pennies, nickels, quarters, whatever. It was on [a] Saturday night. On Sunday, I went straight to the store and bought candy for my brothers and sisters.

When I was in my teens, I used to tune in to American country music, and I used to listen to rock & roll when rock & roll started. So I decided it's good to change conjunto a little — it's still going to be conjunto, but it's going to sound a little more rockish, jazzier and bilingual. Just because [we're of] Mexican descent doesn't mean conjunto music is Mexican. . . . Imagine an accordion player playing "Viva Sagine" in a sombrero — it just doesn't fit. But you put on a Texan hat and play "Viva Sagine" — it tells you it came from the United States.

"THERE ARE JUST NO BOUNDARIES
OR BARRIERS FOR FLACO JIMÉNEZ
WHEN IT COMES TO PLAYING HIS
INSTRUMENT." —LITTLE
JOE HERNÁNDEZ

LEFT: FLACO JIMÉNEZ (CENTER) AT THE RECORDING
SESSIONS FOR DOUG SAHM'S 1973 ALBUM, ALSO
FEATURING BASSIST JACK BARBER (LEFT) AND AUGIE
MEYERS (RIGHT). ABOVE: JIMÉNEZ IN THE NINETIES.

1890 Jesse Walter Fewkes first records the Passamaquoddy Indians. This introduces recording devices to the Native Americans and begins a gradual infusion of more technological aspects into their music. **1890s** The United States government begins an aggressive campaign to "civilize" Native American people. Much of this process involves sending Native American children to boarding schools, forcing Euro-American style and culture upon them, and forbidding them to speak in their native language. Throughout the 1890s and into the early 1900s, Frances Densmore makes recordings of tunes hummed by Geronimo and songs performed by the Chippewa tribe in Minnesota. She goes on to publish twenty-five books on Native American music. **1910** Edward Curtis films 'The Land of the Head Hunters' off the coast of Seattle, Washington. Focusing on the Kwakiutl Indians, the film is perhaps the first documentary made in America and contains footage of musical celebrations. **1924** The Citizenship Act is passed, declaring all Native American people U.S. citizens. Following an investigation by a team of social scientists, it is recommended that Congress increase funding to improve the health and education of Native American people and develop Native American art. **1934** The Indian Reorganization Act encourages Native Americans to "recover" their cultural heritage. **1940s** Reverend Linn D. Pauahty, a Kiowa Methodist minister, forms the label American Indian Soundchiefs. Soundchiefs is the first label to use in-depth recording techniques and to publish albums featuring only one type of song sung by one tribal group instead of compilations of multiple tribes singing a variety of song types. **1947** After World War II, increasing numbers of Native American women become more actively involved in dancing and singing at tribal events. A number form all-female drum groups. **1951** Canyon Records is formed by Ray Boley, who chooses to record both traditional and contemporary Native American artists. **1952** The Termination Policy (a.k.a. Federal Relocation Policy) is adopted, in which federal support of tribes is reduced and some reservations are disbanded. As a result, many tribes are forced to move to urban areas; by 1990, more than 50 percent of all Native Americans live in cities. **Mid-1950s** The influence of both "mainstream" American performers and Canadian artists is found in the music of young Native Americans, who have relocated to urban areas. This influence is also seen in powwows, where the music and dancing have become more upbeat and passionate. **1960s** Intertribal powwow festivals continue to reinvigorate traditional Native American music as well as devise a universal set of rules to judge music and dance competitions that cross tribe lines. **1962** The Institute of American Indian Arts is established in Santa Fe,

New Mexico. **1964** Buffy Sainte-Marie appears at the Newport Folk Festival. **1966** Tony Isaacs and his wife, Ida, form Indian House Records. Their recordings are dedicated to preserving the natural sound of Native music, and they refuse to use synthesizers, sound effects, and many electronic instruments. **1969** Native American singer/songwriter Floyd Westerman releases the LP 'Custer Died for Your Sins.' The American Indian Movement (AIM) forms when a group of Native American students take over Alcatraz Island. **1970** President Nixon formally ends the Termination Policy. **1971** The Ashland Singers, a group of Cheyennes from Montana, refuse to conform to "younger" song styles and commit to singing songs traditionally. **1973** Members of AIM seize Wounded Knee and occupy the village for seventy-one days, putting Native American rights in the spotlight. **1974** Native American band Redbone hits Number Five on the pop chart with the catchy pop-rock single "Come and Get Your Love." **1975** Congress passes the Indian Self-Determination Act, ensuring Native American participation in federal services to Indian communities. The Red Earth Singers, a group of Native American college students who met in Minneapolis, is formed in Bismarck, North Dakota. This diversity begins a "branching out" of single-tribe groups. **1977** Rita Coolidge's album 'Anytime . . . Anywhere' (A&M) peaks at Number Six on the pop chart, propelled by the singles "(Your Love Has Lifted Me) Higher and Higher" (Number Two) and "We're All Alone" (Number Seven) and her concert appearances with her singer/songwriter husband, Kris Kristofferson. **1983** The country album 'Journey to the Spirit World,' by Buddy Red Bow, is released by Etherean Music. Radio station KILI begins broadcasting in Porcupine, South Dakota, eventually becoming the largest Native American–owned and –operated public radio station in America. **1989** Native American label Sound of America Records (SOAR) is formed by Dakota Tom Bee in an effort to strengthen Native culture while making connections with the mainstream. **1994** R. Carlos Nakai, a Native American flutist, is nominated for the Best Traditional Folk Album Grammy for 'Ancestral Voices' (Canyon). **1998** The Native American Music Awards, or Nammys, are established to recognize the accomplishments of America's indigenous music artists. Robbie Robertson, former lead guitarist of the Band, releases 'Contact From the Underworld of Redboy' (Capitol), which features the Six Nations Women Singers, Tudjaat, Verdell Primeaux, and Johnny Mike, among others. **2001** A category for Best Native American Album is introduced during the Grammy Awards telecast. The winner in this first-time category is 'Gathering of Nations Pow Wow' (SOAR), a compilation of songs by various Native American drum groups.

NATIVE AMERICAN MUSIC OF THE TWENTIETH CENTURY

BY WILLIAM K. POWERS

The first voice in America was a Native American voice, and for centuries this indigenous group has followed the edict of its ancestors to celebrate all aspects of its people's lives by singing. For all Natives, music *is* culture, and all musicians are the culture's custodians. Among some tribes, the Native word for *sing* is synonymous with the words *pray* or *heal.* Music is an ancient gift of the spirits, who insist that the past is worthy of keeping. And so, during the past five hundred years, Native cultures have continued to dance and pray to the sounds of ancient voices, defying the potential threats of white domination and the loss of their lifestyle.

Traditional music is still sung by more than three hundred tribal groups, many of which hold common musical traits. Most significant is the nearly exclusive use of the voice, with vocal music ranking above all other forms of Native musical expression. (Sung prayers, for example, are more potent than spoken ones.) Male and female singers vocalize individually or in groups, and dancers cannot perform without an appropriate song to accompany them. Traditional singing remains the most popular style among tribes, and it has kept its characteristic sounds: high-pitched and clear in upper registers, somewhat gruff or raspy in lower ones. Most songs are sung in two- to five-tone scales, but the average range of the singer's voice is about an octave and a half. In group singing, women sing one octave above the men. Primarily, the men sing the sacred music.

Perhaps the most outstanding feature of Native singing is the vocable, a syllable composed of vowel sounds combined mainly with *w*'s and *h*'s (*hay, yay, yah, wi, wo,* etc.), which joins with words to carry the melody. In all parts of the country, vocables may be used to sing an entire song in which the melody is the song's only meaning, symbolizing the inspiration of the composer or the mystical incantations of a spirit. Songs may combine vocables and meaningful words; in rare cases, a song is sung with words only.

OPPOSITE: TRADITIONAL DANCER AT THE OGLALA NATION POWWOW, PINE RIDGE, SOUTH DAKOTA, 1998. ABOVE: UNIDENTIFIED ARAPAHO.

The other near-universal feature of traditional music is its relatively spare instrumentation. Drums predominate, appearing in a variety of sizes and shapes. Rhythm also is limited, with drum accompaniment consisting of steady beats, occasionally accented, with the first beat louder than the second. The High Plains Indians often use triple beats, and southwestern dances occasionally feature improvisational drumming. The relationship between voice and drum is often staggered, the beat slightly anticipating the voice. Second to drums are rattles made from a variety of natural materials such as gourds and pebbles and mainly shaken in time to ceremonial songs and dances.

Two types of flageolets, or flutes, are the other primary instruments played by Indians. Carved from ash or cedar, they are made with a five- or six-holed stem and blown through one end. Indians in the Great Lakes, the Plains, and the southwest traditionally used the flute for courting. The Apache and other Southern California tribes also played another instrument, the one-string fiddle.

What makes Native music distinct is the language of the tribe that sings it, and the similarity of song structure among tribes. Voices generally are higher in the Plains and lower in the Northeast, Great Lakes, Southwest, and Southeast. Traditional music is believed to have remained a constant among each tribe's unique culture. Sacred and secular music, however, is still composed every day, guaranteeing continuity in tribal culture.

Throughout the Twentieth Century, Native American music has undergone a gradual transition, as Indian people and their children have fallen under the sway of the dominant American culture. Exposure to radio and television has made all traditions vulnerable to change, and Native American culture is no exception. Tribal elders have been willing to compromise, however, and accept innovative and sometimes radical changes in their children's music. Native singers and song makers have been willing to take advantage of technological developments, not for the purpose of abdicating their old musical traditions but for strengthening them. Overall, traditional Native cultures have approved of their young participating in the music of America's future while holding on to the songs of their past. Iroquois who sang sacred songs to the accompaniment of water drums and rattles during sacred times have learned to play the accordion and fiddle for "white" dances. Navajo teenagers who pray in all-night sings to cure a relative return home to play rock & roll to entertain younger clan

INSET: OJIBWE SINGERS, CIRCA 1960. OPPOSITE: OMAHA FLAGEOLET PLAYER, 1911.

8

members. Lakota traditional singers who learned to perform in school marching bands still remember the Sun dance. The English language has even been incorporated into Native songs, originally to persuade schoolmasters to permit the singing of "heathen" melodies in class; with new, "civilized" lyrics, many of these songs became romantic "come-ons," sung by boys from their dorm windows to girls across the commons: "My darling, I love you/Why can't I marry you?/*Yah hi yah yah.*"

By the middle of the Twentieth Century, traditional music had changed in other ways, thanks to technology. The availability of electricity on tribal dance grounds allowed for new sound and lighting systems. Only in the Pacific Northwest did tribes such as the Kwakiutl retain indigenous lighting systems made from torches, sound systems constructed from tubes planted under the dance area, and stages and backstages constructed from artistically carved and painted wood. Elsewhere in the country, Native dance areas became larger and singing voices became louder; as the number of dancers and spectators increased, the events were staged at arenas and auditoriums in off-reservation cities. Recording machines — introduced in the Nineteenth Century by ethnologists such as Jesse Walter Fewkes and Frances Densmore for documenting Native American music — were now used by individuals and recording companies to produce traditional and pop music for home listening. Eventually, Native American grassroots companies, such as Ray Boley's Canyon Records and Tony Isaacs's Indian House Records, joined other fledgling regional labels;

BELOW: LAKOTA DANCE HOUSE, AT PINE RIDGE, SOUTH DAKOTA, CIRCA 1890. OPPOSITE FROM TOP: OMAHA DANCE, PINE RIDGE, 1892; NINETEENTH-CENTURY NATIVE AMERICAN GRASS DANCE.

they were soon followed by Native entrepreneurs such as Linn D. Pauahty, a full-blooded Kiowa from Oklahoma, who was the first Native American to produce Plains Indians on his label, American Indian Soundchiefs.

Originally, there were different types of songs to serve varying groups and/or needs of tribal members, including specific songs for children and elders. During the past few decades, singers who had performed exclusively for such cultural needs became popular and professional "entertainers." "Have drum, will travel" became the rallying cry. Song groups, composed of six to ten male singers (and frequently one or several women), would sing these songs while seated or standing around a bass drum, which they played with drumsticks. Initially known only by the neighborhoods where they lived, these groups now took on professional names: Porcupine Singers; Red Cloud Singers; Oglala Juniors; Sioux Travelers from Pine Ridge; Black Lodge Singers from the Blackfeet reservation; and Stoney Park, Assiniboines from Canada. By the 1960s, these singers not only made music for traditional events on reservations and in Native communities but were paid to perform, booking tours and becoming famous far beyond their hometowns. Their records blared on

"OUR SONGS ARE RESOURCES. THEY TELL WHO WE ARE AND WHERE WE CAME FROM, WHAT TYPES OF ACCOMPLISHMENTS WE HAVE HAD. THEY ALSO GIVE YOU A SENSE OF PRIDE, HONOR, AND EMPOWERMENT TO FEEL GOOD ABOUT YOURSELF."
—ROBERT TWO CROW

Arickaree Indians at a "Grass dance"
Presented by Maj. A.J. Gifford, agent at Fort Berthold.

Little Soldier   Lump face   Many bears   Crow Tail   Thunder

reservation cafe jukeboxes; Native disc jockeys played favorite requests for loyal listeners on Native-language radio stations, which between the end of World War II and the mid-1970s began to appear on many of the larger Navajo reservations in Arizona and Lakota reservations in South Dakota. Radio Station KILI, "the Voice of the Lakota Nation," perched high on Porcupine Butte at Pine Ridge, in South Dakota, broadcast over a hundred-thousand-watt FM station to four states.

Several performers helped popularize Native music and traditions. Beginning in the mid-1970s, the late Buddy Red Bow, who played guitar and wrote country & western music with native Lakota lyrics, entertained Indians and non-Indians alike at big-city concerts from Denver to Los Angeles. R. Carlos Nakai, a trained musician who was turned down by Juilliard, adapted his own flageolet technique to Native music and was the first Native American to popularize Navajo music on college campuses and later throughout the world. Kevin Locke, who believed his traditional Lakota music would be accessible to non-Indians if played on a familiar instrument, spent a lifetime transforming his people's vocal music into pieces for the flageolet. Both he and Nakai experimented with flageolet harmony, once unknown in Native American music.

Yankton singers from the eastern part of South Dakota sang two-part harmony in Sunday gospel meetings, then applied their vocal skills to peyote meetings. Kiowa Baptists composed songs in their native language rather than praise Jesus in a foreign tongue. Cree activist Buffy Sainte-Marie joined with folksinger Peter LaFarge and sang to non-Indian audiences, on recordings and at folk festivals, about the federal government's disgraceful treatment of Native Americans. CDs and videotapes introduced Native American music to a global non-Indian audience. Hanay Geiogamah, an Oklahoma-born Kiowa who taught theater at UCLA and sought to bring Native American music and dance to the stage, organized a multitribal troupe featuring the best traditional performers in the country. The resultant American Indian Dance Theatre opened to rave reviews in Europe and continues to perform for theatergoers in New York, Los Angeles, and San Francisco. The Nammys, an annual American Indian music award program established in 1998, presents awards in categories similar to those used by the Grammys to Native Americans or those who have contributed to Indian musical culture. And in 2000, the National Academy of Recording Arts and Sciences established a category for Native American music in its annual Grammy Awards.

The most remarkable development in Indian music during the Nineteenth Century was the powwow. The term is derived from an eastern Algonquian word, *pauau,* which refers to a group of people witnessing a curing ceremony. Colonists adopted the word to mean any gathering of people, and the word's usage soon spread. Originally, the powwow was established as a religious ceremony in the Midwest among the Pawnee, who called it Irushka. It was subsequently adapted into a war dance by the nearby Omaha, who may be credited with introducing it to the tribes of the southern and northern Plains. They in turn adopted it as a social dance, with each tribe adding its own distinct customs to a core of song, dance, and costume.

Initially, around 1850, the dance was mainly for men. First enacted on the naked prairie, it was later performed in circular dance arbors made from wooden uprights over which leafy limbs were placed to give shade to the audience. Men strutted around the dance grounds, encircled by women dancing in place. Some claim the original curing ceremony eventually evolved into a courtship dance, where, as the men say, the women could have a better look at them dancing. The lyrics of the songs, however, spoke of war. The costumes were often symbolic, such as the porcupine headdress — in English called "roach," after the roached mane of a horse — and the feathered bustles that originally denoted slain enemies on the battlefield.

Traditionally, male singers knelt or stood in the center of the arbor around a large bass drum while the rest of the men danced around them, feathers fluttering, and the women bobbed at the periphery. Singers were frequently accompanied by one or two females who sang an octave above the male voices, accenting the words with piercing tremolos to honor returning warriors or those lost in battle. Eventually, handmade drums would be replaced by commercial bass drums traded at forts by members of military marching bands.

At the turn of the Twentieth Century, the powwow was regarded strictly as a Plains dance, with the term used only in Oklahoma. Oklahoma reservations, except for the Osage, were abolished in 1927, but more than sixty tribes continued to live in proximity of each other. Soon, the powwow was the major performance event among Kiowa and Comanche, Cheyenne and Arapaho, Ponca and Pawnee, and other tribes that had never had a powwow tra-

dition, including the Southeast's Seminoles, Cherokees, Choctaws, Creeks, and Chickasaws, as well as others not regarded as Plains, such as the Caddo, Wichita, and Delaware. (Elsewhere on the northern Plains, the powwow was known as the Omaha dance, after the tribe; the Grass dance, after the Omaha custom of wearing grass tucked in their belts to symbolize scalps; the Wolf dance, after the symbol of the warrior; or more playfully the Chicken dance, referring to the headdresses and feather bustles and to a peculiar style of strutting.) Some of the tribes banded together to organize the multitribal American Indian Exposition in Anadarko, Oklahoma, which at one time was the nation's largest powwow. One of the Native Americans' first attempts to convert a cultural performance into an enterprise, it continues to attract thousands of tourists to Indian Country each year. The Gallup Intertribal Ceremonials in Gallup, New Mexico, were also established as a successful commercial venture by non-Indians.

During and after World War I, the powwow took on a patriotic nature. It continued to be a venue in which men, women, and children could dress up in their native attire and join in the music and dance of their parents and grandparents. The lyrics still spoke of early wars with enemy tribes, but with Native Americans volunteering in World War I, the powwow became the appropriate means with which to honor those who fought with the Allies in

ABOVE: NATIVE AMERICAN VETERANS FROM WORLD WAR II PARADING AT PINE RIDGE, CIRCA 1945. OPPOSITE, FROM LEFT: TRADITIONAL DANCER AT THE OGLALA NATION POWWOW, PINE RIDGE, 1998; THE GRAND ENTRY AT THE 1998 PINE RIDGE POWWOW.

Europe. Indians sang mellifluously in their native language about how their boys defeated the Germans, and dancers carried captured Lugers, shooting them into the air to recount their recent victories — just as their fathers and grandfathers had counted coup on their ancient enemies. Dance leaders piped on war whistles, urging the singers to repeat their praises again and again, while dancers' bells clanged cacophonously on Mother Earth. American flags adorned the dance arbors, and women raised their voices, lamenting for the warriors who did not return. The times had changed, but the music remained the same, with old melodic patterns shouldering the emotional weight of a modern era. Warrior societies whose members once carried lances and shields and honored the wolf and buffalo now entered the powwow grounds carrying rifles and American flags and wearing the uniforms of the American Legion and Veterans

of Foreign Wars. Three-gun salutes pierced the sky while the singers sang:

> *Tunkasilayapi tawapi kinhan*
> *Oihanke sni he najin ye*
> *Iyohlate k'un oyate in wanyan*
> *Wicicagin kte ca hecamun welo*
> The flag of the United States
> Shall fly forever without end
> Beneath it the people shall flourish
> That is why I do this.

World War II elicited the same response from Native men and now women, with volunteers and draftees returning home from war to be honored on their reservations and in Indian communities. Around the same time, the powwow began to expand northward from Oklahoma to the northern Plains. By the mid-Fifties, fast and furious dance styles from the southern Plains moved north to collide with song styles entering the United States from Canadian provinces. High-pitched, robust voices singing in clear, sustained tones inundated the Plains, forming an aesthetic bond with the dance movements of the South. While elders clung to the songs of their ancestors, younger people became invigorated with Canada's steel voices and Oklahoma's intricate footwork. Out of the South's fancy and straight dances and the North's cool Grass and Shawl dances was born a new style, which soon mushroomed beyond the Plains, thanks to modern technology. Although popular powwows continued to be held on reservations, they moved with increasing frequency into urban areas, where Native populations had already begun to relocate. At the same time, women, once relegated to the outer limits of the dance arbor, began stepping forward and dancing next to the men. Thus emboldened, women, who once only echoed the voices of the men in song, began leading their own powwow songs and forming all-female drum groups, while others

began composing songs. In the 1950s, young Indians took their musical culture to their new urban homes. They soon established American Indian centers in Los Angeles, San Francisco, Albuquerque, Oklahoma City, Denver, Bismarck, Chicago, New York, and other large cities. During the next fifty years, the pow-wow lost its identity as a phenomenon exclusive to the Plains. Instead, it had become the musical soul of Indian Country. Beginning in the latter part of the 1960s, the drum was used not only for the joy of singing and dancing but for Native politics. Young men and women began to reprise the war songs of their ancestors at the takeover of Alcatraz Island and at confrontations at the Bureau of Indian Affairs and the hamlet of Wounded Knee.

The powwow has erupted into a fast-paced trend that provides music, dance, and costumes to all interested Natives in Indian Country. Powwows take place nearly every week on reservations during the summer and on weekends in cities during the winter. But the powwow has changed, perhaps most dramatically in terms of the costume. At one time, costumes reflected tribal differences. One could actually identify tribes by their attire, particularly by the women's style of dress. During the past century, however, costumes and their attendant dance styles have become uniform, while the music retains its distinct, individual tribal character.

Today there are basically six styles of dance correlated with six types of dance costumes: Men's Traditional, Women's Traditional (also called Ladies'), Men's Grass Dance, Women's Jingle Dress, Men's Fancy, and Women's Shawl Dance. Each boasts different choreographic patterns and related steps. In contrast to the many different dances, there are only two styles of song: "northern drum," characterized by very high-pitched registers for men and slower tempos, and "southern drum," sung by males in lower registers and at faster tempos. Women sing one

octave above the men in both drums. Both northern and southern songs are structurally identical.

Powwows tend to follow a daily pattern. The mornings are occupied with giveaways and special tributes to elders. Participants camp outside the dance arbor, which is surrounded with food stands and vendors selling arts and crafts and sundries. After lunch, the dancers dress in their tents, and the singers take their places in the arbor's shade. As spectators arrange their folding chairs near their relatives and friends, the announcer, directing the activities over a PA system, urges everyone to prepare for the Grand Entry. The dancers line up, usually according to age and costume style, and the singers begin vocalizing. The dancers are led by tribal officials, color guards, flag bearers, tribal dignitaries and their guests, and powwow princesses, or royalty, representing their communities. Since some of the larger powwows attract more than a thousand dancers, after the Grand Entry, the center of the arbor is filled with costumed dancers. After all have entered, the national anthem is sung, usually in the native language of the host tribes, and is followed by a dance honoring veterans of all wars. Intertribal dancing continues for the remainder of the day, interspersed with contest dances for tiny tots, older children, adults, and elders. After supper, the same routine is repeated.

The pattern of the powwow is determined by ancient tribal ceremonies, but some elements, including the Grand Entry, the "day money" fee paid to participants, and the powwow princesses, have been adapted from the rodeo tradition, which has influenced Native Americans for a century and a half. Even though it expands every year, the powwow does not totally detract from traditional tribal music and dance. Traditional music satisfies the individual's need for identity, but the powwow unites artists from many disparate tribes.

At the dawn of the Twenty-First Century, the remarkable thing about Native American music is that it has managed to retain its traditional integrity. More powwow songs are composed today by Native Americans than tunes with words and music adapted to Euro-American instruments. Tracks composed of drums, rattles, and vocables set to modern styles of fusion still do not compare in number to the sacred and secular songs sung on the reservation. Grassroots music in Indian Country nestles deep in Mother Earth, making room for change without ever forsaking tradition, with melodic patterns remaining fixed in age-old spiritual themes. Aware of the joy of singing together, singers compose songs with vocables so that they may be understood by those who speak different languages. There are no strangers at the drum.

Finally, the old people enjoy watching their children and grandchildren sing and dance to rock & roll. That is not to say, however, that they are not worried that their children will fail to carry on their traditions. *"Gluha po!"* a Lakota elder cautions his grandchild. "Hold on to your own ways!" But it appears that the powwow has given young people a new vitality, a renewed recognition of the values of their culture, and a willingness to be a part of it. They realize the first voice in America was a Native American voice. And it is their own.

Opposite, top left: Lakota singers of Pine Ridge, South Dakota, circa 1985.
Both pages, from opposite, center: At the Oglala Nation powwow, 1998: Fancy dancer; jingle dress dancer; singers taking a break; grand entry led by royalty; shawl dancer.

R. CARLOS NAKAI: *When I was still in elementary school, I had a great interest in wanting to pursue some kind of music activity. I spent much of my time listening to music. While living on a farm with my aunt and uncle, I used to order classical recordings. And I really got into Beethoven and Tchaikovsky quite a bit. Much of that time, of course, was [spent] trying to prepare myself with what I could find in libraries and reading up on things, until a man came from Blythe, California, with a truckload of musical instruments. They did a test on our lip formation and the way our teeth were aligned and everything.*

He handed me this instrument, and it looked like a bunch of tubing that you would use either under the sink or somewhere in a plumbing situation. I said, "I don't like this thing; it doesn't look right. I probably won't like it when I make it sound. I'd rather have the thing in the little box over in the corner." And he said, "No, no, no. You're best suited for brass, and men don't play the little things in the box. But you want to play this instrument." And it turned out to be a cornet.

So I spent my time with a cornet, always thinking that it's really the flute that I wanted — the one in the little box. It's not so obvious, you can carry it around with you easily, and all that. So I spent time studying, getting prepared and knowing a little bit about music theory with the aid of my band directors and different high schools, as well as Arizona State College.

I worked with a group called the Navajo Tribal Band, too, which was a professional marching band. We spent our time going to rodeos and parades and all kinds of other activities, nationwide, representing the Navajo tribe. And we decided that maybe I should try my hand at getting [into] a music school. So we wrote a letter to Juilliard. Two band directors in high school and my bandmaster in the Navajo tribal band all wrote letters. And different people in the Navajo tribe wrote letters of support.

We were very hopeful. And then a letter came back, [saying] that although my grade point average and everything was very good at the time — I think it was, "Mr. Nakai would be very hard pressed and would find it very difficult to survive in our school of music, because American Indians do not have a music culture to speak of." And I thought, Wait a minute now, we have all this ceremonial music, we have all these social songs, and things very much like the folk culture of other people in the world. There's a problem here.

So I think much of what I do now is [because] I need to show people that my culture is important. The culture of music that I inhabit in my own traditional world — and the world I am working in today, which is based on a lot of influences impacting me at various points in time — [is] an actual rendition of how I see myself using a philosophy of music in which to communicate.

⌠ LEFT: PAWNEE INDIANS, CIRCA 1868.
⌡ OPPOSITE: R. CARLOS NAKAI, 2000.

1

NATIVE TONGUE: CONTEMPORARY NATIVE MUSIC BY J. POET

To most non-Indians, Native music means the steady drum beat and falsetto cries of the war dance — properly known as powwow music — or the flute music of R. Carlos Nakai. But contemporary Native artists are as experimental and diverse as other modern musicians. There are singer/songwriters like Buffy Sainte-Marie, Bill Miller, and the late Peter LaFarge; jazz musicians like Jim Pepper and Fredrick Whiteface; rappers like Litefoot and Shadowyze; performance artists like John Trudell; and composers like Douglas Spotted Eagle, Brulé, and others who combine Native, rock, and classical European influences. There are also Natives — both full and mixed blood — who have found mainstream success, including Keely Smith, Donna Summer, Jimi Hendrix, Rita Coolidge, and Robbie Robertson of the Band.

Two record companies have played a major role in the mainstreaming of Native music: Canyon, based in Phoenix, Arizona, and Albuquerque, New Mexico's SOAR (Sound of America Records). Canyon Records began in 1951 when Ed Lee Natay, a Navajo singer, asked Ray Boley to record him at Boley's New Mexico recording studio. Boley, who has no Native blood, was impressed by the music; after releasing an album of Natay's songs, he began looking for other Indian singers. Like Moses Asch at Folkways, Boley would record anyone, anywhere, any time, and Native musicians flocked to his label. Canyon sold mostly to Indians and tourists buying albums at trading posts until 1984, when it put out a cassette by flute player R. Carlos Nakai. Canyon has now sold millions of Nakai cassettes and CDs, reaching a large, non-Indian audience with a catalogue of almost five hundred titles. The label has introduced artists like Clan/Destine, one of the best young Native/world/fusion bands, and a wide range of traditional singers including Keith Mahone, Judy Trejo, Delphine Tsinajinne, Sharon Burch, and Joanne Shenandoah.

"We're not a 'Native American record company,' " SOAR's President Tom Bee stresses. "We're a record company [that] records Native artists, to build bridges to the mainstream while strengthening our own culture." SOAR, founded in 1989, signed a distribution agreement with Koch in the early Nineties that made it the first Native label to get its releases on the shelves of mainstream chains; its eye-catching graphics made other Native labels rethink their marketing strategies. SOAR's roster includes Jay Begaye — the godfather of contemporary Native folk music — peyote singer Blackfox, rappers like Natay and Boyz From the Rez, and rockers Tiger Tiger and Xit.

Traditional Native music — what non-Indians call folk music — has an incredible variety of styles. There's the flute music of Nakai, Kevin Locke, Mary Youngblood, and others; the intertribal peyote music of Primeaux and Mike, who have experimented with harmony and song structures adapted from Christian hymns; women's social songs from tribes all across the country; and the "chicken scratch," or *waila* music, of the Tohono O'odham tribe of Arizona, an adaptation of the *norteño* music from the Texas-Mexican border, played without any vocals by groups like Southern Scratch and T.O. Combo.

There are also Native artists working toward mainstream success. Keith Secola (called the Native Springsteen by some) and his Wild Band of Indians make powerful music combining Native perceptions and mainstream rock; Robert Mirabal, from Taos Pueblo, also combines folk, rock, world, and Native music with his powerful — and dark — lyrical vision; Walela — the trio of Rita and Priscilla Coolidge and Laura Satterfield — combines Native, gospel, rock, and pop influences into its beautifully harmonic style; Casper Loma-da-wa, a Hopi reggae artist, has a grasp of roots rock, social consciousness, and dancehall skank equal to that of the artists that inspired him. Topping the list is the blues-rock band Indigenous, led by guitarist Mato Nanji, a player with a style that echoes the power of Hendrix, the attack of Stevie Ray Vaughan, and the dynamics of the Kings — B.B., Albert, and Freddie.

Interest in native music has been growing since the early Seventies. When hippies morphed into the human potential movement, they looked to Native America for spiritual inspiration and began adopting Native music. There has also been a population boom on North America's reservations in recent years, and the current generation is returning to its traditional languages, music, and culture. "Twenty-five years ago, people's perceptions of Native culture were centered on activism; today, it's music," says singer and poet John Trudell. With musicians as powerful as Mato Nanji of Indigenous, and a generation of writers (Sherman Alexie), filmmakers (Chris Eyre), and poets (Joy Harjo) who are not only talented, but also adept at maneuvering through the cultural minefields that are often placed in the way of minority artists, it's only a matter of time before Native artists break out of the underground and into the consciousness of mainstream America.

OPPOSITE, CLOCKWISE FROM TOP LEFT: KEVIN LOCKE, ROBERT MIRABEL (INSET), ROBBIE ROBERTSON, RITA COOLIDGE, PETER LAFARGE

1938 Bill Monroe assembles his Blue Grass Boys, from whom a new offshoot of country music will take its name; they perform at the Grand Ole Opry in October. Roy Acuff christens his band the Smoky Mountain Boys. **1939** Ted Daffan writes the first trucking song, "Truck Driver's Blues." House musician Sam Gill plays the Opry's first electric guitar. **1941** World War II begins; southern recruits introduce country music to their fellow soldiers from various regions of the United States. Okies move to California to work in war-related industries. **1942** Roy Acuff and Fred Rose found Acuff-Rose Publications, Nashville's first and most important publishing company. **1945** Nashville begins its rise as a famous recording center when Decca's Paul Cohen records smooth, Kentucky-born crooner Red Foley. Solo vocalists begin to supplant string bands on the charts. **1947** Ernest Tubb stars in New York's first country-music show, which takes place at Carnegie Hall. **1948** Shreveport, Louisiana's KWKH debuts the Louisiana Hayride. Banjo legend Earl Scruggs and guitarist Lester Flatt leave Bill Monroe's band to form bluegrass powerhouse the Foggy Mountain Boys and, eventually, Flatt and Scruggs. **1949** Hank Williams Sr. debuts at the Opry, performing "Lovesick Blues." KXLA in Pasadena, California, becomes the first all-country radio station. **1952** The future "Queen of Country Music," Kitty Wells, is asked to record an "answer song" to Hank Thompson's "The Wild Side of Life," which contained the lyric "I didn't know God made honky tonk angels." The result, "It Wasn't God Who Made Honky Tonk Angels," will hit Number One on the country singles chart and sell more than eight hundred thousand copies. **1953** After more than a decade of hard living, Hank Williams is pronounced dead on New Year's Day. **1956** Johnny Cash releases his first Number One single, "I Walk the Line." **1959** Bluegrass greats the Stanley Brothers and Their Clinch Mountain Boys play the first Newport Folk Festival. **1960** Flat-picking guitarist Arthel "Doc" Watson and singer/banjoist Clarence Ashley make their first recordings for Folkways. Loretta Lynn has her first country hit with "I'm a Honky Tonk Girl," which reaches Number Fourteen on the country singles chart. **1961** The Country Music Association founds the Country Music Hall of Fame. Jimmie Rodgers, Hank Williams, and Fred Rose are its first honorees. **1963** On March 3, Patsy Cline, Hawkshaw Hawkins, and Cowboy Copas die in a plane crash; Jack Anglin is killed in a car accident en route to Cline's funeral. Texas Ruby dies in a fire. **1964** Jimmy Dean brings country to prime-time television on ABC. **1965** After issuing several independent singles, Merle Haggard releases his first album, 'Strangers' (Capitol), which goes to Number Nine on the country albums chart. **1967** The Country Music Association launches an annual awards show. Crossover pop hits abound: Bobbie Gentry's Number One "Ode to Billie Joe," Roger Miller's "King of the Road," Tammy Wynette's "Stand by Your Man," and Glen Campbell's "Wichita Lineman." **1968** Columbia Records releases the live album 'Johnny Cash at Folsom Prison.' Wandering eccentric Townes Van Zandt records his debut album, 'For the Sake of the Song,' for Poppy Records. **1969** Cash hosts a prime-time television variety show, 'The Johnny Cash Show,' which airs until 1971. He features many new and traditionalist recording artists on the program. **1970** Counterculture-country iconoclast Willie Nelson leaves Nashville and moves to Austin, in his home state of Texas. On July 4, 1973, he holds his first annual Willie Nelson Picnic in the town of Dripping Springs. Within a few years, the festival will become a publicity magnet, attracting some of Nashville's and Texas's most important performers as well as rock artists and fans. **1972** Emmylou Harris shares the vocals on 'GP' (Reprise), the rootsy debut solo album by Gram Parsons, who played in the country-influenced, hippie-era bands the Byrds and the Flying Burrito Brothers. After Parsons's 1973 death, Harris goes on to a successful solo career beginning with 1975's 'Pieces of the Sky.' **1976** RCA releases 'Wanted! The Outlaws,' the first country music album to be certified platinum by the RIAA. It contains recordings by Willie Nelson, Waylon Jennings, Tompall Glaser, and Jennings's wife, Jessi Colter. The record defines the "outlaw country" style, a rough, driving mix of country traditionalism and Southern rock in which artists often record with their touring bands rather than with session players. **1979** The Charlie Daniels Band releases "The Devil Went Down to Georgia," a fusion of traditional fiddling and Southern rock. **1980** Sissy Spacek stars as Loretta Lynn in the hit film 'Coal Miner's Daughter.' Ricky Skaggs adds some bluegrass to Emmylou Harris's album 'Roses in the Snow,' which hits Number Two on the country albums chart and eventually goes gold. **1981** The Oak Ridge Boys and Alabama fuse country pop and rock with "Elvira" and "Feels So Right," respec-

tively. Ricky Skaggs, who in 1969 fronted a teenage bluegrass band with Keith Whitley, releases his major-label debut, 'Waitin' for the Sun to Shine,' which charts four country singles and wins two Country Music Association Awards. George Strait's MCA-released "Unwound" hits Number Six on the country chart; his album 'Strait Country' reveals his nonpop intentions. **1983** The Nashville Network begins broadcasting on cable television. **1986** Steve Earle mixes rock and traditionalism on his MCA album 'Guitar Town,' which hits Number One on the country albums chart and becomes a critical favorite. **1987** Following up the guitarist/singer's Number One debut EP, Dwight Yoakam's 'Hillbilly Deluxe' also goes to Number One on the country albums chart and yields four singles. **1989** Alan Jackson becomes the first artist signed to Arista Records' country division. The title track of his album 'Here in the Real World' hits Number Three on the country chart. **1992** George Strait's 'Pure Country' hits Number Six on the pop albums chart and goes quintuple platinum. He stars in the film of the same name. **1994** Johnny Cash's somber, subdued 'American Recordings' (American) and its single "Delia" introduce acoustic country to the "grunge" generation. Archetypal alternative-country band Uncle Tupelo splits, giving birth to the groups Wilco and Son Volt. **1995** The alternative-country movement gets its voice with the publication of 'No Depression' magazine's premiere issue. Many critics also dub the musical genre "No Depression."

KEEPING IT COUNTRY: TRADITION AND CHANGE, 1940 TO THE PRESENT BY BILL C. MALONE

Country music entered the Forties still bearing the marks of its rural southern origins but with a growing national constituency. In mood, theme, and lyrics, the music reflected the transition being made from a regional to a mass market. The nationalization accelerated by the war had already been launched in the Thirties by an array of fifty-thousand-watt radio stations, radio transcriptions, Hollywood cowboy movies, inexpensive recordings from labels such as Decca, and a growing network of personal appearances. The entertainers were primarily southern good ol' boys and girls who performed increasingly sophisticated styles of music.

Electric instruments gradually moved into the performances of country musicians, altering the sound and ambience of the music and making it more accessible to dancers and a wide array of listeners. Bands that adopted electric amplification dominated the jukeboxes during the war years with sounds born in the honky-tonks and dancehalls of Texas, Louisiana, and Oklahoma. This music reached out to and mirrored the lives of people who were caught up in the social dislocations of the era: military personnel who moved to far-

{ OPPOSITE: HANK WILLIAMS. BELOW, FROM LEFT: GEORGE JONES; SPADE COOLEY.

flung places all over the globe and civilians who took up jobs in defense plants or in other blue-collar occupations. Hillbilly songs began to appear on jukeboxes in cities such as Detroit, Chicago, Cincinnati, and Los Angeles. Although a few important musicians, such as Gene Autry, Woody Guthrie, and the Maddox Brothers and Rose, had been on the West Coast since the mid-1930s, an even greater number of country entertainers relocated there during the 1940s, playing for the large and growing population of Okies whose numbers multiplied because of war-related industries. There the style of music created earlier in Texas and Oklahoma by Bob Wills and Milton Brown flourished in the large dancehalls and on radio broadcasts. By 1946, this upbeat music had acquired a name, when bandleader Spade Cooley (a transplanted Oklahoman) was tagged by promoter Foreman Phillips "the King of Western Swing."

"IT'S THE GREATEST FEELING IN THE WORLD, WHEN YOU'RE A SMALL KID AND YOU FIRST START HEARING THE PEOPLE YOU LOVE TO HEAR SING — WHICH I DID BACK WHEN I WAS A LITTLE BOY, ON THE RADIO — BILL MONROE, ROY ACUFF, AND PEOPLE LIKE THAT WHO REALLY SANG WITH FEELING. [LATER] I MET HANK WILLIAMS ONE AFTERNOON AT A RADIO SHOW IN BEAUMONT [TEXAS] — OH, WHAT A THRILL!" —GEORGE JONES

Despite the growing popularity of swing and other dance styles, star vocalists became preeminent in country music, and "traditional" songs and styles of performance endured, even in the repertoires of the honky-tonk and Western swing bands. The Maddox Brothers and their sister Rose, for example, performed with an exuberance and flamboyance that few groups could equal and popularized everything from shape-note gospel music to honky-tonk and protorockabilly. Roy Acuff clung more closely to oldtime styles than did most prominent performers and, in the process, became a symbol of oldtime America during the war, stressing the values of mama, home, and the old country church. He resisted the use of electric instruments, included a large array of gospel songs and other vintage material in his performances, and still managed to become the most popular country act of the mid-1940s. With songs such as "Wabash Cannon Ball" and "The Great Speckled Bird," Acuff rose to fame with the Grand Ole Opry, as the host of the thirty-minute segment broadcast nationally each Saturday night on NBC.

Country music not only scaled great commercial heights in the fifteen years that followed World War II; in 1949 it even took on the name "country" for the first time, when *Billboard* magazine began describing most-played jukebox recordings with that designation. The word seemed to market a respectability that musicians had always coveted (though *hillbilly* was still embraced by many fans and even musicians in private). Buoyed by a host of radio stations that featured both live and recorded programming and a burgeoning array of small record labels that emerged all over the United States, country music insinuated itself into the consciousness of listeners in every region of the nation.

A long list of singers, such as Eddy Arnold, Carl Smith, and Red Foley, dominated the popularity charts, but a small assemblage of musicians made crucial innovations that shaped the ways in which country entertainers sing and play. When Ernest Tubb, "the Texas Troubadour," joined the Grand Ole Opry in 1942, he introduced his Texas-born honky-tonk style to a national audience and popularized the electric guitar. Before long, even Kentucky and West Virginia hillbillies such as Loretta Lynn and Hawkshaw Hawkins were resolving to become professional singers because of what they heard in Tubb's performances. While Tubb was taking his "Western" style of country music back east, other musicians were making the West Coast a focal point of stylistic change. Kentucky-born Merle Travis, one of several veteran performers who moved to California during the war, popularized his syncopated, two-finger style of guitar playing, influenced the manufacture and availability of electric solid-body guitars, and, with such numbers as "Sixteen Tons" and "Dark as a Dungeon," wrote some of country music's most memorable and enduring songs. When Texan William Orville "Lefty" Frizzell made the California trek in the mid-Fifties, he had already fashioned the warm, nasally resonant singing style, replete with bent and extended notes, that made him one of the most imitated singers in country music history. (He influenced Merle Haggard, Keith Whitley, Randy Travis, and John Anderson, among others.)

By carving out an identity apart from male singers, and by singing songs that dealt with topics not often heard in the music made by women, Kitty Wells (born Muriel Deason) continued the revolution begun in the 1940s by Rose Maddox and Kentucky-born country singer Molly O'Day. Beginning in

ABOVE, FROM TOP: ROY ACUFF AT THE GRAND OLE OPRY, 1939; MERLE TRAVIS, WHO BEGAN HIS CAREER IN THE 1930S, WAS STILL AT IT IN THE 1970S. OPPOSITE: ERNEST TUBB, 1965.

1951, with a song that has often been described as a statement of rebellion, "It Wasn't God Who Made Honky Tonk Angels," Kitty defended the honor of women and spoke also of the temptations that accompany honky-tonk life. The seamy themes that often appeared in her lyrics, however, could never tarnish the ladylike persona that she presented to her fans. In her fifty-plus-year career as the "Queen of Country Music," Kitty Wells remained the embodiment of a faithful wife and homemaker.

Hiram "Hank" Williams did not often sing about the explicit pleasures of drinking and cheating, but he nevertheless conveyed the impression that he was intimately acquainted with those vices and the world that nourished them. Hank Williams's vocal style and the contending impulses of sin and guilt that lent an appealing tension to his music grew out of the churches and honky-tonks of south Alabama. He rode to the top of the country charts in the early 1950s with a haunting voice and a body of songs, both joyous and anguished, that reached across geographic, class, and stylistic categories. The ultimate irony of Williams's career is that he sang with an unmistakable rural and southern inflection but wrote songs that did much to shatter the tenuous walls that had separated country and pop music.

Bill Monroe crafted a sound like no one else's in American music. With his high-lonesome singing, dynamic mandolin style, relentless energy, and talent for finding gifted musicians, he introduced and popularized a style that enabled acoustic string-band music to survive and prosper in a music business increasingly given over to electronic sounds. Between 1945 and 1948, he and guitarist Lester Flatt, fiddler Chubby Wise, string bass player Cedric Rainwater, and the sensational five-string banjoist Earl Scruggs created a supercharged style of music that folklorist Alan Lomax described as "folk music with overdrive." We now call that sound, and its many derivatives, bluegrass.

One of the young fans who thrilled to the high energy and musicianship of Bill Monroe and His Blue Grass Boys was Elvis Presley. Elvis's first Sun record in 1954 included his souped-up adaptation of Monroe's "Blue Moon of Kentucky." "Traditional" country styles suffered temporarily during the rock & roll revolution that Elvis unleashed — fiddles and steel guitars almost vanished from jukeboxes and radio shows. Musicians either adapted to the changes or, in the case of bluegrass, sought new venues for

"BILL MONROE WAS A TEACHER, HE WAS A PHILOSOPHER, HE WAS A GENIUS. AND HE WAS A NATURAL MAN, AND A SOUL MAN. . . . HE WAS A PURE ARCHITECT OF AMERICAN MUSIC."
—MARTY STUART

exposure. Nashville's producers responded in varying ways, seeking to co-opt the revolution either by emphasizing new young talent and absorbing some of the rhythms and techniques of rock & roll, or by effecting a "compromise" that would supposedly preserve the mood and ambience of country music while eliminating its rough, rural edges. Above all, such producers as Chet Atkins and Owen Bradley hoped to retain country music's older audience and to win new fans who wanted a palatable, middle-of-the-road sound. The result was a body of music soon described as "country pop," or the Nashville Sound.

Unleashed by the rock & roll threat and the emergence of country pop, a traditionalist-modernist tug of war has animated country music since the early 1960s. During that decade, for the first time, writers, fans, and a few musicians coined labels to judge styles and rank songs and singers according to their "purity," or closeness to country music's origins. At some point, the term *hard country* came to be applied to any kind of country music that seemed genuinely roots based. The sporadic revitalization of traditional styles has come from within and without the mainstream-country-music world. As witnessed by the folk revival of the early 1960s, old and exotic musical forms periodically fascinate Americans, especially as their way of life becomes more complex and anxiety ridden. The revival inspired a rediscovery of early hillbilly styles, first through the issuance on Folkways of *Anthology of American Folk Music*. People who heard this collection of reissued 78 rpm recordings were not only introduced to people such as the Carter Family, Uncle Dave Macon, and Dock Boggs, but they soon learned that some of these musicians were still alive and could still make music.

Bluegrass also profited from this renewed interest in traditional music. The music had been a refuge for oldtime-music enthusiasts since the mid-Forties, but during the folk revival hosts of young people embraced the style because it seemed to be an expression of the Appalachian South and a contemporary and dynamic extension of hillbilly string-band styles. Led by Mike Seeger, who recorded bluegrass musicians for Folkways, and Ralph Rinzler, who introduced Bill Monroe to urban listeners and produced some of his most important Decca recordings, the folk revival

OPPOSITE: BILL MONROE AT HIS TENNESSEE HOME. ABOVE: BILL MONROE'S HANDS AND HIS BELOVED MANDOLIN, 1994.

provided bluegrass with new venues of college campuses, folk clubs, and festivals. Flatt and Scruggs, the Stanley Brothers, and other bluegrass bands became regular participants at the Newport Folk Festival, and Bill Monroe was recognized as the patriarch of this vital musical style.

With its mixture of superb instrumentation and pastoral imagery — the vision of "the little cabin home on the hill" — bluegrass built the most broadly based spectrum of listeners enjoyed by any subgenre of country music. It never lost its original following of rural and blue-collar workers, but during the folk revival it won a new constituency of students, hippies, and college-educated professionals — a fan base that has stuck with it ever since. Although Earl Scruggs probably did the most to awaken the interests of urban, educated fans, the Country Gentlemen were the first bluegrass musicians to take the music into new dimensions of style and song choice. Organized in Washington, D.C., in 1957, the Gentlemen clung closely to acoustic instrumentation

and the traditional high-harmony style of singing but experimented with jazz, blues, pop, Bob Dylan's songs, and oldtime country music. They were the first of the "progressive bluegrass" bands, and a prime force in establishing Washington, D.C., as the nation's bluegrass capital.

Although bluegrass profited from its identification with the folk revival, the most important consequence of the folk boom was the "discovery" of Arthel "Doc" Watson, from Deep Gap, North Carolina. Watson was playing electric guitar in a country-swing band when Ralph Rinzler met him in 1960 at the famous oldtime fiddlers' contest in Union Grove, North Carolina. Watson, however, also played oldtime styles of country music on the five-string banjo and acoustic guitar, and was playing with Clarence "Tom" Ashley when Rinzler came to North Carolina. He introduced Watson to northern folk-music fans and encouraged him to perform traditional music. Folk-music audiences soon learned that Watson could present to them the

full range of Anglo-American folk music, from balladry to gospel to blues, with a warm and expressive voice and a flat-picking style of guitar-playing that had no equals. He has inspired an entire generation of acoustic-guitar players, including Clarence White, Norman Blake, Dan Crary, Tony Rice, and other luminaries of the flat-top guitar. America's thriving, vibrant acoustic-music scene, represented today by such musicians as David Grisman, Sam Bush, Béla Fleck, and Chris Thile, owes much to the improvisations made by Doc Watson and other rural-oriented musicians who found outlets for their art in the realms of bluegrass and old-time revival music.

Faithfulness to country music's roots, albeit with important and commercial variations, has also been expressed in the "hitmaking" world of country music. Singers, musicians, and songwriters with strong affinities for hard country appear periodically, experience much public exposure, then fade before the onrushing

tide of country pop. None of these "traditionalists," however, are mere throwbacks to an earlier period or slavish imitators of their predecessors. From Merle Haggard and Loretta Lynn in the mid-1960s to Ricky Skaggs and George Strait in the 1980s, and on to Dwight Yoakam and Alan Jackson in the 1990s, these performers have succeeded with updated versions of traditional sounds or by fusing many styles. A select array of women singers, for example, exhibited their links to southern working-class culture while also breaking new ground for their sisters. The most prominent of the group, Loretta Lynn, Dolly Parton, and Tammy Wynette (born Virginia Wynette Pugh), easily conveyed the evidence of their southern working-class origins in their speech, demeanor, and singing styles. Lynn and Parton celebrated those origins in such songs as "Coal Miner's Daughter" and "Coat of Many Colors." Wynette unfortunately became typecast for one recording, "Stand by Your Man," but the song's lyrics were hardly autobiographical. Even with several failed marriages, her highly successful career revealed her to be a woman of independent means and purpose. Loretta Lynn and Dolly Parton sometimes seemed willing to play the role of simple mountain girls, but their masterful performances, rapport with their audiences, and shrewd promotional acumen gave them an edge that most men could only envy. And in such songs as Lynn's "The Pill" and Parton's "To Daddy," they voiced a plea for women's freedom that had scarcely been present in country songs before. Best of all, they emboldened young women to pursue their own independent paths in show business, suggesting in the subtext of their lives and songs: "We made it, and so can you."

All hard-country singers have worked within the context of a music business that has grown increasingly corporate and given over to assembly-line production. Since the 1970s, veteran singers have found themselves discarded in order to make room for newer, usually younger, and more photogenic performers. Some performers, such as George Jones and Johnny Cash, through force of personality, courage of conviction, and charismatic performance, have managed to preserve distinctive, tradition-based styles. Jones's voice has deepened and mellowed during a career that has spanned fifty years, and he no longer shows the influence of his mentors, Roy Acuff and Bill Monroe. But in many ways his is still the voice of blue-collar east Texas, and it preserves the marks of a life molded by Pentecostal, hardscrabble beginnings, innumerable honky-tonk gigs, and too much time consuming the beer sold at those gigs. Despite often-smothering arrangements and trivial material, Jones still manages to convey the ultimate hallmark of the great country singer: a sincere performance that communicates the sense that he has lived the life he sings about.

Johnny Cash also has endured, with a sound and style not far removed from his rockabilly beginnings: spare, honest, intensely

ABOVE: JOHNNY CASH, 1964. OPPOSITE, CLOCKWISE FROM TOP: CASH, CIRCA 1960; BUCK OWENS AND THE BUCKAROOS, CIRCA 1964; MERLE HAGGARD, 1994.

rhythmic, and faintly ominous. Cultivating an air of mystery as "the Man in Black" and exhibiting a receptivity to all kinds of songs not usually associated with country music, Cash has built a following far broader than that of any other country singer. Beginning with his appearance at the Newport Folk Festival in 1964, and continuing through his friendship with Bob Dylan and other country-rock stylists, he has consistently impressed young listeners who have little affinity for most country music. No longer heard on country radio, Cash remains popular on "Americana" stations and with the readers of *Rolling Stone*.

Alvis Edgar "Buck" Owens, Merle Haggard, and Willie Nelson created their updated versions of traditional country music in Bakersfield, California, and, in Nelson's case, in Austin, Texas. Born in Texas, Owens served his apprenticeship as a musician in the thriving clubs of Bakersfield, an oil and cotton town in Southern California. Haggard, mean-

while, was born right outside Bakersfield in Oildale, as the son of Okie migrants. The possessor of a pleading tenor voice, Owens took elements of the Texas honky-tonk style, fused them with the energy of rockabilly, and, along with guitarist/sidekick Don Rich, produced a sparkling electric sound irresistible to both dancers and listeners. Haggard, on the other hand, wasted much of his youth in brushes with the law and periodic incarcerations in reform schools and San Quentin, but he received an invaluable education as a musician at the Lucky Spot, Blackboard, and other Bakersfield clubs. Few singers have been as respectful of country music's roots or as immersed in its history as Haggard, whose indebtedness is displayed in his splendid song poetry and in tribute albums made to Jimmie Rodgers, Bob Wills, and Lefty Frizzell. And in "Mama's Hungry Eyes," a semiautobiographical song set in a Depression-era labor camp, he paid poignant tribute to the culture that produced both him and his music.

Willie Nelson was already respected as a singer and songwriter when, frustrated

with the corporate mentality of Nashville, he moved in 1970 from that city to Austin. There in Texas's capital he found an already thriving music scene — a synthesis of cowboy and countercultural elements (described by local writer Jan Reid as "redneck rock"). Nelson adapted easily to his new environment, letting his hair and beard grow and sporting raiment borrowed from cowboy, Indian, and hippie cultures. Often joined in the city by other maverick entertainers, such as his old friend Waylon Jennings (long known for his rebellious spirit and musical experimentations), Nelson and his partners were sometimes described as "outlaws" because of their lifestyles and resistance to musical standardization. Like Cash, Nelson impressed his young listeners with his integrity, tolerance for unorthodox ideas and musical styles, and solid musicianship. Synthesizing elements of honky-tonk, Western swing, blues, gospel, and vintage pop, he came closer to bridging the gap between rock and country than anyone had ever done, and he also achieved superstardom in the larger country music scene. Beginning in 1973, Nelson's Texas "picnics" attracted enormous crowds of longhairs and traditional country fans and featured such diverse entertainers as Tex Ritter, Roy Acuff, and Leon Russell. He also publicly supported family farmers through the musical extravaganza known as Farm Aid, first held in 1985.

Nelson, Cash, and Haggard were generous in their tributes to the country entertainers who had come before them, and their music often exhibited its debts to bygone traditions. But they did not explicitly link their music to any kind of mission to revive "authentic" styles. Neotraditionalism, as the style came to

be called, emerged later in the Seventies, when Emmylou Harris recorded her 1975 hit version of a Louvin Brothers tune, "If I Could Only Win Your Love," and lasted into the Eighties, when Ricky Skaggs and George Strait paid successful tributes to bluegrass, honky-tonk, and Western swing. Harris had been a coffeehouse folksinger when country-

CLOCKWISE FROM TOP: RICKY SKAGGS (RIGHT) VISITING BILL MONROE AT HOME, 1982; TEENAGE MUSICAL PRODIGY MARTY STUART, CIRCA 1975; LEFTY FRIZZELL, CIRCA 1953. OPPOSITE: EMMYLOU HARRIS, 1975.

rock pioneer Gram Parsons introduced her to the Louvins, a harmony-singing brothers duo from Alabama, and other exemplars of hard-country music. She served a splendid apprenticeship with Parsons, recording with him such heart-wrenching duets as "Love Hurts" and "Hearts on Fire," and then moved into the country field with her commercial fusion of folk, country, and rock.

Ricky Skaggs acted as Harris's frontman in her Hot Band but was already committed to hard-country music when he teamed up with her. He had grown up with bluegrass and, along with Keith Whitley, had played in Ralph Stanley's Clinch Mountain Boys. But in 1981 he forayed into mainstream country with an updated version of a Flatt and Scruggs song, "Don't Get Above Your Raising," which seemed to be an admonition to other country artists who were straying from the music's roots.

George Strait, on the other hand, prospered with a sound that drew upon both the shuffle beat heard in the dancehalls of his native state of Texas and the swinging fiddle rhythms of Bob Wills. His smooth voice and handsome cowboy demeanor vaulted him onto the country charts, where he has remained ever since. Randy Travis and Keith Whitley emerged a few years later with sonorous singing styles reminiscent of Lefty Frizzell. The new traditionalists who have appeared since that time have not always remained committed to oldtime styles, and their relationship with hard-country music sometimes involves little more than the wearing of cowboy hats and boots. A few performers, however, such as Ricky Skaggs, Dwight Yoakam, and Marty Stuart, have militantly affirmed their respect for and loyalty to hard-country styles and have not been reluctant to resurrect the word *hillbilly* to describe their music. In the 1990s, Skaggs abandoned his quest for Top Forty acceptance, going back to his first love, the bluegrass style he learned from his mentors, Bill Monroe and the Stanley Brothers. Stuart came to Nashville in 1971 as a thirteen-year-old mandolin player for Lester Flatt, then went on to play guitar in Cash's band. As a solo artist, Stuart showed his affinity for rockabilly and bluegrass and has since infused his music with both sounds. A tireless promoter of classic country, and its most eloquent spokesman, he has remained an enthusiastic and passionate hillbilly nationalist, although he has lost radio airplay in the process.

Indeed, mainstream country — the kind played on Top Forty radio stations — has generally been aimed at the broadest possible spectrum of listeners. The Country Music Association (founded in Nashville in 1957) has diligently encouraged the creation of radio stations that play only country music. Ironically, a proliferating body of country stations have played a narrowing list of recordings with an increasingly diluted country content. Many have looked to country music as America's new "pop music," a music shorn of its most obvious rural and working-class content and an alternative to hard rock and hip-hop. At the same time, country has gradually absorbed rock elements into its mix, especially evident beginning in the 1980s, via the music of the Eagles, the Allman Brothers Band, and similar groups. Modern country music has built a massive constituency that values the superb musicianship, state-of-the-art production, and bedrock sentiments found on contemporary recordings.

A growing chorus of listeners has argued, however, that while the music may be well performed and well produced, contemporary country is neither "country" nor rooted in working-class experiences. Again and again during the last forty years, many fans (both young and old) have revealed a hunger for or fascination with sounds that are perceived as roots based and therefore truly working class: Ralph Stanley's high-lonesome sound, Johnny Cash's rugged honesty, Merle Haggard's workingman's poetry, or Willie Nelson's rebel spirit. These artists, along with Skaggs, Harris, Yoakam, and Stuart, have increasingly found common ground with musicians on the fringe who have been described as "alternative country." Some of these "outsiders" are singer/songwriters such as the late Townes Van Zandt, Guy Clark, Nanci Griffith, John Prine, Iris DeMent, Lucinda Williams, and Steve Earle, who have carried on the tradition of Woody Guthrie, Pete Seeger, and other socially conscious artists associated with folk music. Like Dylan, who has influenced them all, these singers have freely fused the sounds of country, rock, and folk to create songs that comment intelligently on the human condition. Earle's music, for example, is a smooth mixture of rock, country, Celtic, and bluegrass components, filled with incisive and biting lyrics aimed at the death penalty and other acts of social injustice and presented with gritty intensity.

Alternative country is impossible to define precisely, because it encompasses wildly diverse musicians, but it can probably be best described as any country-based style that exists outside Top Forty. Alt-country musicians seek venues on Americana, college, and public radio stations and in clubs that generally cater to edgy

entertainers. In 1990, inspired by the old Carter Family song "No Depression in Heaven," the country-punk band Uncle Tupelo recorded the album *No Depression,* which in turn inspired an impressive magazine and Web site with the same name. The magazine has been an uncompromising advocate of many forms of music — country rock, bluegrass, "old timey," rockabilly, gospel, hard country — that exist outside the mainstream.

Many kinds of country music, then, have contended for the affection of American listeners during the past sixty years, and musicians have dealt with tradition in a variety of ways. Country is much more than the music made by superstars or performers with great public visibility. Hank Thompson and Ray Price are only two of the veterans who continue to make the rounds of taverns, dancehalls, and theaters. Throughout America, thousands of people play music on weekends, or even during the week, and then go to their day jobs as mechanics, salesmen, factory workers, or beauticians. They have never been able to give up their wage-earning occupations (some in fact work only to support their love of music). Still others participate in weekly jam sessions at someone's house or at the

local VFW or American Legion Hall. Others take part in fiddle contests or festivals or play in church or at local barn dances. Some take time out each year to learn traditional music arts at workshops or through instructional tapes or videos. This truly down-home form of music making *is* roots music, and as long as this kind of democratic participation persists, country music will endure and remain healthy.

"IN LATE 1994, I DISCOVERED THAT THERE WERE THESE KIDS WHO HAD BEEN MAKING MUSIC THAT WAS ABOUT SONGS, WHICH THE MUSIC INDUSTRY AND THE MAINSTREAM HAD MOVED AWAY FROM IN A BIG WAY. AND THEY ALL KNEW WHO TOWNES [VAN ZANDT] WAS, THEY ALL KNEW WHO A.P. CARTER WAS, THEY KNEW ABOUT BOB DYLAN BEFORE *BLOOD ON THE TRACKS.* THEY WERE TAKING A PIECE OF MUSIC THAT THEY'D HEARD, AND IT WAS IMPORTANT TO THEM TO GO BACK TO WHEREVER IT CAME FROM, TO TRACE IT BACK. AND I THINK THAT'S THE IMPORTANT PART ABOUT [ALTERNATIVE COUNTRY]: IT'S ABOUT SONGS, AND IT'S ABOUT THE WAY PEOPLE FEEL, AND IT'S ABOUT TRADITIONS BEING IMPORTANT BUT ALSO NOT BEING THE BE-ALL AND END-ALL AND A BARRIER. IT'S ABSOLUTELY OPEN-ENDED MUSIC." —STEVE EARLE

OPPOSITE: JOHN HARTFORD, STEVE EARLE, MARK SCHATZ, AND MARTY STUART (FROM LEFT) PRESERVING ROOTS TRADITION ONSTAGE IN THE MID-NINETIES. ABOVE: EARLE (LEFT) AND TOWNES VAN ZANDT, 1995.

KITTY WELLS: *I was born and raised in Nashville. My dad played the guitar and used to sit around and sing the oldtime songs like "The Preacher and the Bear." I always liked to listen to guitar music and singing, so when I got up old enough, I learned the chords on the guitar. I had a girlfriend, and the boy she was going with played the guitar, and he taught me some chords. After I learned to play, my dad brought his guitar in and gave it to me to start playing. And we used to sing folksongs like "The Crawdad Song," "Can I Sleep in Your Barn Tonight Mister," "My Little Southern Home in Tennessee," and all those type songs. And of course we sang a lot of gospel songs like "Old Rugged Cross" and "Amazing Grace." We all used to sit around and sing songs like that — my mother and my two sisters. I used to go to church and sing, and my girlfriends and I used to sing at the churches.*

The Grand Ole Opry was here in Nashville, and when I was old enough, my mother and sisters and I used to go up to [it]. We'd get our tickets from our insurance man. There weren't too many [girl singers] on the Opry then. There was Alcyone Bate, who played piano with her father, Dr. Humphrey Bate. Texas Daisy and Texas Ruby came somewhere in the Thirties. There weren't too many women on the show at the time. And when Roy Acuff came to Nashville in '37, he added a girl on the show called Rachel. She played a banjo and sang — it was Rachel and Her Bashful Brother Oswald. They weren't really brother and sister. Back in those days you had to be really careful, you know — people would get the wrong idea.

My cousin lived in Nashville, and she and I started singing together. We got a radio program on Saturday afternoon called the Old Country Store. That was before Johnny [Wright] and I got married. Then when we got married, we both started singing on the same radio station. We had an early morning program, I think about six o'clock in the morning, for fifteen minutes, and we would do the show, then he would go to his job, then I would go to mine.

We moved from Shreveport back [to Nashville] in December of '51, and Johnny and Jack [Anglin], his partner and brother-in-law, started to work on the Opry, and I had decided I was going to stay home, you know, and not travel anymore, just stay home with the children [and] take care of them. And then when I recorded "It Wasn't God Who Made Honky Tonk Angels" and it started making a hit, I had to go back to work. Of course, that was an answer to "The Wild Side of Life." Hank Thompson had a big hit on that record and it was already in the charts, and I think that was one reason that helped the song make a hit. And another thing is [the lyrics were] kind of the women folk telling the men folks off, you know. Kind of getting back at them. Before that, they didn't write any songs for women. All the songs I'd been singing on the radio were written for men. After I made a hit on the Decca label, the other record companies started recording girl artists, and things began to get better.

OPPOSITE AND ABOVE: KITTY WELLS AND JOHNNY WRIGHT, 1994. BOTTOM: WELLS'S EARLY PUBLICITY PHOTO. FOLLOWING: FLATT AND SCRUGGS (TOP), EARL SCRUGGS (BOTTOM), 1969; SCRUGGS (OPPOSITE), 1972.

EARL SCRUGGS: *When I was growing up, we didn't have a radio or anything, but the family played music. We all picked banjos, guitar, Autoharp, or some instrument. My father played banjo a little, the old frailing style — but he died when I was four, so I don't remember any of his playing. I started playing when I was five or six. I was playing local tunes that were played around that part of the country. Real oldtime picking tunes like "Sally Gooden," "Sally Ann," "Cripple Creek," "Home Sweet Home" — strictly rural tunes. That's what I grew up hearing and playing and what I worked on because I didn't know anything else to pick, other than church songs. I played a lot of church songs, because I didn't know that many instrumental tunes or other types of tunes. Some of them played real well; I didn't try to jazz them up. You'd sit around and sing and play.*

I started out playing two-finger style. When I was about ten, I started playing the three-fingered style I now play. I worked on it, and it seemed to enable me to play most any type of music, slow or fast, with a more even flow or roll.

My brothers and sisters were pretty good at playing awhile and then going off and forgetting about it, but I couldn't get it off my mind. I'd always go back and keep trying to pick. When we got a radio and I started hearing commercial playing, that got on my mind, and I wanted to make a career out of it. I started thinking seriously about it, but I was so confused I didn't know how to get into it. When I was about twelve or thirteen, doing my daily chores, I'd dream of playing on the radio.

I started participating in [local] contests and in plays at the high school and things of that nature. Occasionally they'd have a fiddlers' convention, and I'd participate in that. I played so much around local people until they just took it for granted. There were some pretty good pickers around. After I got fourteen or fifteen years old, they started having a radio station out in Spartanburg [South Carolina], and some of us local guys would do a Saturday radio program.

With my father being dead, I was the breadwinner. I had to be very careful to make a strong attempt to go with somebody that was stable in the business where I was pretty well assured of keeping a job.

When I went to work with Bill [Monroe], he had an accordion in the group, and though he was the singer of his own style of music, the band sounded altogether different from what it would become. None of the groups were using the banjo then — except some of the old groups, but it wasn't a featured instrument. Comedians like Uncle Dave Macon used the banjo mainly as a clown's instrument. Then Bill settled down with a five-piece group with my style of banjo picking and kept it ever since.

MERLE HAGGARD: *There was a place where we used to all go park above Bakersfield, out north of town. You could look out up there. We used to take guitars and ice the beer down and go up there and sing Lefty Frizzell's "Mom and Dad's Waltz" all night long, you know. The girls would dance, and we called it Beer Can Hill.*

Thirty, thirty-five years ago [when I took up a country music career], it was sort of like going in the army. You make up your mind when you go in the army that you're putting yourself in harm's way, so to speak. And I guess some people call it fate, you just kind of like put your life in the hand of the Almighty. I've traveled in this bus without a safety belt for thirty, thirty-five years. We've flown more miles than most airline pilots. I've rode freight trains, passenger trains, ships, boats, horseback. I've traveled just about every way you can travel.

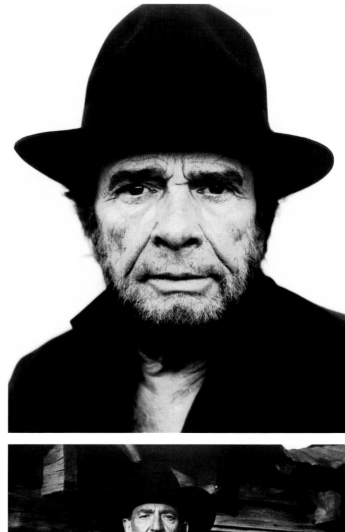

I've written a lot of stuff, probably 320 songs that I've copyrighted and recorded or somebody has recorded. And of all those songs there's just four or five that I can even remember what was going on when they were written. Most of them just telepathically come through me. I don't sit down and say, "Well, I'm going to write a song." They come to me and they come to me fast, and if I don't have somebody around that can write pretty fast, sometimes I lose them if I don't get it down. That's the way I write. It's sort of sporadic, and sometimes it's a long period between things that's worth talking about. Sometimes I make the mistake of trying to force it to come in, and it never works. So I just quit doing it and sit and wait. It's like waiting for a phone call.

WILLIE NELSON: *My grandparents raised me from the time I was six months old, and my grandfather started teaching me guitar when I was five. The first guitar I ever owned was a Stella, a Sears Roebuck guitar that cost six dollars. I was writing a few poems then — all of a sudden I was putting some of the chords I'd learned to the words of the poems I'd written. My grandmother, who played piano and organ, taught my sister Bobbie how to read music. She got some sheet music, and I would learn from her. When she'd learn a song, she'd teach it to me. There were always people coming by the house and wanting us to play a song for them, and we always did. And at school at study hall or for special programs, we'd play. Back then, I thought we'd always be together and always be playing.*

"Merle Haggard is the heart and soul of country music and Western swing." —Ray Benson, Asleep at the Wheel

∫ Opposite: Merle Haggard in the 1960s. From top: Haggard, 2000; Willie Nelson, 1993.

1940 Broadcast Music Incorporated (BMI), a more blues-friendly alternative to ASCAP, becomes a music publisher. 1941 Alan Lomax documents a twenty-six-year-old tractor driver named McKinley "Muddy Waters" Morganfield for the Library of Congress. In Helena, Arkansas, harmonica player Aleck "Rice" Miller (a.k.a. Sonny Boy Williamson) debuts on KFFA's new radio show, King Biscuit Time. Nervous about a proposed march on Washington, D.C., the government passes federal legislation that bans racial discrimination in defense industries. 1942 'Billboard' debuts its "Harlem Hit Parade," its first R&B chart. 1943 In May, Muddy Waters leaves Clarksdale, Mississippi, for Chicago. He carries only an eleven-dollar Sears, Roebuck—brand guitar and a suitcase. 1944 The advent of the mechanized cotton picker drastically changes the cotton industry; by the Sixties, only 5 percent of Delta cotton is picked by hand. 1946 B.B. King moves from Mississippi to Memphis. Arthur "Big Boy" Crudup releases "That's All Right," which is later covered by Elvis Presley. 1947 Jackie Robinson enters major-league baseball. Aaron "T-Bone" Walker releases the huge blues hit "Call It Stormy Monday." 1948 WDIA, a future place of employment for B.B. King, becomes the first all-black format radio station. John Lee Hooker begins his career in Detroit, releasing "Boogie Chillen." 1952 B.B. King tops the R&B chart for five weeks with a cover of Lowell Fulson's "Three O'Clock Blues." Little Walter also scores a Number One R&B hit with "Juke." The electric blues enjoys a brief golden age on black radio and in the record industry. 1954 Schools become desegregated thanks to Brown v. the Board of Education. Muddy Waters's biggest R&B hit, "I'm Your Hoochie Coochie Man" (Number Three), is released by Chess. 1955 Big Bill Broonzy and Yannick Bruynoghe publish Broonzy's autobiography, 'Big Bill Blues.' Outraged citizens refuse to ride the segregated buses of Montgomery, Alabama. 1956 Howlin' Wolf scores two R&B hits, "Smoke Stack Lightning" and "I Asked for Water," both of which reach Number Eight. 1957 The Southern Christian Leadership Conference (SCLC) is formed. Its president is the Reverend Dr. Martin Luther King Jr. 1962 German promoter Horst Lippman and talent coordinator/songwriter/musician Willie Dixon organize the first American Folk Blues Festival, an annual European tour that introduces the Continent to such talents as Sonny Boy Williamson, Muddy Waters, and Howlin' Wolf. **1963** On August 28, Dr. King incites a racially mixed crowd of 250,000 with his "I Have a Dream" speech in Washington, D.C. On September 16, the Sixteenth Street Baptist Church in Birmingham, Alabama, is bombed; four black schoolgirls are killed. **1964** The 1964 Civil Rights Act is passed in response to pressure from the civil rights movement, which has pervaded the public conscience. Three civil rights workers are murdered during the Mississippi Freedom Festival. The Rolling Stones insist that Howlin' Wolf appear with them on television's 'Shindig.' **1965** Malcolm X is assassinated in New York City. Congress passes the Voting Rights Act. Race riots occur in Watts. **1966** Koko Taylor scores a Number Four R&B hit, "Wang Dang Doodle," written by Willie Dixon. **1968** Congress passes the Fair Housing Act. **1969** B.B. King and Muddy Waters play the Fillmore East in New York; by now, the blues has become embraced almost exclusively by white rock, roots, and folk enthusiasts. **1970** 'Living Blues' becomes the first magazine of its kind published in the United States. Blues ambassador B.B. King's mainstream pop hit "The Thrill Is Gone" spends fourteen weeks on the chart, peaking at Number Fifteen. **1971** Alligator Records gets under way with the self-titled, rollicking LP by Hound Dog Taylor and the House Rockers. **1972** Congress passes the Equal Opportunities Act. **1980** 'The Blues Brothers,' John Landis's hit movie starring comedians Dan Aykroyd and the late John Belushi, spawns a real-life, touring Blues Brothers Band and symbolizes the acceptance of the blues by white, suburban America. **1984** Stevie Ray Vaughan, the biggest name in white crossover blues, releases his first hit LP, 'Texas Flood.' **1986** Robert Cray's 'Strong Persuader' reaches Number Thirteen on the pop chart and yields the Number Twenty-two single "Smoking Gun." Cray is one of the few young, contemporary black performers still embracing the blues form. **1989** John Lee Hooker releases a surprise hit, the star-studded, Grammy-winning album 'The Healer.' **1994** Keb' Mo' releases his self-titled debut blues album. **2000** Reprise Records issues 'Riding With the King,' B.B. King's collaboration with blues-indebted British guitar icon Eric Clapton. The record will win a Grammy for Best Traditional Blues Recording.

MOJO WORKING: THE BLUES EXPLOSION BY ROBERT SANTELLI

In the 1940s, when blacks began leaving the fields down south for the factories up north, the blues followed. Mojo men, mannish boys, juke-joint sharpies, guitar players, shouters, and other assorted country bluesmen joined sharecroppers, common laborers, housemaids, levee workers, even entire families in a mass migration northward. Spurred by economic opportunities brought on by the onset of World War II, nearly three million African-Americans left the South between 1940 and 1960.

Some made it only as far as Memphis or St. Louis or Kansas City, where they settled in black neighborhoods and began new lives. Thousands upon thousands more reached Chicago, Detroit, Cleveland, Pittsburgh, Philadelphia, Newark, and New York. Still others headed west to Los Angeles, Oakland, San Francisco, and Seattle. All of this movement dramatically reshaped the nation's cultural map and the way racial issues would be viewed for the next fifty years. Leaving behind the old cotton plantations and the shotgun shacks in the small hamlets in which they had lived, southern blacks came north by train, car, or bus. They traveled with a rare hope and their own small part of the American Dream tucked neatly in the back of their minds. They took with them whatever cherished rural customs they could, mostly as a means of keeping in touch with their old way of life and of dispelling homesickness. But it wasn't long before country traditions originally cultivated in places like the Mississippi Delta and the Piedmont region on the eastern seaboard succumbed to a new, more demanding urban sensibility. One of the best places to witness this transformation was in music, particularly the blues. Almost overnight, it got louder, harder edged, and bigger sounding – just like the cities where it now resided. In the process, a brand-new blues form – urban, or electric, blues – developed, ushering in a period of unparalleled popularity and influence and launching the careers of some of the greatest bluesmen ever.

OPPOSITE: B.B. KING'S FIRST PUBLICITY
PICTURE, TAKEN BY THE HOOKS
BROTHERS AT THEIR BEALE STREET
PHOTOGRAPHY STUDIO, 1949

This new style of the blues was inspired in part by the jump-blues combos of the mid- and late 1940s. These groups created quite a stir on the dance floor with their hot rhythms, honking saxophones, and racy lyrics that were more often shouted than sung. Small and tight, these groups were led by black emigrants from the big-band swing scene, such as Louis Jordan, and included stalwarts Roy Brown, the Liggins brothers (Joe and Jimmy), Wynonie Harris, Amos Milburn, and Big Joe Turner.

Like these popular jump-blues outfits, the new blues bands formed by transplanted country bluesmen contained backbeats and bass riffs. In place of the jump-blues saxophone was the amplified harmonica, dubbed a "Mississippi saxophone" by some, and the electric guitar, which, with the volume turned up, could turn a simple solo into a screeching avalanche of blues angst.

What also separated a jump-blues combo from the emerging urban blues band was the depth and detail of the blues performed and the overall rawness of the music. Polished and slick, jump-blues bands often included liberal doses of jazz and pop in their sound. By contrast, the raw, new blues bands stuck to the deep and down-home blues, but electrified.

In the North, these new blues bands quickly replaced in popularity the acoustic sounds of solo bluesmen. Such traditional country-blues artists could keep a crowd content at a southern juke on the edge of a plantation, but they could not compete at crowded, boisterous house parties or in the noisy neighborhood clubs that sprouted on Chicago's South Side or along Hastings Street in Detroit. Amplification increasingly became a blues necessity, and the more visionary bluesmen quickly found that plugging in meant rocking out — something black crowds embraced with unbridled enthusiasm.

Thus a dramatic metamorphosis of the blues was under way in the Forties and Fifties as the old styles of Charley Patton, Son House, and Robert Johnson were transformed into the more vigorous styles of younger, hungry bluesmen such as Muddy Waters, Little Walter, Howlin' Wolf, and Willie Dixon. It was a new blues day, and there was a new blues way.

OPPOSITE: IN THE 1930S, BIG BILL BROONZY (RIGHT) WAS ONE OF THE FIRST BLUESMEN TO LEAVE MISSISSIPPI FOR CHICAGO. PICTURED HERE IN THE EARLY 1940S WITH LITTLE BILL GATHER AND MEMPHIS SLIM (SEATED). LEFT: FELLOW MISSISSIPPIAN JOHN LEE HOOKER MADE DETROIT HIS NEW HOME IN 1943.

Chicago became the hub of this electric-blues revolution. Uprooted country-blues musicians, mostly from the Mississippi Delta, wound up there, carrying on an early urban-blues tradition that had begun in the 1930s with the arrival of Big Bill Broonzy, Memphis Minnie, Tampa Red, and others looking for recording opportunities. Mississippi-born Broonzy adapted well to the big city. Proving that country-blues styles could easily include influences from the jazz bands he heard all around him, Big Bill sang and played his acoustic guitar against an instrumental backdrop that often included piano, horns, and drums. In 1938 and 1939, the popular Broonzy was invited to perform at John Hammond's From Spirituals to Swing concerts at New York City's Carnegie Hall and became one of the top blues recording artists of his time.

Broonzy wasn't the only bluesman to experiment with an ensemble before the urban-blues onslaught. The Harlem Hamfats played ensemble-style blues in Chicago in the mid-Thirties, and Memphis jug bands were early antecedents of the modern blues band. Down in Helena, Arkansas, in 1941, a singer/harmonica player, Aleck "Rice" Miller — better known as Sonny Boy Williamson (a nickname he appropriated from John Lee Williamson, another harp player who went by the same moniker) — and a guitarist, Robert Junior Lockwood (the stepson of the legendary Robert Johnson), approached the radio station KFFA with the idea of having their own blues show on the air. Recognizing an

opportunity to satisfy companies that wanted to reach black radio audiences with product information, KFFA created King Biscuit Time, a fifteen-minute show that aired daily at 12:45 p.m., with the Interstate Grocery Company as its sponsor.

Eventually MC'd by Sonny Payne, a white radio announcer fond of the blues and a boyhood friend of Lockwood's, the show was a smash with black listeners. Williamson and Lockwood turned their duo into a full-fledged blues band, adding Peck Curtis on drums and Dudlow Taylor on piano. Later pianists Pinetop Perkins and Willie Love and guitarist Houston Stackhouse would play the King Biscuit show, depending on who was in Helena at the time. This unit was the prototype for the modern blues band: Both Lockwood and Stackhouse played electric guitars, Williamson used the microphone not just as a means of amplification but also as a way to broaden the sonic textures of the blues harp, and drummer Curtis and the pianists he played with created rhythms that would be emulated over and over again in Chicago and elsewhere up north.

The King Biscuit band also proved that blues belonged on the radio. The show Sonny Boy and friends performed on each day aired all over the Mississippi and Arkansas deltas and up through Memphis and West Memphis. It had a profound influence on emerging area bluesmen, many of whom would ultimately wind up in the Windy City, creating their own bands. Although Williamson ended his regular performances on the show in 1944, he often returned to the airwaves when passing through Helena. His popularity was such that his image was even printed on the bags of King Biscuit cornmeal. Still on the air today, King Biscuit Time is one of the longest-running daily radio shows in history.

A young Mississippi bluesman taken by the music he heard on KFFA was Riley B. King. Born in Indianola, Mississippi, King was a farmhand and tractor driver who yearned to play the electric guitar the way Lockwood and two other seminal black guitarists did, namely Charlie Christian and Aaron "T-Bone" Walker. Walker had met Christian in the early 1930s, when the electric guitar was just beginning to make its presence heard. These two pioneers — Christian in jazz and Walker in the blues — permanently altered the role of the guitar in a band setting, taking it from a solely rhythm stance to one that emphasized rhythm and lead. Walker's single-string solos harked back to Blind Lemon Jefferson's country-blues style, but with amplification the former's leads sounded cleaner, crisper, cooler. Walker also

incorporated complex chords and carefully crafted tones into his guitar style, thanks to Christian's influence and Walker's never-ending fascination with jazz. Virtually every bluesman who picked up an electric guitar from the Forties onward could not help but be moved by Walker's amplified string genius.

Riley King, a cousin of famed country bluesman Bukka White, quit the Mississippi Delta farm he was working on in 1947, moved to Memphis, formed a band, and began playing the clubs on Beale Street, the city's most notorious bluesway. Soon after arriving in Memphis, King met up with Sonny Boy Williamson, who landed him a performance on West Memphis radio station KWEM. Eventually King got his own radio show on WDIA, across the Mississippi River in Memphis, plugging Pepticon, an alcohol-based, cure-all tonic. Calling himself the Beale Street Blues Boy, B.B. King, as he later became known, spun records over the air, gaining a broad blues knowledge that he put to use onstage with his band.

King played with a loose assortment of Memphis blues musicians – including Roscoe Gordon, Bobby "Blue" Bland, and Johnny Ace – informally known as the Beale Streeters. Aided by his daily

appearance on the radio, King's popularity grew, leading to a recording contract in 1949 with the Bullet label. King also recorded at Sam Phillips's Memphis Recording Service (which would later become Sun studios), as did blues harp player James Cotton and Chester Burnett, a big, strapping blues singer from the Delta, more commonly known as Howlin' Wolf. In 1951, King had his first major hit, "Three O'Clock Blues," which lodged itself in the Number One position on the rhythm & blues chart and transformed King into a blues star who would criss-cross the country with his big band and, in the 1950s, record many blues and R&B hits. The hard work paid off; King ultimately became an international blues icon, whose stature as a blues ambassador is without rival today.

In 1943, four years before King departed the Delta, a young singer/guitarist named McKinley Morganfield headed for Chicago after a 1941 field recording session with Alan Lomax, which resulted in a second session the following year. Like B.B. and Wolf, Morganfield also had a nickname: Muddy Waters was the tag his grandmother had given him as a child growing up on the Stovall Plantation, just outside Clarksdale, Mississippi. Waters believed his chances of becoming a commercial recording artist were better up north than in Mississippi or even Memphis, so he joined the black movement out of the South, arriving in Chicago determined to make his blues mark.

It didn't take long. A singer with a rough-hewn voice that belied his youth, Waters also played a mean, slashing guitar that was at once angry and arrogant. His chords and bottleneck slide-guitar riffs were direct descendants of the sounds he heard from Son House, Willie Brown, Charley Patton, Robert Johnson, and other first-generation Delta bluesmen. Yet, something in Muddy Waters's delivery was new and refreshing, something that came from the past but was now clearly lodged in the blues present — and future.

It was one thing for Muddy Waters, who had met and befriended Big Bill Broonzy, to play house-rent parties and the occasional club with his acoustic guitar as accompaniment. It was clearly another when Waters got hold of an electric guitar and began playing with a band. What resulted made American blues history: the true transformation of the music, from a singular, lonely rural sound to a lively urban one that filled dance floors in South Side clubs, that ripped the heart out of any blues sentimentality that might have been wafting in the air, and that opened the door to a brand-new blues sound. In time, Muddy's blues redefined the music in contemporary terms, helping to give birth to rock & roll in the early Fifties, to inspire countless young British guitarists to play the blues in the early Sixties, to keep the blues alive in the Seventies — one of its leanest decades — and to forever change the face of American music, since no pop or roots form could escape the blues' reach for long.

Waters couldn't have become the catalyst for change without a recording contract. Like country-blues fans down south, many black blues fans up north also relied on recordings to hear the latest blues sounds, even though they also had numerous bars and clubs that featured live blues. Owning blues records meant that the music could enter one's home — and stay there. A relationship was begun with that particular artist or song, and it grew increasingly intimate each time the record was played on the phonograph.

The first time Waters stepped into a Chicago studio was in 1946, to cut some songs for veteran black talent scout and producer Mayo Williams and Columbia Records. But these records weren't released until many years after Waters had become a star. His recording career really got going the following year, when blues pianist Sunnyland Slim arranged for Waters to record for Leonard and Phil Chess, two Jewish immigrant

"MUDDY WATERS IS THE CONSUMMATE CONNECTION BETWEEN THE DELTA AND CHICAGO." —KEB' MO'

brothers who had recently started a record company called Aristocrat, which later became Chess. Although Waters was fronting his own band at the time and recorded his first Chess sides in an ensemble setting, his earliest Chess tracks somehow missed the mark.

But Leonard Chess, who would form a tight relationship with Waters and guide his career throughout the Fifties, was not discouraged. In 1948, he cut Waters as a traditionally styled Delta bluesman with only bass player Big Crawford adding bottom; the resulting single, "I Can't Be Satisfied" with the flip side "I Feel Like Going Home," was a smash in the black community. Clearly, the record was a throwback to the Mississippi Delta blues tradition from which Waters had come; homesick blacks longing for family and friends down south found solace in Waters's solo sound. But as much as Waters kept his link with the Delta, he was more moved by the bigger, nastier blues style he created when surrounded by a band.

ABOVE: WILLIE DIXON, CIRCA 1955

LEFT: MUDDY WATERS, 1962.
BELOW: BUDDY GUY, 1965.

"[MUDDY WATERS SHOWED UP AT MY FIRST GIG.] HE SLAPPED ME AND MADE ME GET INTO A RED CHEVROLET STATION WAGON, MADE ME EAT [A] SANDWICH. I STARTED CRYING, TELLING HIM I'M GOING BACK HOME, BECAUSE I DIDN'T KNOW ANYBODY AND I WAS ABOUT TO STARVE. HE SAID, 'NO, YOU'RE NOT GONNA STARVE, AND YOU'RE NOT GOING BACK. YOU'RE GONNA PLAY THIS GUITAR, BECAUSE EVERYBODY TELLS ME HOW GOOD YOU IS. I'M HERE TO HEAR YOU, AND WHEN I HEAR YOU PLAY, YOU AIN'T GOIN' NO-DAMN-WHERE.' " —BUDDY GUY

It helped that Muddy Waters knew a good blues musician when he heard one. That was why his band was full of first-rate players, many of whom enjoyed acclaimed solo careers: Guitarist Jimmy Rogers, pianist Otis Spann, and harp players Little Walter Jacobs, Junior Wells, and James Cotton were all blues stars in their own right by the mid-Sixties. Original drummer Elgin Evans backed numerous Chicago blues musicians after his stint with Waters, while another Waters drummer, Fred Below, went on to become the house drummer at Chess, backing everyone from Little Walter to Chuck Berry.

And then there was Willie Dixon, who often played bass behind Waters. A big, round man with a warm heart and a comforting smile, Dixon also had the best ears in the blues business. Born in Vicksburg, Mississippi, Dixon came to Chicago in 1936 and pursued a career as a professional boxer before turning to music full time. He had stints with the Five Breezes and the Big Three Trio, but he made his biggest contribution after the Chess brothers hired him in 1948. During the next decade or so, Dixon's role at Chess was indispensable. In many ways, he defined the Chess sound.

A superb songwriter, Dixon supplied Waters with the material that became his biggest Chess hits, including the 1954 landmark number "Hoochie Coochie Man." Another Waters signature song, "I Just Want to Make Love to You," also came from Dixon, as did "I'm Ready" and lesser known but equally potent numbers such as "Young Fashioned Ways," "You Shook Me," and "You Need Love."

Phil Chess told noted blues historian Mary Katherine Aldin that "Willie used to come and hang around Chess. And then we used him on blues dates, not every time, but the majority of the dates, especially if it was his songs; he would rehearse them with the artist, be it Muddy or one of the others. Then he became sort of like a house band. We'd say, 'Willie, we got a session coming up with so-and-so, you got anything for him that would suit him?' Muddy came in with some stuff of his own, too, but really the most powerful stuff was Willie's."

Dixon had a knack for dealing with the stylistic nuances of just about every artist on the Chess roster, and he used that talent to great advantage. Dixon also wrote songs for artists other than Waters, arranged them, added the necessary bass parts, secured musicians for the sessions, led the house band, acted as a mediator when things got heated in the studio, found new talent, wrote more songs, penciled in more sessions. In short, Willie Dixon was the quintessential behind-the-scenes Chicago bluesman.

"THE BLUES IS ACTUALLY SOME KIND OF DOCUMENTARY OF THE PAST AND THE PRESENT AND SOMETHING TO GIVE PEOPLE INSPIRATION FOR THE FUTURE. BLUES HAS WISDOM. . . . IT'S ALWAYS BEEN THERE." —WILLIE DIXON

Dixon also helped Howlin' Wolf find his blues muse. Dixon wrote such Wolf wonders as "Evil," "Spoonful," "I Ain't Superstitious," "Little Red Rooster," and "Back Door Man." Like Dixon and Waters, Wolf had come to Chicago from Mississippi, where he blended the coarse sounds of Delta blues with a rocking backbeat. Two things set Wolf apart from Waters and the rest of the Chicago blues crowd: his vocal delivery and his onstage showmanship. Wolf's voice sounded as if it had been brutally tortured, then left in the Mississippi sun to dry out, crust up, and blow away. It was shrieky and scary and as mysterious as a full moon at midnight at the crossroads. The moment he stepped onstage and had an audience in front of him, Wolf carried on like a man possessed. Rolling and tumbling, wailing and shouting, thumping and pumping, Wolf brought a radically new dimension to live blues.

{ OPPOSITE: WILLIE DIXON, MEMPHIS SLIM, AND BIG JOE WILLIAMS (FROM LEFT), IN NEW YORK CITY AFTER A RECORDING SESSION FOR FOLKWAYS, 1961

As wild as Wolf was, Little Walter Jacobs was smooth and suave. A ladies' man, a big-time boozer, and a charmer who could con a drink or a dollar from most everyone he met, Walter Jacobs gave new meaning to the blues harp by extending its tonal reach. Walter was brilliant in the way he controlled the air that flowed through his instrument; he emphasized dynamics, and he curved his notes with the kind of teasing, sexual tension rarely achieved by other blues harp players.

Born in Louisiana, Jacobs began his career after arriving in Chicago around 1946. He learned the rudiments of the blues harp from two masters, Big Walter Horton and Sonny Boy Williamson. After showing his performing talents on Chicago's Maxwell Street, where bluesmen young and old came on Sundays to play for tips and spare change, Little Walter joined Muddy Waters's band and at once gave the group a harp style that could contrast or complement Muddy's singing and slide-guitar playing, depending on the song.

Little Walter struck out on his own in 1952, after he recorded a romping blues harp instrumental, "Juke," that was a big hit for Chess. He was replaced in Waters's band by another up-and-coming Chicago blues harp player, Junior Wells. When Wells left his group, the Aces, to join Waters, Little Walter, leaving Waters, took Wells's place in the Aces — which now included Robert Junior Lockwood, who had come to Chicago from the Delta. Eventually, Little Walter renamed the group the Jukes, and it quickly became one of the hottest blues bands in Chicago.

Sonny Boy Williamson arrived in Chicago in the summer of 1955 to record some sides for Chess, giving competition to Little Walter's claim of being the best blues harp player in town. Walter was a better singer than Williamson, who had a tendency to mumble his lyrics or utter little more than a lazy slur. But no blues harmonica player, not even Little Walter, had a bigger bagful of harp sounds or tricks. Sonny Boy could insert the harp into his mouth, playing his instrument as if he were speaking through it. He also could blow notes on the harp with his nose. Despite the gimmicks, Sonny Boy Williamson was not a blues clown. Such Sonny Boy songs as "Nine Below Zero," "One Way Out" (later covered by the Allman Brothers Band), and "Bring It On Home," all from Sonny Boy's classic *Down and Out Blues* on Chess, rank with the greatest of all blues harp recordings.

While the blues were flying high in Chicago during the late Forties and Fifties, other northern cities filled with southern

THIS PAGE, FROM TOP: LITTLE WALTER, IN 1964, NEARLY TWENTY YEARS AFTER HE ARRIVED IN CHICAGO; THE POPULAR PEPPERS LOUNGE, CHICAGO.

"[IN CHICAGO,] WE'D HAVE A BLUE MONDAY PARTY OR A SUNDAY MATINEE, AND A LOT OF THE MUSICIANS THAT WASN'T PLAYING ANYPLACE, IF YOU HAD A GIG, THEY'D COME BY YOUR GIG AND JAM. ONE WOULD START IT, SAYING, 'WELL, [LITTLE] WALTER'S COMING IN THE HOUSE. JUNIOR SAYS THAT YOU COULD'VE LEFT YOUR HARMONICAS BACK HOME.' THE GUITAR PLAYERS WOULD START TALKING ABOUT WHO COULD BEAT THE OTHER ONE PLAYING THE GUITAR. OH, MAN, YOU TALKIN' ABOUT A GOOD TIME!" —JUNIOR WELLS

black transplants were also enjoying healthy blues scenes. In nearby Detroit, one Mississippi singer/guitarist, John Lee Hooker, became the city's biggest blues star. His monumental blues record, "Boogie Chillen," was one of the top postwar blues tunes, elevating Hooker to the heights enjoyed by Muddy Waters, Little Walter, and Howlin' Wolf. "Boogie Chillen," a primal one-chord vamp, carried a mysterious spirit. As much as the song made you want to dance or boogie, it also brought you into musical contact with the underbelly of the blues, that uncharted territory where demons prowled in the darkness.

In New York, the blues took a different turn. Many of the blues musicians who wound up there came from Virginia, the Carolinas, and Georgia, where the blues bore more rag and finger-picking folk influences than they did in the Delta. Unlike Waters, Wolf, Little Walter, and the rest of their Chicago colleagues who embraced amplification and electrified the blues, the Reverend Gary Davis, Sonny Terry and Brownie McGhee, and Josh White, along with Louisiana bluesman Huddie Ledbetter — more popularly known as Lead Belly — opted to keep their acoustic blues sound intact. Embraced by white folk artists living in New York at the time, such as Woody Guthrie, Pete Seeger, and Lee Hays, New York blues artists moved easily from the streets of Harlem to white intellectual circles in which radicalized folksingers were welcome and socialist politics prevailed.

The Reverend Gary Davis swung from secular blues to sacred gospel numbers with ease, bridging the gap that many presumed existed between the pulpit and the juke joint. Originally from South Carolina and blind, Davis was a salt-of-the-earth singer and a master guitarist whose filigreed finger picking brought out the richness of the blues from the Southeast. Whether performing on street corners, at parties, or on the concert stage, Davis played a repertoire that was the perfect composite of black American roots music.

Also blind, harp player Sonny Terry formed one half of the most enduring duo in blues history, with guitarist Brownie McGhee. Born in North Carolina, Terry met McGhee, originally from

Tennessee, in the early 1940s. Recording opportunities inspired the pair to move to New York, where they became friends with Josh White and Lead Belly, both of whom peppered their blues song lists with black folk songs and spirituals. Terry and McGhee were more true to the Piedmont blues popular in the Carolinas — Brownie playing guitar and Sonny blowing the harp. Playing to black as well as white audiences, the duo spread the blues in a city where jazz and pop were the more popular musical choices.

Josh White and Lead Belly made the greatest inroads with white audiences. White had moved from his native South Carolina to New York in the early 1930s and performed both as a solo artist and the leader of the Josh White Singers. He was also an actor, often onstage with Paul Robeson, and a gifted performer who entertained President Franklin Roosevelt and recorded for the Library of Congress. With a warm and embracing delivery, White's acoustic and homespun blues were a long way from those of Muddy Waters. Yet they penetrated places where Chicago blues could never have gone in the early postwar period.

In 1934, Lead Belly was released from prison and went to work for the Lomax family in New York City. Lead Belly fell in with Woody Guthrie, Pete Seeger, and other New York City folkies who saw the ex-convict as the perfect picture of blues authenticity. Some of his songs were folk-blues in origin, such as "Rock Island Line," "The Midnight Special," and "Goodnight Irene," but Lead Belly also penned political protest songs. "Bourgeois Blues" and "Scottsboro Boys" carried messages that were not unlike those heard in the songs of Guthrie and Seeger. Few blues artists in the Forties and Fifties were willing to incorporate left-

"T-BONE WALKER WAS, TO ME, THAT SOUND OF BEING IN HEAVEN. IT SEEMED LIKE WHENEVER HE PLAYED A NOTE, IT JUST WENT THROUGH ME LIKE A SWORD."
—B.B. KING

of-center political themes into their music and raise the wrath of Cold War America. Lead Belly bucked that trend and, when inspired, played songs that reflected social, political, and racial injustice in America until his death in 1949.

Despite their richness, postwar New York blues never really competed with the music coming out of Chicago. By the mid-1950s, Chess Records had a remarkable roster of blues recording artists, including the masters already mentioned, plus lesser known but equally vital artists such as J.B. Lenoir and Lowell Fulson, and the blues-influenced rock & rollers Chuck Berry and Bo Diddley. Still, there was plenty of talent to go around in Chicago. Vee-Jay Records signed Jimmy Reed. Short-lived Cobra Records had a stable of young guitarists — Otis Rush, Buddy Guy, and Magic Sam — all of whom would come to epitomize Chicago blues in the Sixties. The great slide guitarist Elmore James lived in and worked out of Chicago. Pianists such as Sunnyland Slim, Jimmy Yancey, Blind John Davis, Little Brother Montgomery, Chess session player Lafayette Leake, and, for a while, Roosevelt Sykes worked Windy City clubs and made records. Old-timer Big Bill Broonzy continued to call Chicago home until his passing in 1958.

Leading the pack always, though, was Muddy Waters. In 1960, Waters was invited to perform at the Newport Jazz Festival in Rhode Island. Much has been made of the electric performance of Bob Dylan (backed by the Chicago-based Paul Butterfield Blues Band) at the Newport Folk Festival in 1965, which allowed the perceived unholy alliance of folk and rock to occur. But in 1960, Waters had the white Newport crowd on its feet, dancing to the electrified sound of Chicago blues, before Dylan had even ventured east from Hibbing, Minnesota.

After more than a decade of countless club gigs and a batch of hit

19

records, the Muddy Waters Band peaked at Newport in 1960. The live album that followed, *Muddy Waters at Newport,* became one of the most influential blues records of its time, particularly in England, where young Brits were eagerly embracing the blues. But looming on the horizon back home in America were increasingly smaller black audiences for blues as soul, a new R&B-derived black pop music, drew young music fans into its camp. With the onset of the folk-revival movement in the early Sixties, Waters began recording acoustically; his album *Folk Singer* (1964) saw him return to his Mississippi roots, as did the followups, *The Real Folk Blues* and *More Real Folk Blues.* In Chicago, however, Muddy could still work out with a band and did so in clubs such as Sylvio's, the Checkerboard Lounge, and Theresa's — all mainstays of the city's electric-blues scene.

The black audience for electric blues might have been dwindling, but young whites began frequenting these black clubs in the Chicago ghetto, finding the music the perfect alternative to the Beatles and the Beach Boys, and the pop schlock of the teen idols and girl groups. Steve Miller, Boz Scaggs, Charlie Musselwhite, Paul Butterfield, Mike Bloomfield, and Elvin Bishop — all young white kids with a passion for the blues — sat in Chicago clubs and learned the music from the masters. Butterfield, a harp player and singer who had meticulously studied the sound and style of Little Walter, and guitarists Bloomfield and Bishop formed the

Paul Butterfield Blues Band, which not only played true Chicago blues but also racially integrated itself, enlisting bass player Jerome Arnold and drummer Sam Lay from Howlin' Wolf's band. In Chicago, the Butterfield Blues Band gained acceptance by many black blues musicians, mostly for its dedication to blues detail and its intense passion for both the music and its culture.

British interest in Chicago blues began after Muddy Waters performed in England in 1958 with his pianist Otis Spann, following the path blazed by Big Bill Broonzy earlier in the decade. Young British blues bands led by Alexis Korner, Cyril Davies, and John Mayall (which between them included such members as Mick Jagger, Brian Jones, Jeff Beck, Eric Clapton, Mick Fleetwood, and Jack Bruce) imitated the Chicago blues sound. When the Rolling Stones first came to America, the band's primary goal was to visit Chicago and record at the Chess studios at 2120 South Michigan Avenue, which it did. The Animals and the Yardbirds, like the Stones and Mayall's Bluesbreakers, believed Chicago to be the center of the electric blues universe — which it remained through the 1960s. Although Elmore James died in 1963, Sonny Boy Williamson in 1965, and Little Walter in 1968, Waters and Wolf continued to record and perform, playing as much outside Chicago as at home. By the late Sixties, however, a new generation of blues musicians began to share the spotlight.

SEVERAL NEARLY FORGOTTEN BLUESMEN WERE REDISCOVERED IN THE 1960S AND EMBRACED BY A NEW GENERATION OF FANS WHO SAW THEM PERFORM AT FOLK FESTIVALS. AMONG THEM WERE (ABOVE, FROM LEFT) THE REVEREND GARY DAVIS AND SON HOUSE, SKIP JAMES, AND MISSISSIPPI JOHN HURT. OPPOSITE: FROM CHICAGO, HOWLIN' WOLF BROUGHT HIS BAND — INCLUDING GUITARIST HUBERT SUMLIN AND BASSIST ANDREW "BLUEBLOOD" MCMAHON — TO NEWPORT IN 1966.

Guitarists Otis Rush, Buddy Guy, Magic Sam, and Freddie King; harp aces Junior Wells and James Cotton; and singer Koko Taylor, who took a Willie Dixon tune, "Wang Dang Doodle," and turned it into a bestseller, were new blues stars, although all stepped aside when Waters and Wolf were around.

Beyond Chicago, B.B. King played three hundred dates a year and scored a 1970 breakthrough hit with "The Thrill Is Gone," while Albert King (no relation to either Freddie or B.B.) hit pay dirt with "Born Under a Bad Sign." Blues broke into rock in a big way, too, with such acts as the Blues Project, the Stones, Cream, Fleetwood Mac, the Allman Brothers Band, Canned Heat, Big Brother and the Holding Company with Janis Joplin, Johnny Winter, Bonnie Raitt, and Led Zeppelin serving to introduce blues – even if it was at times diluted – to a new, mostly young white audience.

As rich and exciting as urban electric blues were in the Fifties and Sixties, the music in the next decade suddenly turned fallow and the audience fan base meager. Black blues audiences, except in Chicago, Memphis, and the South, had all but disappeared as younger listeners absorbed first soul, followed by funk, then disco, and finally hip-hop. Believing the blues to be caught in a time warp and not relevant to contemporary black culture, young

blacks respectfully turned their backs on the music, leaving white fans to support it. In the Seventies, however, even the white audience shrank, as blues-based rock ran its course and more progressive rock styles and, later, punk took its place. Although the British group Pink Floyd took its name from old bluesmen Pink Anderson and Floyd Council, its music, arty and adventurous, was a far cry from the true blues.

Many black blues artists survived the Seventies by performing in Europe and those American clubs where the blues somehow had managed to hang on. Chicago-based Alligator Records produced recordings of Hound Dog Taylor, Koko Taylor, and others, but it would not be until the mid-Eighties that urban electric blues would make a comeback. Although Chicago was still the spiritual home of the blues, with the exception of Buddy Guy, most leaders of this revival resided elsewhere. Robert Cray came from the Pacific Northwest; Albert Collins, though he recorded for Alligator, was from Texas, as was Stevie Ray Vaughan, the great white hope of the blues, who would die tragically in a 1990 helicopter crash, just as he was poised for superstardom. Vaughan's base was Austin, Texas, where his brother Jimmie's band, the Fabulous Thunderbirds, also lived and played clubs such as Antone's. By the late Eighties, the blues attention that Austin received almost equaled that of

Chicago, which had kept its blues legacy intact via the huge, free Chicago Blues Festival held each June and the city's relentless public relations charge that if it was blues you were after, Chicago was the place to find it.

Today blues fests and concerts around the country celebrate both rural and urban blues, as evidenced by the success of the latest generation of artists including Keb' Mo', Alvin Youngblood Hart, Corey Harris, Kenny Wayne Shepherd, Jonny Lang, Susan Tedeschi, and the North Mississippi All-Stars. They often share concert bills with longtime blues artists Buddy Guy, Taj Mahal, R.L. Burnside, Bonnie Raitt, John Lee Hooker, and B.B. King. These artists and others continue to draw thousands of fans to the music and its colorful history. Dozens of independent record labels release hundreds of blues recordings each year. The Memphis-based Blues Foundation supports "blues in the schools" programs, and institutions such as Cleveland's Rock and Roll Hall of Fame and Museum and Seattle's Experience Music Project regularly pay tribute to the blues as the great American roots form it is. The blues has also been commercialized like never before — you can hear it on beer commercials and in the restaurant/nightclub chain House of Blues.

Appropriately, the blues have crossed over into the Twenty-First Century, pulling in new fans, reconnecting with old ones, and celebrating a roots style that remains a vital part of the American music treasury.

LEFT, FROM TOP: BUDDY GUY, AT CHICAGO BLUES CLUB THERESA'S, 1971; JOHNNY WINTER, JAMES COTTON (CENTER), AND MUDDY WATERS IN THE LATE 1960S AFTER A RECORDING SESSION. OPPOSITE: ONE OF THE NEW GENERATION OF BLUESMEN, KEB' MO'.

B.B. KING: *I started to like blues when I was about six, seven years old. My mother's aunt bought records by people like Lonnie Johnson, Robert Johnson, Blind Lemon Jefferson, a few others. Some of them I liked — Lonnie Johnson was one, Blind Lemon was two. It was something about [the fact that] nobody else played that kinda music. All you heard was country music at the time. I liked some of it, but I didn't like it as well as I liked hearing Blind Lemon and Sonny Boy Williamson.*

When I was a teenager and used to sit on the street corners in Indianola [Mississippi] playing, I'd have my hat out there. People that would request a gospel song would always praise me highly when I finished the song, pat me on the head or shoulders and say, "Go ahead, son, that's great. You gonna be great one day." But they never put nothing in the hat. People that would ask me to do a blues song would always put something in the hat. And that's what started me to be a blues singer in the first place.

When I left Mississippi, the first thing I did was go over to West Memphis. Sonny Boy Williamson was at a station [there], so that's where I went to try to get, shall we say, into this business. I got there and I asked him if he would let me go on his program. Sonny Boy was a great big, tall guy, and he looked down at me and says, "What can you do?" And I'm half scared to death. So I said, "I can sing, and I can play." "Let me hear you," he said, and I [played]. He liked it, so he put me on.

Sonny Boy had a place in West Memphis that he played where [the owner] got a little part of [the money made off the cover charge], but [he] got most of it. But this particular day, he had another offer where he had a guarantee of maybe $150 or $200. So he asked the lady who worked at the first place, did she hear me that day? She said yes. He said, "Well, I'm gonna send this boy to work in this place." He hadn't asked me anything, but when I looked up at him, I said, "Yeah, I'll go." And that's how it started off.

When I sing the blues today, I still get some of the spiritual feeling; it's a thin line between blues and gospel, in my opinion, and the roots of all music that I hear, especially in the Western world, seem to fit into the music that I play. So if I border the line of rock, or soul, country, or any other kind of music, I can incorporate it into the blues because there's a place there.

{ OPPOSITE: B.B. KING, 1969. THIS PAGE, FROM TOP: KING AT THE TRIANON BALLROOM, IN CHICAGO, 1963; THE AMBASSADOR OF THE BLUES WAILING ON HIS GUITAR, LUCILLE, IN 1998.

JAMES COTTON: *We came out of the field [one day] for to eat lunch, and I went in my sister's room, playin' around with the radio. And I heard Rice [Sonny Boy Williamson] when he came on the air [on King Biscuit Time]. And I said, "What the world is that? What this come on this radio?"*

My uncle hooked me up with Sonny Boy. He take me to Sonny Boy to tell Sonny Boy that I didn't have no people. And I caught Sonny Boy's eye when I played the [harmonica] for him — he looked at this little kid, and I played it just like him. [And Sonny Boy] said, "Ah, I'll take him."

[I] stayed with him six years. In the end I wanted to be just like Sonny Boy. I watched every move he make, every word he said — if he play it tonight, I play it tomorrow.

Must have been 1949 or '50. Was playin' at a place called the Bebop Hall in West Memphis, Arkansas. Sonny Boy walked up to me just before closin' time with a half a pint. And he put his finger in the bottle, turned it, drink it, notched his finger and hand it to me and said, "Now you drink to us." I looked at him, and he said, "You got the band, son. I'm gone."

And he called [the band]. Said, "This is your bandleader for now on," said, "I'm gone, I'm goin'." He went to Milwaukee. I stayed here with a band, which broke up in a couple of months by me being young and

crazy and all the older peoples was in the band knowed better than what I was doin'. So they each went their own way.

[In 1954] I was over in West Memphis. Muddy Waters had been down through south Georgia, Florida, wherever, and had [harmonica player] Junior Wells with him. Some kinda way Junior quit the band, and then they heard I was in West Memphis somewhere, so they came over there lookin' for me. I had another job — I was drivin' a truck. And when I walked through the door, somebody pointed me out to 'em. Muddy walked up to me and said, "Hello, my name Muddy Waters." I yelled, "And my name's Jesus Christ!" 'cause I didn't believe him. And he, you know, he said, "I come to give you a job." And me and him talked — I still didn't believe him. And he said, "I'm playin' at 500 Beale Street tomorrow night at the Hippodrome." Said, "Be there at eight o'clock."

So then I showed up, and Jimmy Rogers and Otis Spann was in his band. Jimmy Rogers showed me where to put my amplifier, and we went up, played two songs. The minute Muddy opened his mouth, I know it was him. And I said, "Well, this is it." So I went to Chicago with him and stayed there twelve years.

ABOVE: JAMES COTTON AT JIMMY'S BBQ IN CHICAGO, 1993. OPPOSITE: COTTON IN 1963, THREE YEARS BEFORE HE LEFT MUDDY WATERS'S BAND TO START HIS OWN GROUP.

KOKO TAYLOR: *I left Memphis on a Greyhound bus with fifteen cents in my pocket and a box of Ritz crackers. When that bus got to Sixty-third and Cottage Grove in Chicago, I looked up and saw all of those bright lights. I had never saw that many lights before in my life. And I said, "Good God, this must be heaven." I heard people talking about, "Yeah, you know the old Howlin' Wolf, he's singing down there at the Blue Dog, Muddy Waters's place." And I found out where all them was, and on the weekend when I wasn't working, I would go to these different places. Howlin' Wolf and them, they heard that I wanted to sing. They'd say, "We got little Koko in the house tonight. We going to get her up here and let her do one for us." That's how I got my enjoyment on the weekends, just going out listening to the blues. I was sitting in one night with Howlin' Wolf and when I finished singing, he came down with this big*

man. He said, "You know, I like that voice you got. That's the kind of voice that the world needs today. We got plenty mens out here singing the blues but not enough women. Are you under contract?" I said, "Contract?" It scared me because I always heard down south when somebody got a contract on you they want to kill you. He said, "Well, I'd like to take you down to Chess Records, because I believe that they would like what they hear in your voice, the same as I did." And he took me down to Chess Records, where I auditioned, and

Leonard Chess said, "Yeah, this is who we've been looking for."

Willie Dixon called me up [at] twelve o'clock one night, [while] I'm in bed: "Koko, come down here. I just wrote this song called 'Wang Dang Doodle,' and we want to rehearsal on it while it's fresh in my mind." I said, " 'Wang Dang Doodle'! Why we got to rehearsal on it tonight? What's so important about it we can't do it tomorrow?" He said, "Koko, we got to pick the chicken while the water is hot."

OPPOSITE: KOKO TAYLOR, LIVE IN CHICAGO, 2000. BELOW: TAYLOR BELTS THE BLUES IN LONDON IN 1967.

1929 Les Paul invents one of the first electric guitars when he puts the needle from his record player into the wood of his acoustic guitar. When sound erupts from the phonograph, the amplification needed for rock & roll is born. 1949 The 45 rpm single is introduced by RCA. 1950 Sam Phillips opens Memphis Recording Service at 706 Union Avenue in Memphis. 1951 "Rocket '88' " by Jackie Brenston, featuring Ike Turner's Kings of Rhythm, is cut at Phillips's studio. Arguably the first rock & roll recording, it hits Number One on the R&B chart. 1952 A riot breaks out at Alan Freed's Moondog Coronation Ball in Cleveland and the rock & roll frenzy officially begins. Bob Horn's 'Bandstand' (which will later become 'American Bandstand') is broadcast for the first time from Philadelphia. Sam Phillips debuts his label, Sun Records. 1953 "Crazy Man Crazy" by Bill Haley is the first rock & roll hit by a white artist. 1954 Alan Freed's radio show, Moondog's Rock & Roll Party, moves to WINS in New York City and becomes the city's Number One radio show. Sam Phillips signs Elvis Presley and releases his first single "That's All Right" a song written by Arthur "Big Boy" Crudup; the flip side, "Blue Moon of Kentucky," is a bluegrass number written by Bill Monroe. 1955 "Rock Around the Clock" by Bill Haley and His Comets is the first rock & roll song to reach Number One. It stays there for eight weeks. Chuck Berry debuts on the pop chart. 1956 Little Richard reaches the Top Forty with "Tutti Frutti." Elvis explodes onto the scene: "Heartbreak Hotel" stays at Number One for eight weeks; the double hit "Don't Be Cruel"/"Hound Dog" — at the time the biggest hit in music history — stays at Number One for eleven weeks. Fellow Sun artist Carl Perkins's first hit, "Blue Suede Shoes," comes out the same year, losing the top spot to Elvis. Chuck Berry's "Roll Over Beethoven" is also popular and tells of the new focus on rock & roll. 1957 ABC airs the first episode of 'American Bandstand' with Dick Clark as host. The first song played is Jerry Lee Lewis's "Whole Lot of Shakin' Going On." Buddy Holly enters the spotlight when "That'll Be the Day" reaches Number One. 1958 Elvis is drafted into the Army. 'Billboard' debuts its Hot 100 singles chart. 1959 Bo Diddley debuts on the pop chart. Buddy Holly, Ritchie Valens, and J.P. Richardson (a.k.a. the Big Bopper) are killed in a plane crash during their tour. Fifty percent of all chart hits are somehow related to rock. 1963 The Philips Company introduces the compact audio cassette. 1964 The Beatles appear on 'The Ed Sullivan Show,' launching the British Invasion. From January to March, the Beatles are responsible for 60 percent of all record sales; by the end of the year they will have scored nineteen Top Forty hits. The two-year-old Rolling Stones record at Chess studios; Muddy Waters,

Buddy Guy, and Chuck Berry drop in for a visit. The Top Ten pop charts reflect the lowest number of records by black artists since 1950.

1965 Backed by the Paul Butterfield Blues Band, Bob Dylan performs an electric "Maggie's Farm" at the Newport Folk Festival. The Byrds record Dylan's "Mr. Tambourine Man," resulting in a Number One hit. **1966** Bob Dylan and the Band record their frequent jams in the basement of the Band's "Big Pink" house in Woodstock, New York; the sessions will become an LP, 'The Basement Tapes.' British guitarist Eric Clapton works on 'Bluesbreakers' during his brief stint with John Mayall's band; it will be his final all-blues album until his 1994 solo release 'From the Cradle.' **1967** The Monterey Pop Festival, featuring the Mamas and the Papas, Janis Joplin, Jimi Hendrix, and the Who, gives birth to the open-air rock festival. **1968** Country and roots influences infuse a number of hit albums: the Byrds' 'Sweetheart of the Rodeo,' Bob Dylan's 'John Wesley Harding,' and the Band's 'Music From Big Pink.' The Grateful Dead's 'Workingman's Dead' (1970) and Neil Young's 'Harvest' (1972) will continue in this tradition. **1969** The original Woodstock Festival is held, attracting nearly half a million rock enthusiasts. "Proud Mary" becomes Creedence Clearwater Revival's first Top Ten smash. The song will become a hit for Ike and Tina Turner in 1971. Robert Plant, the singer in the British hard-rock band Led Zeppelin, quotes Blind Lemon Jefferson and Robert Johnson in the bluesy, proto-metal anthem "Whole Lotta Love." **1973** The movie 'American Graffiti' launches a nostalgic craze for 1950s music and style. Bruce Springsteen's first album, 'Greetings From Asbury Park, NJ,' is released. **1976** First in America, then in England, punk rockers call for a return to rock's rudimentary roots. **1982** The Stray Cats release their first American album, 'Built for Speed,' starting the rockabilly revival. **1985** Bob Dylan, Willie Nelson, B.B. King, and many others perform at the first Farm Aid Concert, bringing rock, country, and blues together to benefit America's farmers. **1995** In the tradition of 1982's 'Nebraska' — a collection of folk-rock demos produced entirely in the singer's home — Bruce Springsteen invokes the spirit of Woody Guthrie for 'The Ghost of Tom Joad,' a folk-inspired album dedicated to the plight of the American workingman.

ROOTS MUSIC BEGATS ROCK & ROLL BY DAVID McGEE

In the America of 1954, with the pace of life quickening in step with the nation's heady postwar optimism and growing affluence, a template was being forged that not only would affect the immediate future, but would continue to resonate even today. The template's pattern was defined by roiling forces at loose in the land that would ignite and explode two years later, in 1956, in a thunderous blast that signaled in its intensity a symbolic breaking free from an unsettling past in which the national psyche had been upended by two world wars, a "conflict" in Korea, and the Great Depression. It was born in the midst of sweeping cultural, scientific, and technological change embracing a wide scope of developments: the Rust brothers' invention of a mechanical cotton picker; Dr. Jonas Salk's development of a vaccine aimed at wiping out the crippling disease of polio; the introduction into everyday life of a cathode-ray-based box that beamed into homes live and filmed entertainment and news from all over the world. What had happened to that point was, in retrospect, mind-boggling. In 1954 Dr. Martin Luther King Jr. accepted the pastorship at Dexter Avenue Baptist Church, in Montgomery, Alabama, the pulpit from which he would lead the civil rights movement into the modern era. The United States Supreme Court outlawed school segregation in *Brown* v. *Board of Education of Topeka.* Following the defeat of French forces in Indochina, which had been renamed Vietnam and partitioned into North and South, U.S. Secretary of State John Foster Dulles promised the government in the South that America would not abandon it to the Communist forces occupying the northern part of the tiny Southeast Asian nation.

> "When I was a disc jockey some time ago on WDIA, there were white college kids that always wanted to come on my show at night. I came on at midnight and they'd come in with me and sit down till three, sometimes six in the morning when the other disc jockey came. Their parents still did not want them to listen to the blues, so they learned it on their own."
>
> —Rufus Thomas

From a musical standpoint, Memphis, Tennessee, circa 1954, was the locus of events that would later alter the world as surely as those in the

{ Opposite: Entertainer and DJ Rufus Thomas at Memphis radio station WDIA, 1965

political, scientific, and technological arenas. The Bluff City had long been the destination for black artists migrating northward from Mississippi to test their music on the tough, savvy audiences that filled clubs on the city's Beale Street ("the Main Street of Black America," so called owing to its preponderance of black-owned businesses catering largely to the black population). But Memphis was a melting pot for renegade musicians black and white, harboring within its boundaries country artists, pop artists, and a whole breed of left-field musicians (later described by a local journalist as having ridden into town on "the midnight train from nowhere"), whose propulsive, rhythm-rich approach, replete with whimsical lyrics, bridged stylistic categories without ever falling clearly into one or another. All of it, the whole intoxicating brew, could be heard twenty-four hours a day on radio station WDIA, the "Mother Station of the Negroes," which employed an all-black disc jockey team, two of whom were also making their marks as blues artists: B.B. King, who spiced his Sepia Swing Club and Heebie Jeebies shows with live, on-air performances, and Rufus Thomas, a veteran entertainer in his early thirties who had entered show business right out of high school as a member of the Rabbit Foot Minstrels and had honed his singing and dancing on the southern circuit, playing minstrel and amateur shows whenever and wherever anyone would pitch a tent.

As a disc jockey, Thomas was a most egalitarian personality, his playlist knowing no limits with regard to style or color. "I played it all on my show," he told writer Peter Guralnick. "Every type of music. . . . Frankie Laine, Vaughn Monroe, Nat 'King' Cole. My family and I were raised on the Grand Ole Opry. Every Saturday night we'd run home to catch the Opry on the radio."

In pursuing careers as musical artists when they weren't being disc jockeys, both King and Thomas crossed paths with an enterprising entrepreneur named Sam Phillips, who, in 1950, had opened a recording studio in town after relocating from his native Florence, Alabama, where he had been a radio engineer. In the same way that Thomas embraced music according to quality, not color, so did Phillips have a hunch that the major labels were dead wrong in segregating the music of black artists into the category of "race" records. "I knew there were city markets to be reached, and I knew that whites listened to blues surreptitiously," he told writers Colin Escott and Martin Hawkins.

So Phillips hung out his shingle, so to speak, at his new facility, the Memphis Recording Service, at 706 Union Avenue, only a couple of miles east of the WDIA studio: "We Record Anything-Anywhere-Anytime" was the studio's motto. Following a failed label venture, Phillips hit upon the idea of recording the wealth of blues artists in the area and then leasing the masters to other labels. Signed to the West Coast–based RPM label in 1950, B.B. King cut his early, dynamic sides at Phillips's studio. In 1951, on the strength of King's recommendation, Phillips recorded a powerhouse combo known as the Kings of Rhythm, led by a prodigiously talented multi-instrumentalist, songwriter, arranger, and vocalist from Mississippi named Ike Turner. One of the Kings of Rhythm sessions produced a landmark recording, "Rocket '88,' " a supercharged paean to the sleek, powerful Oldsmobile of the same name, sung with fierce conviction by Turner's cousin Jackie Brenston. "Rocket '88' " topped the R&B chart, and years later was referred to by Phillips as the first rock & roll recording. Over the next three years, Phillips would cut and lease out memorable sessions with blues moaner Howlin' Wolf; with Little Junior Parker, he of the rough-edged voice that could sell a blues lament like no one else's; with harmonica virtuoso James Cotton; and with the rocking one-man band Joe Hill Louis.

In 1952, Phillips formed a new label, Sun; a year later, his first releases produced a couple of R&B hits, the first in the form of Rufus Thomas's "Bear Cat," an answer record to a rowdy blues called "Hound Dog" cut almost at the same time for another label by Big Mama Thornton; and "Feelin' Good," by Little Junior Parker. Phillips also had in his stable a lively country & western band, Doug Poindexter and the Starlite Wranglers, which featured an inventive guitarist named Scotty Moore and a rambunctious bass slapper named Bill Black.

Come 1954, a nineteen-year-old truck driver for Crown Electric, Elvis Presley, walks into Sun studios with

"ELVIS PRESLEY APOLOGIZED TO ME FOR DOING 'BLUE MOON OF KENTUCKY.' IT WAS THE FIRST SONG HE RECORDED. AND I TOLD HIM, 'IF IT HELPED YOU GET YOUR MUSIC STARTED AND EVERYTHING, I'M FOR YOU 100 PERCENT. GO RIGHT AHEAD AND SING "BLUE MOON OF KENTUCKY." ' "
—BILL MONROE

"LITTLE RICHARD, FATS DOMINO, ALL OF THESE PEOPLE WERE THE FOUNDERS OF ROCK & ROLL. LITTLE RICHARD WAS THE KING OF ROCK & ROLL, NO DOUBT ABOUT IT. BUT THEY DIDN'T GIVE IT TO HIM: [THEY MADE] ELVIS PRESLEY THE KING OF ROCK & ROLL. WHY DOES IT HAVE TO BE WHITE TO BE RIGHT?" —RUFUS THOMAS

designs on cutting a single as a birthday present for his mother. The Tupelo, Mississippi, native came into Sun having absorbed just about everything American music had to offer up to that point: In a rare moment of braggadocio, he said he thought he knew almost every gospel song ever written and often convinced his fellow musicians of the same during casual interludes around the piano; he was enthralled by the blues, traditional country, bluegrass, and classic pop music. Phillips teamed Presley with Scotty Moore and Bill Black – another Phillips hunch that worked out pretty well – and the trio produced a single that reflected both the catholic nature of Presley's taste and the boldness that informed Phillips's vision. One side featured a rousing version of blues artist Arthur "Big Boy" Crudup's "That's All Right," the other a lively uptempo reading of "Blue Moon of Kentucky," a song written and originally recorded as a melancholy bluegrass ballad by Bill Monroe.

That same year, Phillips also had a hunch about a raw-boned cotton picker from Tiptonville, Tennessee, Carl Perkins, and signed him, too. He would come to have hunches about Johnny Cash, who had deep roots in folk music and desired to cut gospel songs; about Jerry Lee Lewis, whose extraordinary artistry – whether he was recording stone country, gospel, blues, or this new uptempo music – was matched by an ego as large as his native land.

What all these artists had in common was a reverence for the music that had shaped their own. Perkins's uptempo style, for example, was an amalgam of honky-tonk, blues, and rhythm & blues, with a gospel underpinning. His musical frame of reference spanned from Jimmie Rodgers to Hank Williams, with verbal exhortations to his band inspired by the theatrics of Bob Wills. His guitar playing was more difficult to pin down, and because it came from so many sources it seemed the most wholly original of all the architects of rock & roll guitar. Perkins himself would point to Ernest Tubb's guitarist, Billy Byrd, as someone he admired. It's likely that some of his double-string runs sprang from T-Bone Walker and some of his single-string solos from Lonnie Johnson. As a songwriter, Perkins had absorbed the *curriculum vitae* of country music: the Carter Family, Roy Acuff, Bob Wills, Ernest Tubb, and especially Hank Williams. Along with Presley's early Sun singles, Perkins's regional hits had been identified as "rockabilly" music – a name whose origin is in dispute to this day. Some credit Johnny and Dorsey Burnette of Memphis's wild-eyed Rock 'n' Roll Trio, who supposedly coined it in homage to their sons Rocky and Billy Burnette; others who have studied the word's etymology ascribe its coinage to still-

"THAT WHOLE [ROCKA-BILLY] SOUND STOOD FOR ALL THE DEGREES OF FREEDOM. IT WOULD JUST JUMP RIGHT OFF THAT TURNTABLE; LIVE, IT WOULD CREATE SUCH A THUMP IN YOUR BELLY. EVERYTHING – THE VOCABULARY OF THE LYRICS AND THE SOUND OF THE INSTRUMENTS. IT WAS ALMOST LIKE ANOTHER PARTY IN THE ROOM. WE WANTED TO GO WHERE THAT WAS HAPPENING." —BOB DYLAN

unidentified southern disc jockeys anxious to find a new label for the day's new sounds.

Whereas Perkins brought all types of rhythmic influences to his style of rockabilly, Presley spiced his version with pop music. He was deeply enamored of Dean Martin, to Phillips's consternation, but he was also indebted to the aching, falsetto flights of the Ink Spots' lead singer, Bill Kenny. The style of rockabilly Presley constructed in the studio with Moore and Black was more ornate than what Perkins would surface with in 1954. Playing a semi-hollow-bodied Gibson electric guitar, the versatile Moore fashioned robust, intricate solo runs in stark contrast to the steely, angular lines and double- and triple-string flourishes Perkins favored on his Gibson Les Paul. Moore's rather baroque approach was the ideal complement to a vocalist like Presley, who could call upon countless stylistic techniques to get a song over.

The South was rife with artists (including a young George Jones) advancing various forms of the music called rockabilly, but Presley and Perkins were the exemplars of the new style – the two artists whose recordings evinced the highest standards of writing, playing, and singing. For two years they were labelmates at Sun, sitting in on each other's recording sessions and touring the southern circuit together. But in 1955, desperate for cash to prop up his failing label, Phillips sold Presley's contract to RCA for $35,000. Traveling apart now – Presley in Nashville, Perkins in Memphis – the two lit the rock & roll fuse in January of 1956, Presley with his first RCA single, "Heartbreak Hotel," Perkins with his fourth Sun single, "Blue Suede Shoes." The two recordings vied with each other for the top spot on the national chart, with Presley's eventually prevailing. Perkins's, meanwhile, became not merely a song, but a treatise that codified certain attitudes and a sense of style developing among America's youth, especially its teenagers. "Blue Suede Shoes" quickly became a musical landmark; Elvis Presley soon grew into the living embodiment of America's postwar brio and cultural upheaval, a hip-swiveling, greasy-haired, sideburn-sporting, white-bucks-shod avatar of a new sensibility among young people, who for the first time in this country's history had the disposable income and their own music with which to advance their agenda of personal freedom and individual expression.

OPPOSITE, FROM TOP: RICHARD PENNIMAN, A.K.A. LITTLE RICHARD (AT PIANO), CONSIDERED BY MANY TO BE THE GREATEST SHOWMAN OF ROCK & ROLL; RECORD SALES BOOMED IN THE 1950S AS TEENAGERS BEGAN SPENDING THEIR CASH ON RECORDINGS BY EXCITING NEW ARTISTS.

In one fell swoop, rock & roll barged in on the entire country, attacking a stodgy popular culture from all sides – the South, the North, the East, and the West. Following Presley's and Perkins's breakthroughs came a host of other inspired artists, whose new music was built on the solid foundation of Twentieth-Century American roots music. This was the culmination of virtually every innovation in every field of roots music in the century: traditional country, exemplified by the haunting, harmonized Appalachian-style folk ballads of the Carter Family and the country-blues fusions of Jimmie Rodgers; the various strains of Mississippi Delta blues, all marked by complex, percussive guitar stylings and lyrics that often spoke to the dark side of the human condition as experienced by black artists growing up in a system of entrenched, institutionalized racism; hard-charging, high-lonesome, technically demanding bluegrass, as developed by Bill Monroe; Western swing, refined by Bob Wills from the scintillating blend of musics he had grown up with in Texas; honky-tonk, traditional country's raw-boned offspring; boogie-woogie, as perfected in Kansas City in the 1930s, foremost by Big Joe Turner and his gale force of a piano player, Pete Johnson; the electric blues of Muddy Waters and Howlin' Wolf; Louis Jordan's jump blues; the populist, socially conscious folk balladry of Woody Guthrie; gospel, whether it was found in the shape-note, heartfelt confessions of Roy Acuff or the ethereal harmonies and sanctified testifying of black groups such as the Soul Stirrers. Even classic pop from the great songwriters of the Thirties and Forties found its way into this volatile mix. It came from New Orleans. It came from Georgia. It came from Mississippi by way of Chicago. It was rooted in the past, but spoke to the future.

"IT BOTHERED ME THAT PEOPLE WAS COVERING MY MATERIAL. I DIDN'T LIKE IT, SEE? I THOUGHT MAYBE THEY SHOULD WRITE THEIR OWN. BUT I LEARNED DIFFERENT, THAT IT WAS VERY GOOD TO HAVE SOMEBODY THINK ENOUGH OF YOUR STUFF TO DO IT. WHEN I UNDERSTOOD THAT, IT WAS A GOOD FEELING. IT LET ME KNOW THAT I HAD SOMETHING SPECIAL."
—BO DIDDLEY

FROM TOP: BORN IN MISSISSIPPI, BO DIDDLEY HELPED INVENT ROCK & ROLL IN CHICAGO; LLOYD PRICE (RIGHT) WITH HIS FATHER, 1953; NEW ORLEANS PIANO MAN FATS DOMINO, ONE OF EARLY ROCK & ROLL'S BIGGEST STARS. OPPOSITE: CHUCK BERRY, PERFECTING HIS FAMOUS DUCK WALK.

When Presley and Perkins broke into the mainstream in 1956, a number of independent labels were particularly well prepared to take advantage of the explosion in new music sweeping the land. Leaving the dwindling white, adult pop market to the majors, they rushed in with the artists the kids could relate to and the sounds the kids were jumping for. Los Angeles was home to Art Rupe's Specialty label, founded in 1946 and specializing in black popular music. In the late Forties and early Fifties, Rupe signed and developed an amazing roster of artists whose styles were equally influenced by gospel, blues, and rhythm & blues. Chief among these were Guitar Slim, a brilliant guitarist and singer/songwriter whose towering single, "The Things That I Used to Do," spent fourteen weeks atop the R&B chart in 1954 and featured a young Ray Charles on piano; Percy Mayfield, "the Poet of the Blues," whose smooth-voiced, romantic crooning and intelligent, topical original songs set him apart from the moon-June-spoon balladeers on the pop charts; Roy Milton, a swing drummer directing a powerhouse combo whose nineteen Top Ten R&B singles, beginning with 1946's "R.M. Blues," sounded suspiciously like what would later be called rock & roll; and, not least of all, Sam Cooke, the charismatic lead singer of the Soul Stirrers, who would go on to sanctify popular music as one of soul's founding fathers.

Early on, Rupe recognized New Orleans as an unmined mother lode of talented black artists looking for a break. On a talent-scouting trip there in 1952, he signed vocalist Lloyd Price, whose original song "Lawdy Miss Clawdy" wound up topping the R&B chart and became a rock & roll standard after being covered by Elvis Presley.

By far, Rupe's most commercially significant signing came not from New Orleans but from Macon, Georgia — although New Orleans would be his launching pad to international stardom. Richard Penniman had been recording blues ballads and novelty jump blues for various labels since 1951, without success, when he sent an audition tape to Rupe in 1955. Impressed, Rupe sent his A&R man "Bumps" Blackwell to New Orleans to record Penniman with a crack band that included drummer Earl Palmer and tenor saxophonist Lee Allen. Between September 1955 and October 1957, Penniman — now called Little Richard — blazed across the firmament, his gospel whoops and jet-fueled R&B exploding into one glorious rock & roll moment that left behind monuments: "Tutti Frutti," "Long Tall Sally," "Rip It Up," "Ready Teddy," "Lucille," "Jenny, Jenny," "Keep a Knockin'," and "Good Golly, Miss Molly."

Imperial Records had been founded in 1947 in Los Angeles by former semipro baseball player Lew Chudd, but its heart, and its best prospect for solvency, lay in New Orleans. There, under the aegis of a brilliant bandleader, musician, arranger, songwriter, and producer named Dave Bartholomew (whom Chudd had hired as his talent scout), five-foot-five, 220-pound local artist Antoine Domino had been seeing his Imperial singles land in the upper reaches of the R&B chart since his first hit in 1950, "The Fat Man." Fats Domino, as he was called, was first and foremost inspired by the jump blues of Louis Jordan, but his expressive piano playing betrayed the influence of Crescent City legends such as Professor Longhair and Champion Jack Dupree; his muscular vocal style was clearly beholden to big-voiced shouters such as Big Joe Turner and Roy Brown. Together, Domino and Bartholomew concocted an intoxicating gumbo that blended the ebullient spirit of the Mardi Gras with R&B propulsion in establishing New Orleans as home to a style of rock & roll as exciting, as fertile, as rich in historical resonance as the one coming out of Memphis. Bartholomew would be the architect of the best New Orleans recordings of the Fifties, and the band he assembled to back Domino and other artists on the Imperial label comprised musicians who ranked among the finest of their day in any genre: Palmer, wailing tenor saxophonist Herb Hardesty, guitarist Ernest McLean, and Bartholomew him-

"GROWING UP IN DYESS, ARKANSAS, I WAS ONLY A FEW MILES FROM THE MISSISSIPPI. THE RADIO SHOWS I LISTENED TO AS A BOY PLAYED WHAT THEY CALLED RACE MUSIC. I LISTENED TO BLACK GOSPEL AND WHAT THEY CALLED HILLBILLY AS WELL, WHICH BECAME MY FORTE. I NEVER DID TRY TO GET [MY MUSIC] HEARD IN NASHVILLE. I WAS DETERMINED THAT I WAS GOING TO RECORD IN MEMPHIS. I LIKED THE WAY THE MUSIC WAS COMING OUT OF THAT TOWN, THE FEEL AND THE SOUND." —JOHNNY CASH

self on trumpet. For ten years — from 1952 through 1962 — Domino was a regular on the pop charts, usually making the Top Twenty, and when his run ended, he had left behind a batch of songs that defined New Orleans–style rock & roll: "Blueberry Hill," "I'm Walkin'," "Valley of Tears," and "Whole Lotta Loving," to touch on a handful of gems.

Even before Presley burst into the mainstream, Chuck Berry had served notice that he was an artist to be reckoned with, a singer, songwriter, and instrumentalist of rare prowess, with deep roots in blues, R&B, and traditional country. A St. Louis, Missouri, native, he had come to Chess Records in Chicago with his redoubtable piano-playing partner, Johnnie Johnson; with an endorsement from Muddy Waters, Berry was signed by Phil and Leonard Chess. In 1955, he hit the pop Top Ten with a fanciful original rocker titled "Maybellene." The song was modeled on "Ida Red," an old country fiddle tune that had been oft-recorded over the years (by Bill Monroe and others) since surfacing in 1927 on a Tweedy Brothers 78 rpm disc. Berry's distorted, searing guitar sound harkened not only to the electric flourishes pioneered by T-Bone Walker, but also to honky-tonk styles. A gifted storyteller and acute observer of the developing youth culture, Berry emphasized these attributes in songs that spoke to issues close to the hearts of the new teen audience: fast cars, mating rituals, school day drudgery, and so forth. His body of work includes an entire subgenre that might best be identified as folk music for teens: "School Day," "Johnny B. Goode," "Sweet Little Sixteen," "Almost Grown, "No Particular Place to Go" — songs limning a world with its own language, symbols, and customs, built on musical styles from the past reconstituted for and reflecting a world in transition.

One of Berry's labelmates, Bo Diddley, dug deep into his heritage for inspiration and, in turn, continues to exert an influence on would-be rock guitar gods. His stage name (he was born Ellas Bates), for one, when reversed denotes a primitive, guitar-like,

OPPOSITE: LOUISIANA NATIVE JERRY LEE LEWIS WAS KNOWN FOR HIS WILD ANTICS ONSTAGE. ABOVE: JOHNNY CASH CROSSED ALL MUSICAL BOUNDARIES WITH HIS MUSIC, BEGINNING IN THE 1950S.

{ ABOVE: STARTING OFF SINGING GOSPEL, JAMES BROWN HELPED
TO CREATE THE EMOTION-DRENCHED R&B CALLED SOUL, AND
LATER PIONEERED FUNK. OPPOSITE: BROTHERS PHIL (LEFT) AND
DON EVERLY BROUGHT LOVELY HARMONIES TO ROCK & ROLL.

African-American, one-stringed instrument, the diddley bow. His signature shave-and-a-haircut-six-bits rhythm has been traced back to the African-Cuban clave pattern. To his unassailable beat he added elements of gospel and blues, a sure feel for black street culture, and an engaging way with self-aggrandizing lyrics to create as singular and complex a style of rock & roll as played by any artist to set foot on a stage or in a recording studio.

The same year that saw "Heartbreak Hotel" and "Blue Suede Shoes" also saw the debut of another Sun artist of stature, Johnny Cash, whose first single, the foreboding "I Walk the Line," reached the pop chart's Top Twenty. Born into a sharecropping family in Arkansas, Cash wandered into Phillips's studio in 1955, shortly after completing a stint in the air force. While he had absorbed the same country, blues, and gospel influences that defined Presley and Perkins, Cash also had embraced folk music in a significant way. He reveled in tall tales and mythology of a distinctly American bent and immersed himself in the romance of the steel rail. His first Sun album would include such original compositions as "Folsom Prison Blues," an early, acerbic salvo expressing his view of prisons as dehumanizing facilities. At Columbia, Cash would realize the muted ambitions of his Sun years. Ever conscious of history, he championed the work of promising young songwriters with whom he found common ground, and in this way introduced to the country audience the music of Bob Dylan, Kris Kristofferson, and Bruce Springsteen — like Cash, each a descendant of Woody Guthrie. It was his own way of answering the question posed by the family he married into, the Carters: Will the circle be unbroken?

Although the full scope of Jerry Lee Lewis's artistry during his Sun tenure would not be fully evident until the extensive release in the Seventies and Eighties of tracks stored in the studio's vault, the musical palette of Ferriday, Louisiana's homegrown wild man was as broad as his labelmates'. His three white-hot hit singles — 1957's "Whole Lot of Shakin' Going On" and "Great Balls of Fire" and 1958's "Breathless" — were full-frontal rock & roll assaults that benefited from the honky-tonk machismo apparent in Lewis's vocal approach but otherwise betrayed little debt to what had come before them, so seamlessly had the Killer, as he was known, melded his influences into something fresh. The recordings were, sui generis, rock & roll, the call of a new day.

A more telling moment for the Sun legends came on December 4, 1956, when a Perkins recording session, with Lewis sitting in on piano, was interrupted by a surprise visit from Presley, recently returned from his first, disastrous performances in Las Vegas. Cash, too, was hanging around, killing time before he had to pick up his wife from work. Elvis sat down at the piano, and in short order they were into a community sing. Cash had to bow out after singing two songs with the group, but during the next hour-plus the remaining three essentially toured their roots in songs that reflected their mutual immersion in the spiritual life and were reflective of their rural upbringing and values. Gospel figured most heavily in the repertoire that day, from "I Shall Not Be Moved," "Down by the Riverside," "As We Travel Along on the Jericho Road," to Thomas A. Dorsey's classic "Peace in the Valley." When Jerry Lee took over the piano, he made his own statement in a series of songs that included not only his first Sun single, "Crazy Arms," but also a taste of Jelly Roll Morton's "Black Bottom Stomp" and Gene Autry's "You're the Only Star in My Blue Heaven." It was, all in all, a short course in the roots of rock & roll by four young men — dubbed "the Million Dollar Quartet" by a local newspaper writer — whose work in the Sun studio had done much to transform the roots music of their youths into a new genre.

It would seem that the Million Dollar Quartet had the waterfront covered when it came to building new music on a foundation of American roots music. But there was one area that none of them, not even Cash with his folk leanings, addressed. The most direct link to Appalachian folk music, from which had sprung traditional country and bluegrass, was Kentucky's Don and Phil Everly, sons of successful folk and country artists (their father, Ike Everly, was especially well regarded as a guitarist). When they were signed as songwriters by Roy Acuff's music publishing company in 1955, they were still in their teens. But they had grown up in the business, having been regulars on their family's radio show, and were remarkably self-assured performers for their age. Signed to a recording contract by Cadence Records in 1957, the brothers broke out with a Number Two single, "Bye Bye Love," written by the Nashville husband-wife team of Felice and Boudleaux Bryant, who wrote epics of teen misery. Over the next five years, the Everlys landed twenty-three singles in the Top Thirty, including four chart-toppers. They began clicking with their own songs in 1959, when Don's "('Til) I Kissed You" peaked at Number Four, followed in 1960 by Phil's "When Will I Be Loved," which reached Number Eight. Unlike the other rock & rollers of their day, the Everlys built their sound around their twin acoustic guitars, often tuned to an exotic open G, and their high, keening bluegrass-style harmonies. When fused to a rockabilly-derived rhythm, their plaintive harmonizing and acoustic-based sound was yet another rock & roll subgenre that leaned on the past in pointing the way to the future. The Everlys were the first to find mainstream success with a form of pop rockabilly, but others, such as Buddy Holly, Ritchie Valens, and Eddie Cochran, would follow and take the music that had come out of the Sun studio in 1954 in new directions.

Pop made an incursion into rock & roll in the early Sixties, and though the roots musics that had informed its earliest styles began to diminish in influence, they never completely disappeared. Gospel, for one, continued to exert a powerful influence, especially among the popular black artists whose audiences were as much white as they were black. Sam Cooke had left Specialty to form his own label and was laying the foundation for a new style of black music that embraced gospel fervor and pop romanticism. After signing with Atlantic Records in 1952, Ray Charles had abandoned his early Charles Brown/Nat "King" Cole–style crooning for a more boisterous, jubilant amalgam of hard R&B and pulpit sermonizing, complete with call-and-response choruses. James Brown's frenetic, hoarse-voiced testimonials, soul-shaking rhythmic assault, and impeccable sense of showmanship were beholden to the unbridled spectacles common to Julius Cheeks and the Sensational Nightingales' live shows. With a style rooted in gospel and legitimate swing, Ruth Brown did nothing less than put the Atlantic label on the map with her 1949 hit, "So Long," and over the next decade racked up more than twenty R&B hits, almost all of them with at least one foot in the church.

Post-1958 saw the advent of manufactured teen idols, who were chosen more for their looks and style than for their musical ability, performing material written for them and designed to reinforce their clean-cut, all-American boy images. But this would soon pass, as all fads do; bubbling under the surface, meanwhile, was the music that had been there throughout the Twentieth Century. It would resonate most profoundly in the folk revival of the early Sixties, with a group of artists whose bible was the *Anthology of Folk Music*. Disenfranchised by rock & roll's pop turn — or never attracted to rock & roll in the first place — a new generation of artists was cutting its teeth on the *Anthology* and bringing folk music to mainstream prominence.

Bob Dylan, the preeminent practitioner of the *Anthology*'s sensibility, energized the folk movement with his vivid, eloquent, socially conscious writing and an untrained voice that carried a tremendous emotional wallop, much like the rustic vocalists he had heard on the *Anthology*. Since discovering rock & roll in its infancy, he had been increasingly drawn to folk music's populist sympathies and soon discovered and absorbed every nuance of Woody Guthrie's *oeuvre*, while at the same time firing his imagination with the work of the Beat writers and French Symbolist poets. The influence of the oldtime texts of the *Anthology* and Guthrie's powerful songs of protest and wry social commentary lit a path that led Dylan literally to Guthrie's side, when they met during Guthrie's hospitalization for the Huntington's chorea that would soon kill him. Dylan was, in his own words, "a Woody Guthrie jukebox." As he shook up the folk world with his early albums and songs seemingly designed to comment on the frenzied cultural and

NEWP

4

RT **FOLK FESTIVAL**

2

{ ABOVE: BOB DYLAN (IN POLKA DOTS), BACKED BY MEMBERS OF THE PAUL BUTTERFIELD BLUES BAND (GUI-
TARIST MIKE BLOOMFIELD, DRUMMER SAM LAY (HIDDEN), BASSIST JEROME ARNOLD, AND ORGANIST AL
KOOPER, FROM LEFT), SHOCKED THE 1965 NEWPORT AUDIENCE BY PLUGGING IN — AND IN THE PROCESS LED
THE WAY TO FOLK ROCK.

political environment in early-Sixties America — "The Times They Are a-Changin'," "The Lonesome Death of Hattie Carroll," "Blowin' in the Wind," "A Hard Rain's a-Gonna Fall" — so did he upend rock & roll in 1965 when he began splitting his sets between acoustic and electric music and released his first Top Ten rock & roll hit record, "Like a Rolling Stone." That was a year and a half after the Beatles had conquered America with new variations on Fifties templates and opened the door to a host of British bands purveying American roots music — especially blues — in electrified form.

With Dylan's breakthroughs, a host of musical artists schooled in roots rock & roll and folk found common ground, and commercial music took on new depth in its lyrics and arrangements. In Chicago, a lively folk scene had been brewing, centered around the Earl of Old Town club. Among its alumni, Roger McGuinn took a distinctive approach to folk music that he had learned while studying with the veteran traditional folk artist Bob Gibson. McGuinn relocated to California, founded the Byrds, and brought Dylan's work into the mainstream in 1965 with "Mr. Tambourine Man." At the end of the decade, the Byrds pioneered a compelling fusion of country and rock that drew on the past for its fresh sound. The Byrds' landmark *Sweetheart of the Rodeo* album featured Dylan's "You Ain't Going Nowhere" and "Nothing Was Delivered," bookending songs by Woody Guthrie and Merle Haggard, as well as an original composition by the band's new member, Gram Parsons — whose understanding of traditional country music was so deep it made him seem like a time traveler from an earlier era.

On the East Coast in the early and mid-Sixties, the New York City–Boston axis was producing a heady brew of folk music informed by the intellectual iconoclasm of the Fifties Beat Generation and the oldtime forms found on the *Anthology*. Jug bands proliferated, the most prominent being Boston's Jim Kweskin Jug Band, which approached the old songs with a jazz musician's improvisational mind-set. "If we couldn't murder a song," Kweskin founding member Geoff Muldaur once said, "we weren't interested in it." In New York, John Sebastian (son of a classical harmonica player, a true musical rarity) and Zal Yanovsky were deeply enmeshed in the folk scene, through jug bands and various configurations of acoustic groups, when they plugged in and became the Lovin' Spoonful, purveyors of folk-rooted rock & roll of the most tuneful and accessible sort in the mid-Sixties. That same fertile New York folk scene also begat the Mugwumps and the Journeymen, some of whose members later metamorphosed into the Mamas and the Papas. As the group's principal songwriter, the late Papa John Phillips melded gentle folk-rock rhythms and melodies to producer Lou Adler's complex, multilayered, Phil Spector–style soundscapes, the result being one of the most commercially successful and beloved groups of the decade.

In San Francisco, the Grateful Dead was founded by musicians who had grown up immersed in oldtime music a la Harry Smith's *Anthology*. The band was led by guitarist Jerry Garcia, who had cut his musical teeth on the *Anthology* and in a variety of Bay Area jug and string bands. Another group member, keyboardist "Pigpen" McKernan, was a blues fanatic. Teamed with bassist Phil Lesh, rocking guitarist Bob Weir, and drummer Bill Kreutzmann, the Dead became the preeminent jam band of its day, given to angular, languid instrumental excursions into a multitude of musical styles. But when everything else was stripped away, the Dead's roots in oldtime music were obvious, particularly on the two albums considered the band's landmarks, 1970's *Workingman's Dead* and *American Beauty*, both betrayed a strong country strain in the band's harmony singing and instrumental arrangements and in Garcia's

FROM TOP: THE BYRDS DURING THE RECORDING OF 'SWEETHEART OF THE RODEO' IN 1968: GUEST BANJOIST JOHN HARTFORD, GRAM PARSONS, CHRIS HILLMAN, AND ROGER MCGUINN (FROM LEFT); THE 1970-ERA BYRDS: MCGUINN, SKIP BATTIN, GENE PARSONS, AND CLARENCE WHITE (FROM LEFT). OPPOSITE: THE GRATEFUL DEAD IN THEIR HOMETOWN, 1967: JERRY GARCIA, PIGPEN, PHIL LESH, BOB WEIR, AND BILL KREUTZMANN (FROM LEFT).

steel-guitar work. Never satisfied solely with the framework the
Dead provided him for musical expression, Garcia frequently
broke off from the band to pursue side projects such as Old and
In the Way, which also featured bluegrass mandolin master David
Grisman. Also in the Bay Area, beginning in 1966, Janis Joplin,
with her band, Big Brother and the Holding Company, added
rock & roll backbone to a repertoire filled with traditional and
contemporary blues.

In the mid-Sixties, the Sir Douglas Quintet, led by Doug Sahm,
came out of Texas looking very British but sounding like no one
else, thanks to Sahm's penchant for eccentric fusions of country,
rock & roll, blues, folk, and Tex-Mex. Other Texas rock, country,
and folk artists have regularly reached across the border for inspiration, even to the point of importing the great Mexican accordion player Flaco Jiménez for their recording projects, such as the
Doug Sahm—led roots music "supergroup," the Texas Tornados.
One of the finest of the younger generation of multicultural
artists, Austin-based Tish Hinojosa spices her songs with refer-
ences to Hispanic cultural and historical events, employs the *conjunto* style as her primary frame of reference as a songwriter, and
periodically records entire albums in Spanish.

8

The persistence of memory. No matter the commercial character rock &
roll (and popular music in general)
takes as time goes on, it seems an artist
or group of artists emerges from the fray with music that draws
from ancient wells and reasserts the timelessness of sacred texts.
Creedence Clearwater Revival, for example, began a steady run of
hits in 1969, at the dawn of bubblegum pop and the sunset of
psychedelic rock, with a sound that was geographically located
somewhere between the Sun studio in Memphis and the dark
heart of the Mississippi Delta. CCR's voice, literally and figura-
tively, was John Fogerty, whose songs' relentless rhythms betrayed
his debt to the early rock & rollers; as a lyricist, his use of
metaphor in tracks such as "Who'll Stop the Rain" and the
scabrous "Fortunate Son" revealed an antiestablishment bent that
harkened back to the leftist politics of Woody Guthrie and his
acolytes. Tellingly, following CCR's breakup in 1972, Fogerty's
first solo project was a one-man-band album, *The Blue Ridge Rangers,*
a collection of bluegrass, country, and gospel songs.

Like Fogerty, Bruce Springsteen stepped into and elevated a tepid
commercial rock scene. Both released in 1973, his first two
albums embraced influences as varied as Dylan, Phil Spector, and
British Invasion—era rock. *Born to Run,* his third album, represented the apex of his fascination with epic songs depicting the rituals and rites of restless youths with wheels for wings. His fourth

album, *Darkness on the Edge of Town,* was raw and merciless in its execution, adult in its themes of betrayal and loss, while evincing a fine-tuned sense of empathy for the working-class roots of his New Jersey upbringing. All signs were pointing to a sea change as Springsteen widened his research into the human condition and listened more intently to the music that America had produced in the decades before his birth in 1949. Deeply moved by Guthrie's work, and knowledgeable about the sort of people who populated the world Guthrie described, Springsteen got off the arena-rock treadmill in 1982 with the stark, foreboding, solo acoustic *Nebraska,* originally recorded on his home four-track recorder — as bold a move as any artist of Springsteen's rank has made in the history of rock & roll. Although his next album, *Born in the U.S.A.,* sold in the multimillions and made him, unequivocally, a superstar capable of selling out stadiums all over the world, Springsteen's personal journey was underway, as he aligned himself with worthy causes that aided the poor and disenfranchised.

While he has never turned his back on rock & roll — witness the joyous celebrations that attended his 2000 reunion tour with his E Street Band — Springsteen has periodically asserted his core values in projects ranging from the folk album *The Ghost of Tom Joad* to the haunting, Oscar-winning theme song he wrote for the film *Philadelphia.*

Springsteen and Fogerty aren't the sole exemplars of roots music's enduring influence on contemporary music, but they are, arguably, two of the most important ones. Bonnie Raitt, Bob Seger, John Mellencamp, Melissa Etheridge, the Indigo Girls, Sheryl Crow, and others could all bear witness to the importance of the early templates in their own work. The spirits of Bill Monroe, the Carter Family, Jimmie Rodgers, Hank Williams, Woody Guthrie, and Sam Cooke endure, not so much in the mainstream anymore, but under the surface, beating like Poe's telltale heart and nurturing numerous variations on the original themes. Steve Earle, a Nashvillian by way of Texas, couples fundamental rock & roll drive with a flinty political consciousness that would make Woody Guthrie smile. Gillian Welch and Iris DeMent craft beautiful, fragile melodies and express a God-fearing worldview that seems channeled from Mother Maybelle Carter. Lucinda Williams has outgrown the novelty of being a woman singing Robert Johnson songs to come

into her own, with a razor-edged blend of blues and country fueling original songs that unflinchingly explore relationships from a female perspective. And a host of bands are out there in America reminding anyone who comes to their shows that the past is a living entity energizing their contemporary twists on honky-tonk, country, and rock & roll: BR5-49, Son Volt and Wilco (offspring of Uncle Tupelo), the Derailers. Emmylou Harris, confidante of Gram Parsons, will cut adventurous, atmospheric albums with producers such as Daniel Lanois that virtually defy categorization, but in her public pronouncements and performances she remains a staunch, unrelenting advocate for the traditional in country music. And as rock & roll has embraced a host of indigenous American musics in its mix, it has over the years broadened its boundaries with multiethnic strains such as Los Lobos's blending of Mexican folksongs with traditional rock & roll styles (realizing the promise implicit in the music Ritchie Valens was shaping out of Hispanic and American sources in the months prior to his death at age seventeen) and Los Super Seven's amalgam of traditional country, honky-tonk and Hispanic influences. While not the persistent chart presence it was in the 1950s, the spirit of New Orleans lives on in the celebratory sounds of the Neville Brothers, in the second-line rhythms ever present in Mac "Dr. John" Rebennack's eloquent piano playing, and in the spirited, heartfelt Cajun and zydeco stylings of the long-standing band Beausoleil and the distinctive solo artist Buckwheat Zydeco.

The list is broad and deep, and its names will not always be found on the Hot 100 chart. But they are out there, and so is this music, speaking to those who grew up with it, and beckoning those too young to have experienced it firsthand, but who are now rummaging through history for something that speaks to the deepest part of their beings, and to the human condition. The past, indisputably, is prologue.

OPPOSITE: BRUCE SPRINGSTEEN, ONSTAGE WITH THE E STREET BAND IN THE EARLY EIGHTIES. ABOVE: CREEDENCE CLEARWATER REVIVAL, CIRCA 1970: JOHN FOGERTY, DOUG CLIFFORD, TOM FOGERTY, AND STU COOK (FROM LEFT).

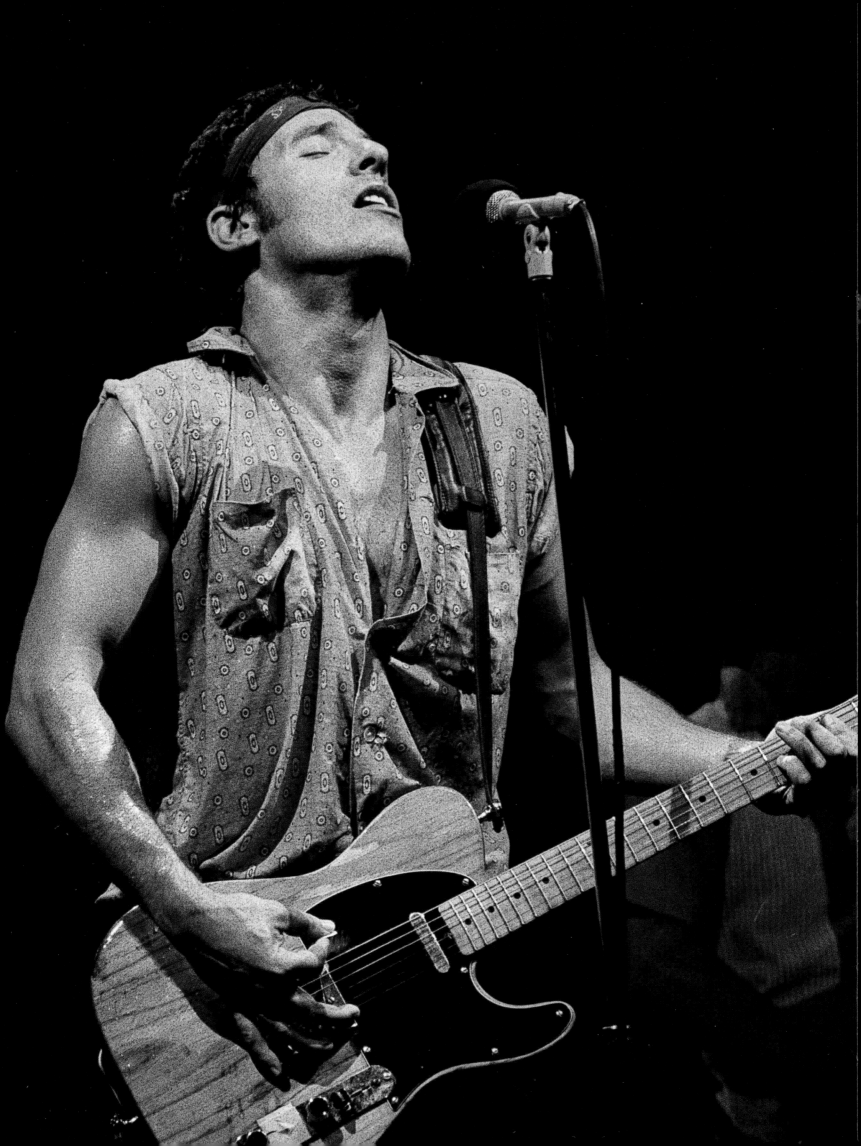

SAM PHILLIPS: *I was born in 1923 and raised in Florence, Alabama, which is about 150 miles east of Memphis, Tennessee. By 1929, the crash came, and the Great Depression set in up until World War II in 1941. So, as a child on the farm, I saw the value of the songs as a respite from hard labors. Everybody worked from before sunup until pitch-black dark. Radio wasn't in [our home] yet, so the black church become the single most important respite from the storm of life. The same type of feel existed among white country churches — the folk music from the soul, so to speak, talk[ing] about true-life experiences.*

[Beginning in 1950] I did a lot of auditions at my little studio in Memphis, Tennessee, called Memphis Recording Service, and after that I started my label [Sun]. When rock & roll came in, it was really white people playing the blues. The next thing you know, preachers [were] jumpin' on us and mamas and daddies [were] jumpin' on us. It was a radical change. I'm talking especially about rhythm & blues, "race" records, as they were called then. What we were doing with blacks and whites was to a degree overlooked for a long time by the major labels. [My goal] was to broaden the base for [their] airplay. I absolutely made sure to the best of my ability that nobody tried to mimic a black man, but, for God's sake, if you can sing with that feel and that soul and that touch that he or she has got, the Lord would sure wanna try that.

[Elvis Presley's first record] "That's All Right" was really the beginning of broadening that base of black and white [music]. Rock & roll, to me, is greater than any other music on the face of the earth because it represents so much from all different stratas of life: country, blues, gut-bucket blues, [and] to an extent pop. I just had to do everything that I could with it, because if I did it would either succeed or it would fail. [Rock & roll] music did more [than anything else] to soften the racial divide in our country — and ultimately around the world.

BELOW: SAM PHILLIPS MANS THE BOARDS AT HIS LEGENDARY SUN STUDIO, 1958.
OPPOSITE: PHILLIPS (RIGHT) AND HIS BRAND-NEW DISCOVERY, JERRY LEE LEWIS, CIRCA 1957.

CONTRIBUTORS

JIM BROWN is a three-time Emmy and Cable Ace Award–winning producer and director whose musical documentaries and television concerts include: *The Weavers: Wasn't That a Time!*; *Musical Passage*; *Woody Guthrie: Hard Travelin'*; *American Guitar Heroes*; *A Vision Shared: A Tribute to Woody Guthrie and Lead Belly*; *We Shall Overcome*; *In the Hank Williams Tradition*; *The Songs of the Civil War*; *Child of Mine: The Lullaby Project*; *Pete Seeger Family Concert*; *In the Spotlight: Jubilee at Wolftrap With Mary Chapin Carpenter*; *An Evening With Harry Belafonte and Friends*; and *Keeping the Music Alive*. He also heads Ginger Group Productions and is an associate professor at New York University's Tisch School of the Arts.

DAVID EVANS is professor of music at the University of Memphis, where he directs the Ph.D. program in ethnomusicology with a focus on Southern folk and popular music. He has been involved in blues research since the mid-1960s and produced many albums of field and studio recordings of blues. He is the author of *Tommy Johnson* (1971) and *Big Road Blues: Tradition and Creativity in the Folk Blues* (1982) and the editor of the American Made Music series of books for the University Press of Mississippi.

HOLLY GEORGE-WARREN is the editor or coeditor of numerous books on music, including *The Rolling Stone Album Guide*, *The Rolling Stone Illustrated History of Rock & Roll*, and *The Rolling Stone Encyclopedia of Rock & Roll*, for which she won the 1996 ASCAP-Deems Taylor Award. Her writing appears in *The Rolling Stone Book of Women in Rock*; *Rock, She Wrote*; *The Encyclopedia of Country Music*; *Country on Compact Disc*; *The Rolling Stone Jazz and Blues Album Guide*; and *Classic Country*, among others. The coauthor of *How the West Was Worn*, she also has written for *Rolling Stone*, the *New York Times*, the *Village Voice*, the *Journal of Country Music*, *The Oxford American*, *Country Music*, and *No Depression*. In 2001, she received a Grammy nomination (for Best Historical Recording) for coproducing Rhino Records' five-CD box set *R-E-S-P-E-C-T: A Century of Women in Music*.

ALAN JABBOUR is a Floridian by birth and a violinist by early training. The folk revival drew him into studying folklore and folk music as a graduate student at Duke University in the 1960s, when he documented and apprenticed with oldtime fiddlers in the Upper South. He taught at UCLA before becoming head of the Archive of Folk Song at the Library of Congress (1969–74), director of folk arts at the National Endowment for the Arts (1974–76), and director of the American Folklife Center at the Library of Congress (1976–99). A longtime performer of and writer about folk music, he has returned to both activities enthusiastically since his retirement.

BILL C. MALONE is a retired professor of history from Tulane University in New Orleans. He now lives in Madison, Wisconsin, where he hosts a recorded program of classic country music (Back to the Country) each Wednesday morning on WORT-FM. Malone is the author of *Country Music, USA*, the first published general history of the subject, and was the compiler and annotator of the *Smithsonian Collection of Classic Country Music*, a box set of historic country music recordings. His latest book is *Don't Get Above Your Raising: Country Music and the Southern Working Class*.

DAVID MCGEE is the author of *Go, Cat, Go! The Life and Times of Carl Perkins, the King of Rockabilly*, and also serves as country music editor for barnesandnoble.com. A veteran *Rolling Stone* and Rolling Stone Press contributor, he has written the book for the Broadway musical *Save the Last Dance for Me*, a celebration of the life and songs of the legendary songwriter and Rock and Roll Hall of Fame member Doc Pomus.

MANUEL PEÑA is a specialist in the folklore and music of the Hispanic Southwest. He has written three books, *The Texas-Mexican Conjunto*, *The Mexican American Orquesta*, and *Música Tejana*. Peña has been professor of anthropology and music at the University of Texas at Austin and professor of music at California State University, Fresno.

CLAUDIA PERRY is a music writer who has written for the *Star-Ledger* of Newark, New Jersey, the *Houston Post*, the *Real Paper* of Cambridge, Massachusetts, *Stereo Review Sound and Vision*, and *Texas Monthly*. She was a 1999 Grammy nominee in the album notes category for her essay "Digging Country's Roots," part of *From Where I Stand: The Black Experience in Country Music*. She is a member of the Rock and Roll Hall of Fame nominating committee.

J. POET, music editor of *Native Peoples* magazine, writes about Native, world, folk, blues, Americana, and other musics for dozens of magazines, newspapers, and Web sites, including *Pulse, Grammy,* and the New York Times Syndicate. He lives in San Francisco with a rabbit, hundreds of houseplants, and his psychologist partner, who keeps him fairly sane.

WILLIAM K. POWERS spent fifty-two years on the Pine Ridge Indian reservation in South Dakota studying Lakota music, dance, language, and religion. He is the author of twenty-five books and monographs on Native Americans, including *Oglala Religion, Yuwipi: Vision and Experience in Oglala Ritual,* and *War Dance: Plains Indian Musical Performance.* He also has published more than two hundred articles in American and European journals of anthropology, history, humanities, and popular magazines, winning numerous literary awards. He currently is editor and publisher of Lakota Books, which specializes in publications and educational tools in Native American culture/history and bilingual education. Powers holds a Ph.D. in anthropology from the University of Pennsylvania and has lectured at major universities in the United States and Europe. He frequently collaborates with his wife, Dr. Marla N. Powers, who also is an anthropologist.

The author of *The Big Book of Blues* and *The Best of the Blues,* ROBERT SANTELLI has been writing about American roots music, reggae, and rock & roll for more than twenty years in such publications as *Rolling Stone, Downbeat,* the *New York Times,* and the *Asbury Park Press.* Before moving to Seattle in 2000 to become the deputy director of public programs for Experience Music Project, Santelli was the vice president of education and public programs at the Rock and Roll Hall of Fame and Museum in Cleveland. Santelli is the executive editor of the American Music Masters series published by Wesleyan U. Press. He coedited *Hard Travelin': The Life and Legacy of Woody Guthrie* (Wesleyan/1999) and edited *Bruce Springsteen's Songs* (Avon/1999). Santelli lives on Bainbridge Island with his wife, Cindy, and their three kids.

ANN ALLEN SAVOY is an author, musician, and record producer. In addition to numerous CD booklets and articles about Cajun music, she wrote the Botkin Prize–winning book *Cajun Music: A Reflection of a People.* As a musician, she has played guitar, fiddle, and accordion and traveled throughout the world with her husband, accordionist Marc Savoy, and fiddler Michael Doucet in the Savoy Doucet Cajun Band. Recently she has recorded and traveled with her all-woman band, the Magnolia Sisters. She has recorded six CDs on the Arhoolie and Rounder labels, has appeared in many documentaries on the subject of Cajun music, and with her husband was the subject of Les Blank's film *Marc and Ann.* She also works as an executive record producer for Vanguard Records.

A three-time Grammy nominee, CHARLES WOLFE is the author of more than twenty books on American music, including *Classic Country* and *A Good-Natured Riot: The Birth of the Grand Ole Opry,* a winner of both the ASCAP-Deems Taylor and Ralph J. Gleason–music book awards. He teaches at Middle Tennessee State University near Nashville.

SOURCES FOR MARGINAL QUOTES

EARLY COUNTRY: TREASURES UNTOLD

Page 16   Marty Stuart: Interview with Bill Malone, for the film *American Roots Music,* 2000.

Page 19   Tammy Wynette: Interview with Holly George-Warren, 1994.

Page 20   Johnny Cash: Johnny Cash with Patrick Carr, *Cash: The Autobiography* (New York: HarperSanFrancisco, 1997).

Page 21   Earl Scruggs: Interview with Jim Brown, for the film *American Roots Music,* 2000.

Page 23   Bob Dylan: Liner notes to *The Songs of Jimmie Rodgers: A Tribute Album* (Egyptian/Columbia, 1996).

Page 23   Jimmie Rodgers: Nolan Porterfield, *Jimmie Rodgers* (Champaign: University of Illinois Press, 1992).

Page 25   Buck Owens: Interview with George-Warren, 1995.

Page 26   Doug Green: Interview with Brown, 2000.

Page 30   Bill Monroe: Interview with George-Warren, 1994.

Page 30   Ricky Skaggs: Interview with Brown, 2000.

Page 32   Ralph Stanley: Interview with Brown, 2000.

THE BIRTH OF THE BLUES

Page 39   Honeyboy Edwards: Paul Trynka, *Portrait of the Blues* (London: Hamlyn, 1996).

Page 45   John Sebastian: Interview with Brown, 2000.

Page 54   Robert Junior Lockwood: Interview with Brown, 2000.

THE FLOWERING OF THE FOLK REVIVAL

Page 65   Harold Leventhal: Interview with Brown, 2000.

Page 65   Steve Earle: Interview with Brown, 2001.

Page 69   Pete Seeger: Interview with Brown, 2000.

Page 78   Alan Lomax: Interview with Brown, 1988.

Page 80   Pete Seeger: Interview with Brown, 2000.

Page 80   Peter Yarrow: Interview with Brown, 2000.

Page 83   Doc Watson: Interview with Malone, 2000.

HALLELUJAH: THE SACRED MUSIC OF BLACK AMERICA

Page 87   Erskine Lytle: Interview with Sam Pollard, for the film *American Roots Music,* 2000.

Page 97   Aretha Franklin: Aretha Franklin and David Ritz, *Aretha: From These Roots* (New York: Villard, 1999).

Page 97   Geneva Gentry: Interview with Pollard, 2000.

Page 99   Al Green: Al Green with Davin Seay, *Take Me to the River* (New York: HarperEntertainment, 2000).

Page 101   Marabeth Gentry: Interview with Pollard, 2000.

Page 102   Matthew Kennedy: Interview with Pollard, 2000.

Page 102   Cissy Houston: Interview with Brown and Pollard, 2001; Cissy Houston with Jonathan Singer, *How Sweet the Sound: My Life With God and Gospel* (New York: Doubleday, 1998).

CAJUN AND ZYDECO: THE MUSICS OF FRENCH SOUTHWEST LOUISIANA

Page 107   Luderin Darbone: Ann Allen Savoy, *Cajun Music: A Reflection of a People* (Eunice: Bluebird Press, Inc., 1984).

Page 109   Steve Riley: Interview with Brown, 2000.

Page 118   D.L. Menard: Savoy, *Cajun Music: A Reflection of a People.*

Page 123   Clifton Chenier: Ibid.

Page 124   Marc Savoy: Interview with Brown, 2000.

BOTTOM, BOTH COURTESY OF BLUEBIRD PRESS; {123} TOP ANN SAVOY COLLECTION; JOHN FAGO; {124} RICK OLIVIER; {125} TOP, LEFT ANN SAVOY; TOP, RIGHT PHILIP GOULD; BOTTOM ANN SAVOY. **MÚSICA TEJANA: THE MUSIC OF MEXICAN TEXAS** {126-127} MICHAEL OCHS ARCHIVES; {128} TOP LEE RUSSELL/LIBRARY OF CONGRESS; HOLLY GEORGE-WARREN COLLECTION {129} TEXAS STATE LIBRARY & ARCHIVES COMMISSION; {130} MANUEL PEÑA COLLECTION; {131} MANUEL PEÑA COLLECTION; {132} PHILIP GOULD; {133} CLOCKWISE FROM TOP LEFT ALAN LOMAX/LIBRARY OF CONGRESS; MANUEL PEÑA COLLECTION; LEE RUSSELL/LIBRARY OF CONGRESS BELOW MANUEL PEÑA COLLECTION; {134} PHILIP GOULD; {135} TOP PHILIP GOULD; DENNIS KEELEY/REPRISE RECORDS, COURTESY OF JAY BELL; {136} FRANK DRIGGS COLLECTION; {137} RAMON HERNANDEZ ARCHIVES, COURTESY OF MANUEL PEÑA; {138} LITTLE JOE HERNANDEZ COLLECTION, COURTESY OF MANUEL PEÑA; {139} COURTESY OF EMI LATIN; {140} RAMON HERNANDEZ ARCHIVES, COURTESY OF MANUEL PEÑA; {141} PHILIP GOULD; {142-143} DAVID GAHR; {143} PHILIP GOULD. **NATIVE AMERICAN MUSIC OF THE TWENTIETH CENTURY** {144-145} EDWARD CURTIS/LIBRARY OF CONGRESS; {146} MARLA N. POWERS; {147} COURTESY OF THE SMITHSONIAN INSTITUTION, DEPARTMENT OF ANTHROPOLOGY/WILLIAM K. AND MARLA N. POWERS COLLECTION; {148} MARLA N. POWERS; {148-149} COURTESY OF THE SMITHSONIAN INSTITUTION, DEPARTMENT OF ANTHROPOLOGY/WILLIAM K. AND MARLA N. POWERS COLLECTION; {150} COURTESY OF THE SMITHSONIAN INSTITUTION, DEPARTMENT OF ANTHROPOLOGY/WILLIAM K. AND MARLA N. POWERS COLLECTION; {151} BOTH COURTESY OF THE SMITHSONIAN INSTITUTION, DEPARTMENT OF ANTHROPOLOGY/WILLIAM K. AND MARLA N. POWERS COLLECTION; {152-153} DAVID GAHR; {154} COURTESY OF SMITHSONIAN INSTITUTION, DEPARTMENT OF ANTHROPOLOGY/WILLIAM K. AND MARLA N. POWERS COLLECTION; {155} BOTH MARLA N. POWERS; {156} ALL MARLA N. POWERS; {157} ALL MARLA N. POWERS; {158} COURTESY OF SMITHSONIAN INSTITUTION, DEPARTMENT OF ANTHROPOLOGY/WILLIAM K. AND MARLA N. POWERS COLLECTION; {159} JOHN RUNNING/CANYON RECORDS; {160} CLOCKWISE FROM TOP PAUL SLAUGHTER/COURTESY OF HAWKSONG PRODUCTIONS; DAVID JORDAN WILLIAMS/COURTESY CAPITOL RECORDS; MICHAEL OCHS ARCHIVES; DAVID GAHR; ©PETER NASH/MICHAEL OCHS ARCHIVES; **KEEPING IT COUNTRY: TRADITION AND CHANGE, 1940 TO THE PRESENT** {162-163} LES LEVERETT {CARTERS}; HOLLY GEORGE-WARREN COLLECTION; {164} LES LEVERETT; {165} LEFT LES LEVERETT; MICHAEL OCHS ARCHIVES; {166} TOP CHARLES WOLFE COLLECTION; DAVID GAHR; {167} LES LEVERETT; {168} DAVID GAHR; {169} MARK SELIGER; {170} TOP JOHN COHEN; DAVID GAHR; {171} TOP JIM HERRINGTON; ©FDR/MICHAEL OCHS ARCHIVES; {172} DAVID GAHR; {173} CLOCKWISE FROM TOP MICHAEL OCHS ARCHIVES; HOLLY GEORGE-WARREN COLLECTION; MARK SELIGER; {174} CLOCKWISE FROM TOP LES LEVERETT; LES LEVERETT; CHARLES WOLFE COLLECTION; {175} DAVID GAHR; {176} RAEANNE RUBENSTEIN; {177} JIM HERRINGTON; {178} MARK SELIGER; {179} TOP MARK SELIGER; HOLLY GEORGE-WARREN COLLECTION; {180} TOP MICHAEL OCHS ARCHIVES; LES LEVERETT; {181} LES LEVERETT; {182} COURTESY OF CAPITOL RECORDS; {183} TOP JIM HERRINGTON; FRANK OCKENFELS[3]/COURTESY OF COLUMBIA RECORDS. **MOJO WORKING: THE BLUES EXPLOSION** {184-185} VAL WILMER; {186} LEFT DAVID GAHR; VAL WILMER; {187} MICHAEL OCHS ARCHIVES; {188} ©FDR/MICHAEL OCHS ARCHIVES; {189} MICHAEL OCHS ARCHIVES; {190} MICHAEL OCHS ARCHIVES; {191} BOTH FRANK DRIGGS COLLECTION; {192-193} JOHN COHEN; {193} TOP MICHAEL OCHS ARCHIVES; VAL WILMER; {194} DAVID GAHR; {196} TOP VAL WILMER; ©RAY FLERLAGE/MICHAEL OCHS ARCHIVES; {197} PETER AMFT; {198} VAL WILMER; {199} DICK WATERMAN; {200} LEFT DAVID GAHR; DICK WATERMAN; {201} DAVID GAHR; {202} TOP VAL WILMER; DAVID GAHR; {203} © 1997 TONY BAKER /MERGE LEFT STOCK; {204} PETER AMFT; {205} TOP ©RAY FLERLAGE/MICHAEL OCHS ARCHIVES; ©SIMON MEAKER/ALL ACTION/RETNA, LTD.; {206} KENJI ODA; {207} FRANK DRIGGS COLLECTION; {208} KENJI ODA; {208-209} VAL WILMER. **ROOTS MUSIC BEGATS ROCK & ROLL** {212} MICHAEL OCHS ARCHIVES; {214} ©COLIN ESCOTT/MICHAEL OCHS ARCHIVES; {215} MICHAEL OCHS ARCHIVES; {216} BOTH MICHAEL OCHS ARCHIVES; {218} ALL MICHAEL OCHS ARCHIVES; {219} MICHAEL OCHS ARCHIVES; {220} MICHAEL OCHS ARCHIVES; {221} MICHAEL OCHS ARCHIVES; {222} MICHAEL OCHS ARCHIVES; {223} MICHAEL OCHS ARCHIVES; {224-225} DAVID GAHR; {226} TOP CHARLES WOLFE COLLECTION; DAVID GAHR; {227} HERB GREENE/WALNUT STREET GALLERY; {228-229} DAVID GAHR; {230} MICHAEL OCHS ARCHIVES; {231} DAVID GAHR; {232} MICHAEL OCHS ARCHIVES; {233} MICHAEL OCHS ARCHIVES. {238} ACKNOWLEDGMENTS: KENJI ODA. LEAD BELLY: BERNARD HOFFMAN/TIMEPIX.

ACKNOWLEDGMENTS

Bringing the film *American Roots Music* to the printed page has been a real labor of love, enriched by the panorama of roots music that has been our soundtrack. We couldn't have done it, though, without the help of some very talented and dedicated souls. We're grateful to our top-notch publisher, Harry N. Abrams — particularly our insightful and knowledgeable editor, Eric Himmel, as well as Michael Walsh and his staff. We also appreciate the unwavering support of our agent, Sarah Lazin, and her staffers Paula Balzer and Dena Koklanaris. Thanks to the *American Roots Music* team: Jim Brown, Robert Santelli, Sam Pollard, Jeff Rosen, Sarah Cullen, Ray Funk, John Cohen, Paul Kingsbury, Elizabeth Snider, Rachel Schneider, and all the writers who've been involved every step of the way. It's been a privilege and a pleasure working with the amazing designer Beth Middleworth, and we couldn't have done it without the help of tireless photo researcher Moira Haney. Our kudos also to the fantastic photographers whose work you see in this book. Those at Wenner Media who have been crucial to our efforts include: Jann S. Wenner, Kent Brownridge, John Lagana, Fred Woodward, Rich Waltman, Mary McDonald O'Brien, Evelyn Bernal, Paul Leung, and Donny Katz. Others who have really gone out of their way to help us include David Gahr, Pamela Stansfield, Les Leverett, Dave Marsh, Elizabeth Gall, Patricia Romanowski, Andrea Danese, Rene Hersey, Paul Buckley, Anthony DeCurtis, Jenny Boyd, Nolan Porterfield, Paul Trynka, Ann Abel, Pam Grossman, Dave Konjoyan, Kim Curry, Dennis Ambrose, Bill Bentley, Marya Garskof, Michael Ochs, Helen Ashford, Jonathan Hyams, Frank Driggs, Jo Rae DiMenno, Adele Hauck, Jami Lopez, Mark Satloff, Camilla and Roger McGuinn, Ben Shaefer, Raeanne Rubenstein, Bob Oermann, Robert Warren, Jim Duffy, Robert Legault, and John Branch. Thank you to the Recording Academy, which originally assigned j. poet to write an essay on contemporary Native American music for its forty-third annual Grammy program. And, finally, I have been truly blessed with a sharpshooting staff of tireless editors at Rolling Stone Press: associate editor Nina Pearlman, assistant editor Jordan Mamone, and editorial assistant Andrew Simon. Without their expertise, this book would not exist. And — I believe I can speak for everyone involved in the creation of *American Roots Music* — the biggest thank you is due to the incredible musicians whose work we celebrate in these pages. Muchas gracias, merci beaucoup, wopila eciciyapi, thanks y'all!

HOLLY GEORGE-WARREN
EDITOR, ROLLING STONE PRESS
APRIL 2001